SIMPLE PROGRAM DESIGN
A STEP-BY-STEP APPROACH
LESLEY ANNE ROBERTSON   FIFTH EDITION

SIMPLE PROGRAM DESIGN
A STEP-BY-STEP APPROACH
LESLEY ANNE ROBERTSON FIFTH EDITION

COURSE TECHNOLOGY
CENGAGE Learning

CENGAGE
Learning™

Simple Program Design
A Step-by-Step Approach
5th Edition
Lesley Ann Robertson

Director of Learning Solutions: Sandy Clark
Managing Editor: Tricia Coia
Marketing Manager: Penny Crosby
Editorial Assistant: Erin Kennedy
Production Editor: Kelly Robinson
Cover Designer: Beth Paquin
Manufacturing Coordinator: Julio Esperas
Editor: Marta Veroni
Compositor: Polar Design

Any URLs contained in this publication were checked for currency during the production process. Note, however, that the publisher cannot vouch for the ongoing currency of URLs.

For product information and technology assistance, in Australia call 1300 790 853; in New Zealand call 0800 449 725

For permission to use material from this text or product, please email aust.permissions@cengage.com

ISBN 978 1 42 390132 7

Cengage Learning Australia
Level 7, 80 Dorcas Street
South Melbourne, Victoria Australia 3205

Cengage Learning New Zealand
Unit 4B Rosedale Office Park
331 Rosedale Road, Albany, North Shore 0632, NZ

For learning solutions, visit cengage.com.au

Printed in China by RR Donnelley Asia Printing Solutions Limited.
4 5 6 7 8 9 10 15 14 13 12 11

Contents

Selection control structures

Expands the selection control structure by introducing multiple selection, nested selection and the case construct in pseudocode. Several algorithms, using variations of the selection control structure, are developed.

Repetition control structures

Develops algorithms that use the repetition control structure in the form of DOWHILE, REPEAT...UNTIL, and counted repetition loops.

Pseudocode algorithms using sequence, selection and repetition

Develops algorithms to solve eight simple programming problems using combinations of sequence, selection and repetition constructs. Each problem is properly defined; the control structures required are established; a pseudocode algorithm is developed; and the solution is manually checked for logic errors.

Array processing

Introduces arrays, operations on arrays, and algorithms that manipulate arrays. Algorithms for single and two-dimensional arrays, which initialise the elements of an array, search an array and write out the contents of an array, are presented.

8 First steps in modularisation

Introduces modularisation as a means of dividing a problem into subtasks. Hierarchy charts and parameter passing are introduced, and several algorithms that use a modular structure are developed.

9 General algorithms for common business problems

Develops a general pseudocode algorithm for four common business applications. All problems are defined; a hierarchy chart is established; and a pseudocode algorithm is developed, using a mainline and several subordinate modules. The topics covered include report generation with page break, a single-level control break, a multiple-level control break and a sequential file update program.

10 Communication between modules, cohesion and coupling

Introduces communication between modules and develops algorithms that pass parameters between modules. Module cohesion and coupling are introduced, several levels of cohesion and coupling are described, and pseudocode examples of each level are provided.

11 An introduction to object-oriented design

*Introduces object-oriented design, classes and objects, attributes,
responsibilities, operations, accessors and mutators, and information hiding.
The steps required to create an object-oriented solution to a problem are
provided and solution algorithms developed.*

12 Object-oriented design for more than one class

*Introduces relationships between classes including association, aggregation,
composition and generalisation. Introduces a simplified UML language,
describes polymorphism and operation overriding and lists the steps required
to create an object-oriented design for a problem with more than one class.*

13 Object-oriented design for multiple classes

*Expands an object-oriented solution to cater for multiple classes, inheritance
and polymorphism and introduces interface and GUI design.*

Appendix 1 Flowcharts

*Introduces flowcharts for those students who prefer a more graphic approach
to program design. Algorithms that use a combination of sequence, selection
and repetition are developed in some detail.*

Appendix 2   Special algorithms

Contains a number of algorithms that are not included in the body of the textbook and yet may be required at some time in a programmer's career.

Appendix 3

Glossary

Index

Preface

With the increased popularity of programming courses in our universities, colleges and technical institutions, there is a need for an easy-to-read textbook on computer program design. There are already dozens of introductory programming texts using specific languages such as C++, Visual Basic, Pascal and COBOL, but they usually gloss over the important step of designing a solution to a given programming problem.

This textbook tackles the subject of program design by using modern programming techniques and pseudocode to develop a solution algorithm. The recommended pseudocode has been chosen because of its closeness to written English, its versatility and ease of manipulation, and its similarity to the syntax of most structured programming languages.

Simple Program Design, Fifth Edition is designed for programmers who want to develop good programming skills for solving common business problems. Too often, programmers, when faced with a problem, launch straight into the code of their chosen programming language, instead of concentrating on the actual problem at hand. They become bogged down with the syntax and format of the language, and often spend many hours getting the program to work. Using this textbook, the programmer will learn how to properly define the problem, how to divide it into modules, how to design a solution algorithm, and how to prove the algorithm's correctness, before commencing any program coding. By using pseudocode and modern programming techniques, the programmer can concentrate on developing a well-designed and correct solution, and thus eliminate many frustrating hours at the testing phase.

The content of the book covers program design in two distinct sections. Chapters 1 to 10 cover algorithm design in the context of traditional programming languages. The section begins with a basic introduction to program design methodology, and the steps in developing a solution algorithm. Then, concept by concept, the student is introduced to the syntax of pseudocode; methods of defining the problem; the application of basic control structures in the development of the solution algorithm; desk-checking techniques; arrays; module design; hierarchy charts; communication between modules; parameter passing; and module cohesion and coupling.

Chapters 11 to 13 cover algorithm design in the context of object-oriented programming. The section introduces the concepts of object-oriented design and the steps involved in creating an object-oriented solution to a problem. Step-by-step algorithms using object-oriented design are provided, as well as material on polymorphism, operation overriding, multiple classes and interfaces.

Each chapter thoroughly covers the topic at hand, giving practical examples relating to business applications, and a consistently structured approach when representing algorithms and hierarchy charts.

This fifth edition has been thoroughly revised, in keeping with modern program design techniques. It includes an improved section on modularisation and communication between modules, and a greatly expanded section on object-oriented design with many more step-by-step examples.

Programming problems of increasing complexity are provided at the end of most chapters, so that teachers have a choice of exercises that match the widely varying abilities of their students. Detailed solutions are available to teachers and students on CD for half of each chapter's problems.

I would like to thank Kim Styles and Wendy Doube, lecturers in Computing at Monash University, for their wonderful input on object-oriented design methodology; Victor Cockrell, Curtin University, for his enthusiastic suggestions and his Quick Reference Chart for translating pseudocode into several computer languages; and my brother, Rick Noble, for his amusing cartoons at the beginning of each chapter.

Lesley Anne Robertson

About the author

Lesley Anne Robertson was introduced to pseudocode and program design methodology when she joined IBM Australia in 1973 as a trainee programmer. Since then, she has consistently used these techniques as a programmer, systems analyst, and lecturer in Computing at the University of Western Sydney, NSW, where she taught computer program design for 11 years.

Lesley now lives on a vineyard and winery in Mudgee, Australia, with her daughters Lucy and Sally and labradoodles Milly and Molly.

Program design

1

Objectives

- To describe the steps in the program development process
- To introduce current program design methodology
- To introduce procedural and object-oriented programming
- To introduce algorithms and pseudocode
- To describe program data

Outline

1.1 Steps in program development

Computer programming is an art. Many people believe that a programmer must be good at mathematics, have a memory for figures and technical information, and be prepared to spend many hours sitting at a computer, typing programs. However, given the right tools and steps to follow, anyone can write well-designed programs. It is a task worth doing, as it is both stimulating and fulfilling.

Programming can be defined as the development of a solution to an identified problem, and the setting up of a related series of instructions that, when directed through computer hardware, will produce the desired results. It is the first part of this definition that satisfies the programmer's creative needs; that is, to design a solution to an identified problem. Yet this step is so often overlooked. Leaping straight into the coding phase without first designing a proper solution usually results in a program that contains many errors. Often the programmer then needs to spend a significant amount of time finding these errors and correcting them. A more experienced programmer will design a solution to the program first, desk check this solution, and then code the program in a chosen programming language.

There are seven basic steps in the development of a program, as follows.

1 Define the problem

This step involves carefully reading and rereading the problem until you understand completely what is required. To help with this initial analysis, the problem should be divided into three separate components:

- the inputs
- the outputs
- the processing steps to produce the required outputs.

A defining diagram, as described in Chapter 3, is recommended in this analysis phase, as it helps to separate and define the three components.

2 Outline the solution

Once the problem has been defined, you may decide to break it down into smaller tasks or steps, and establish a solution outline. This initial outline is usually a rough draft of the solution and may include:

- the major processing steps involved
- the major subtasks (if any)
- the user interface (if any)
- the major control structures (e.g. repetition loops)
- the major variables and record structures
- the mainline logic.

The solution outline may also include a hierarchy or structure chart. The steps involved in developing this outline solution are detailed in chapters 2 to 6.

3   Develop the outline into an algorithm

The solution outline developed in Step 2 is then expanded into an algorithm: a set of precise steps that describe exactly the tasks to be performed and the order in which they are to be carried out. This book uses pseudocode (a form of structured English) to represent the solution algorithm. Flowcharts for every pseudocode algorithm up to and including Chapter 8 are provided in Appendix 1 for those who prefer a more pictorial method of algorithm representation.

4   Test the algorithm for correctness

This step is one of the most important in the development of a program, and yet it is the step most often bypassed. The main purpose of desk checking the algorithm is to identify major logic errors early, so that they may be easily corrected. Test data needs to be walked through each step in the algorithm to check that the instructions described in the algorithm will actually do what they are supposed to. The programmer 'walks' through the logic of the algorithm, exactly as a computer would, keeping track of all major variables on a sheet of paper. The use of a desk check table to desk check the algorithm is introduced in Chapter 3, and many examples of its use are provided.

5   Code the algorithm into a specific programming language

Only after all design considerations in the previous four steps have been met should you actually start to code the program into your chosen programming language.

6   Run the program on the computer

This step uses a program compiler and programmer-designed test data to machine test the code for syntax errors (those detected at compile time) and logic errors (those detected at run time). This is usually the most rewarding step in the program development process. If the program has been well designed, the time-wasting frustration and despair often associated with program testing are reduced to a minimum. This step may need to be performed several times until you are satisfied that the program is running as required.

7   Document and maintain the program

Program documentation should not be listed as the last step in the program development process, as it is really an ongoing task from the initial definition of the problem to the final test result.

Documentation includes both external documentation (such as hierarchy charts, the solution algorithm and test data results) and internal documentation that may have been coded in the program. Program maintenance refers to changes that may need to be made to a program throughout its life. Often, these changes are performed by a different programmer from the one who initially wrote the program. If the program has been well designed using structured programming techniques, the code will be seen as self-documenting, resulting in easier maintenance.

1.2 Program design methodology

The fundamental principle of program design is based on the fact that a program accepts input data, processes that data, and then delivers the data to the program user as output. Recently, a number of different approaches to program design have emerged, and the most common are:

- procedure-driven
- event-driven
- data-driven.

Procedure-driven program design

The procedure-driven approach to program design is based on the idea that the most important feature of a program is *what* it does – its processes or functions. By concentrating on what a program must do, the programmer identifies and organises the processes in the program solution. The flow of data into and out of each process or function is then considered and a strategy developed to break each function into smaller and more specific flows of data. The details about the actual structure of the data are not considered until all the high-level processes or functions of the program have been defined.

Event-driven program design

The event-driven approach to program design is based on the idea that an event or interaction with the outside world can cause a program to change from one known state to another. The initial state of a program is identified, then all the triggers that represent valid events for that state are established. Each of these events results in the program changing to a new defined state, where it stays until the next event occurs. For example, when a program user decides to click the left mouse button, click the right mouse button, drag the mouse or double click the mouse, each action could trigger a different *event* within the program and thus result in a different program state.

Data-driven program design

The data-driven approach to program design is based on the idea that the data in a program is more stable than the processes involved. It begins with an analysis of the data and the relationships between the data, in order to determine the fundamental data structures. Once these data structures have been defined, the required data outputs are examined in order to establish what processes are required to convert the input data to the required output.

The choice between procedure-driven, event-driven or data-driven program design methodologies is usually determined by the selection of a programming language. However, regardless of the program design method chosen, you must develop the necessary basic skills to be able to design a solution algorithm to a given problem. These basic skills include a well-defined and disciplined approach to designing the solution algorithm and adherence to the recommended program development process:

Step 1: Define the problem.
Step 2: Outline the solution (or user interface).
Step 3: Develop the outline into a solution algorithm.
Step 4: Test the algorithm for correctness.
Step 5: Code the algorithm into a specific programming language.
Step 6: Run the program on the computer.
Step 7: Document and maintain the program.

1.3 Procedural versus object-oriented programming

Procedural programming is based on a structured, top-down approach to writing effective programs. The approach concentrates on *what* a program has to do and involves identifying and organising the *processes* in the program solution. The problem is usually broken down into separate tasks or functions and includes top-down development and modular design.

Top-down development

In the top-down development of a program design, a general solution to the problem is outlined first. This outline is then divided gradually into more detailed steps until finally the most detailed levels have been completed. It is only after this process of top-down development (also called *functional decomposition* or *stepwise refinement*) that the programmer starts to code. The result of this systematic, disciplined approach to program design is a higher precision of programming than was previously possible.

Modular design

Procedural programming also incorporates the concept of modular design, which involves grouping tasks together because they all perform the same function (for example, calculating sales tax or printing report headings). Modular design is connected directly to top-down development, as the steps or subtasks into which the program solution is divided actually form the future modules of the program. Good modular design also assists in the reading and understanding of the program.

Object-oriented programming

Object-oriented programming is also based on breaking down the problem; however, the primary focus is on the *things* (or objects) that make up the program. The program is concerned with how the objects behave, so it breaks the problem into a set of separate objects that perform actions and relate to each other. These objects have definite properties, and each object is responsible for carrying out a series of related tasks.

This book looks at both approaches to program design, procedural and object-oriented. It is then left to you and your choice of programming language to determine which methodology you will use. It must be noted, however, that, regardless of design methodology or programming language, all programmers must have the basic skills to design solution algorithms. It is the intention of this book to provide these skills.

1.4 An introduction to algorithms and pseudocode

A program must be systematically and properly designed before coding begins. This design process results in the construction of an algorithm.

What is an algorithm?

An algorithm is like a recipe: it lists the steps involved in accomplishing a task. It can be defined in programming terms as a set of detailed, unambiguous and ordered instructions developed to describe the processes necessary to produce the desired output from a given input. The algorithm is written in simple English and is not a formal document. However, to be useful, there are some principles that should be adhered to. An algorithm must:

* be lucid, precise and unambiguous
* give the correct solution in all cases
* eventually end.

For example, if you want to instruct someone to add up a list of prices on a pocket calculator, you might write an algorithm such as the following:

```
Turn on calculator
Clear calculator
Repeat the following instructions
    Key in dollar amount
    Key in decimal point (.)
    Key in cents amount
    Press addition (+) key
Until all prices have been entered
Write down total price
Turn off calculator
```

Notice that in this algorithm the first two steps are performed once, before the repetitive process of entering the prices. After all the prices have been entered and summed, the total price can be written down and the calculator turned off. These final two activities are also performed only once. This algorithm satisfies the desired list of properties: it lists all the steps in the correct order from top to bottom in a definite and unambiguous fashion until a correct solution is reached. Notice that the steps to be repeated (entering and summing the prices) are indented, both to separate them from those steps performed only once and to emphasise the repetitive nature of their action. It is important to use indentation when writing solution algorithms because it helps to differentiate between the different control structures.

What is pseudocode?

Pseudocode and flowcharts are both popular ways of representing algorithms. Flowcharts are discussed in Appendix 1, while pseudocode has been chosen as the primary method of representing an algorithm because it is easy to read and write, and allows the programmer to concentrate on the logic of the problem. Pseudocode is really structured English. It is English that has been formalised and abbreviated to look like the high-level computer languages.

There is no standard pseudocode at present. Authors seem to adopt their own special techniques and sets of rules, which often resemble a particular programming language. This book attempts to establish a standard pseudocode for use by all programmers, regardless of the programming language they choose. Like many versions of pseudocode, this version has certain conventions:

1 Statements are written in simple English.
2 Each instruction is written on a separate line.
3 Keywords and indentation are used to signify particular control structures.
4 Each set of instructions is written from top to bottom, with only one entry and one exit.
5 Groups of statements may be formed into modules, and that module given a name.

1.5 Program data

Because programs are written to process data, you must have a good understanding of the nature and structure of the data being processed. Data within a program may be a single variable, such as an integer or a character, or a group item (sometimes called an aggregate), such as an array or a file.

Variables, constants and literals

A variable is the name given to a collection of memory cells designed to store a particular data item. It is called a *variable* because the value stored in those memory cells may change or vary as the program executes. For example, a variable called total_amount may contain several values during the execution of the program.

A constant is a data item with a name and a value that remain the same during the execution of the program. For example, the name *fifty* may be given to a data item that contains the value 50.

A literal is a constant whose name is the written representation of its value. For example, the data item may contain the literal '50'.

Data types

At the beginning of a program, the programmer must clearly define the form or type of the data to be collected. The data types can be elementary data items or data structures.

Elementary data items

An elementary data item is one containing a single variable that is always treated as a unit. These data items are usually classified into data types. A data type consists of a set of data values and a set of operations that can be performed on those values. The most common elementary data types are:

integer:
> representing a set of whole numbers, positive, negative or zero
> e.g.   3, 576, −5

real:
> representing a set of numbers, positive or negative, which may include values before or after a decimal point. These are sometimes referred to as floating point numbers
> e.g.   19.2, 1.92E+01, −0.01

character:
> representing the set of characters on the keyboard, plus some special characters
> e.g.   'A', 'b', '$'

Boolean:
> representing a control flag or switch that may contain one of only two possible values, true or false.

Data structures

A data structure is a structure that is made up of other data items. The data items that it contains are its components, which may be elementary data items or another data structure. In a data structure, data is grouped together in a particular way, which reflects the situation with which the program is concerned. The most common data structures are:

record:
> a collection of data items or fields that all bear some relationship to one another. For example, a student record may contain the student's number, name, address and enrolled subjects.

file:
> a collection of related records. For example, a student file may contain a collection of the above student records.

array:
> a data structure that is made up of a number of variables or data items that all have the same data type and are accessed by the same name. For example, an array called *scores* may contain a collection of students' exam scores. Access to the individual items in the array is made by the use of an index or subscript beside the name of the array. For example, scores (3) represents the third score in the array called scores.

string:
> a collection of characters that can be fixed or variable. For example, the string *Jenny Parker* may represent a student's name.

Files

A popular method of storing information is to enter and store data in a file. There are several major advantages of using files:

- Several different programs can access the same data.
- The data can be entered and reused several times.
- The data can be easily updated and maintained.
- The accuracy of the data is easier to enforce.

There are two types of files in which data can be stored:

- sequential or text files, in which data is stored and retrieved sequentially
- direct or random-access files, in which data is stored and retrieved randomly, using a key or index.

Sequential files may be opened to read or to write, but not both operations on the same file. Random-access files can be opened to read and write on the same file.

Data validation

Data should always undergo a validation check before it is processed by a program. Different types of data require different checks and can be quite specific; however, the most common data validation checks are as follows:

- *Correct type:* the input data should match the data type definition stated at the beginning of the program.
- *Correct range:* the input data should be within a required set of values.
- *Correct length:* the input data – for example, string – should be the correct length.
- *Completeness:* all required fields should be present.
- *Correct date:* an incoming date should be acceptable.

Chapter summary

In this chapter, the seven steps in program development were introduced and briefly described:

1 Define the problem.
2 Outline the solution.
3 Develop the outline into an algorithm.
4 Test the algorithm for correctness.
5 Code the algorithm into a specific programming language.
6 Run the program on the computer.
7 Document and maintain the program.

Three different approaches to program design were introduced, namely procedure-driven, event-driven and data-driven program design. Procedural programming and object-oriented programming were introduced, along with top-down development and modular design.

An algorithm was defined as a set of detailed, unambiguous and ordered instructions developed to describe the processes necessary to produce the desired output from the given input. Pseudocode is an English language-like way of representing the algorithm; its advantages and some conventions for its use were listed.

Programmers need to have a good understanding of the data to be processed; therefore, data variables, constants and literals were defined, and elementary data items, data structures, files and data validation were introduced.

Pseudocode

2

Objectives

- To introduce common words, keywords and meaningful names when writing pseudocode
- To define the three basic control structures as set out in the Structure Theorem
- To illustrate the three basic control structures using pseudocode

Outline

2.1 How to write pseudocode

When designing a solution algorithm, it is necessary to keep in mind the fact that a computer will eventually perform the set of instructions you write. If you use words and phrases in the pseudocode that correspond to some basic computer operations, the translation from the pseudocode algorithm to a specific programming language becomes quite simple.

This chapter establishes six basic computer operations and introduces common words and keywords used to represent these operations in pseudocode. Each operation can be represented as a straightforward instruction in English, with keywords and indentation to signify a particular control structure.

Six basic computer operations

1 A computer can receive information

When a computer is required to receive information or input from a particular source, whether it be a terminal, a disk or any other device, the verbs Read and Get are used in the pseudocode. Read is usually used when the algorithm is to receive input from a record on a file, while Get is used when the algorithm is to receive input from the keyboard. For example, typical pseudocode instructions to receive information are:

    Read student name
    Get system date
    Read number_1, number_2
    Get tax_code

Each example uses a single verb, Read or Get, followed by one or more nouns to indicate what data is to be obtained.

2 A computer can put out information

When a computer is required to supply information or output to a device, the verbs Print, Write, Put, Output or Display are used in the pseudocode. Print is usually used when the output is to be sent to the printer, while Write is used when the output is to be written to a file. If the output is to be written to the screen, the words Put, Output or Display are used in the pseudocode. Typical pseudocode examples are:

    Print 'Program Completed'
    Write customer record to master file
    Put out name, address and postcode
    Output total_tax
    Display 'End of data'

Usually an output Prompt instruction is required before an input Get instruction. The Prompt verb causes a message to be sent to the screen, which requires the user to respond, usually by providing input. Examples are:

    Prompt for student_mark
    Get student_mark

3   A computer can perform arithmetic

Most programs require the computer to perform some sort of mathematical calculation, or to apply a formula, and for these a programmer may use either actual mathematical symbols or the words for those symbols. For instance, the same pseudocode instruction can be expressed as either of the following:

```
add number to total
total = total + number
```

Both expressions clearly instruct the computer to add one value to another, so either is acceptable in pseudocode. The equal symbol '=' is used to indicate assignment of a value as a result of some processing.

To be consistent with high-level programming languages, the following symbols can be written in pseudocode:

+ for add
− for subtract
* for multiply
/ for divide
( ) for parentheses

The verbs Compute and Calculate are also available. Some examples of pseudocode instructions to perform a calculation are:

```
divide total_marks by student_count
sales_tax = cost_price * 0.10
compute C = (F − 32) * 5/9
```

Order of operations

When writing mathematical calculations for the computer, the standard mathematical *order of operations* applies to pseudocode and to most computer languages. The first operation carried out will be any calculation contained within parentheses. Next, any multiplication or division, as it occurs from left to right, will be performed. Then, any addition or subtraction, as it occurs from left to right, will be performed.

4   A computer can assign a value to a variable or memory location

There are three instances in which you may write pseudocode to assign a value to a variable or memory location:

1 To give data an initial value in pseudocode, the verbs Initialise or Set are used.
2 To assign a value as a result of some processing, the symbols '=' or '←' are written.
3 To keep a variable for later use, the verbs Save or Store are used.

Some typical pseudocode examples are:

```
Initialise total_price to zero
Set student_count to 0
total_price = cost_price + sales_tax
total_price ← cost_price + sales_tax
store customer_num in last_customer_num
```

Note that the '=' symbol is used to assign a value to a variable as a result of some processing and is not equivalent to the mathematical '=' symbol. For this reason, some programmers prefer to use the '←' symbol to represent the assign operation.

5 A computer can compare two variables and select one of two alternative actions

An important computer operation available to the programmer is the ability to compare two variables and then, as a result of the comparison, select one of two alternative actions. To represent this operation in pseudocode, special keywords are used: IF, THEN and ELSE. The comparison of data is established in the IF clause, and the choice of alternatives is determined by the THEN or ELSE options. Only one of these alternatives will be performed. A typical pseudocode example to illustrate this operation is:

```
IF student_attendance_status is part_time THEN
    add 1 to part_time_count
ELSE
    add 1 to full_time_count
ENDIF
```

In this example the attendance status of the student is investigated, with the result that either the part_time_count or the full_time_count accumulator is incremented. Note the use of indentation to emphasise the THEN and ELSE options, and the use of the delimiter ENDIF to close the operation.

6 A computer can repeat a group of actions

When there is a sequence of processing steps that need to be repeated, two special keywords, DOWHILE and ENDDO, are used in pseudocode. The condition for the repetition of a group of actions is established in the DOWHILE clause, and the actions to be repeated are listed beneath it. For example:

```
DOWHILE student_total < 50
    Read student record
    Print student name, address to report
    add 1 to student_total
ENDDO
```

In this example it is easy to see the statements that are to be repeated, as they immediately follow the DOWHILE statement and are indented for added emphasis. The condition that controls and eventually terminates the repetition is established in the DOWHILE clause, and the keyword ENDDO acts as a delimiter. As soon as the condition for repetition is found to be false, control passes to the next statement after the ENDDO.

2.2 Meaningful names

When designing a solution algorithm, a programmer must introduce some unique names, which will be used to represent the variables or objects in the problem. All names should be meaningful. A name given to a variable is simply a method of identifying a particular storage location in the computer.

The uniqueness of a name will differentiate this location from others. Often a name describes the type of data stored in a particular variable. For instance, a variable may be one of three simple data types: an integer, a real number or a character. The name itself should be transparent enough to adequately describe the variable; for example, number1, number2 and number3 are more meaningful names for three numbers than A, B and C.

If more than one word is used in the name of a variable, then underscores are useful as word separators, for example sales_tax and word_count. Most programming languages do not tolerate a space in a variable name, as a space would signal the end of the variable name and thus imply that there were two variables. If an underscore cannot be used, then words can be joined together with the use of a capital letter as a word separator, for example salesTax and wordCount. For readability, it is not advisable to string together words all in lower case. A name such as 'carregistration' is much harder to read than 'carRegistration'.

2.3 The Structure Theorem

The Structure Theorem revolutionised program design by establishing a structured framework for representing a solution algorithm. The Structure Theorem states that it is possible to write any computer program by using only three basic control structures that are easily represented in pseudocode: sequence, selection and repetition.

The three basic control structures

1   Sequence

The sequence control structure is the straightforward execution of one processing step after another. In pseudocode, this construct is represented as a sequence of pseudocode statements:

```
statement a
statement b
statement c
```

The sequence control structure can be used to represent the first four basic computer operations listed previously: to receive information, put out information, perform arithmetic, and assign values. For example, a typical sequence of statements in an algorithm might read:

```
        add 1 to pageCount
        Print heading line1
        Print heading line2
        Set lineCount to zero
        Read customer record
```

These instructions illustrate the sequence control structure as a straightforward list of steps written one after the other, in a top-to-bottom fashion. Each instruction will be executed in the order in which it appears.

2   Selection

The selection control structure is the presentation of a condition and the choice between two actions, the choice depending on whether the condition is true or false. This construct represents the decision-making abilities of the computer and is used to illustrate the fifth basic computer operation, namely to compare two variables and select one of two alternative actions.

In pseudocode, selection is represented by the keywords IF, THEN, ELSE and ENDIF:

```
        IF condition p is true THEN
            statement(s) in true case
        ELSE
            statement(s) in false case
        ENDIF
```

If condition p is true, then the statement or statements in the true case will be executed, and the statements in the false case will be skipped. Otherwise (the ELSE statement) the statements in the true case will be skipped and statements in the false case will be executed. In either case, control then passes to the next processing step after the delimiter ENDIF. A typical pseudocode example might read:

```
        IF student_attendance_status is part_time THEN
            add 1 to part_time_count
        ELSE
            add 1 to full_time_count
        ENDIF
```

The selection control structure is discussed fully in Chapter 4.

3   Repetition

The repetition control structure can be defined as the presentation of a set of instructions to be performed repeatedly, as long as a condition is true. The basic idea of repetitive code is that a block of statements is executed again and again, until a terminating condition occurs. This construct represents the sixth basic computer operation, namely to repeat a group of actions. It is written in pseudocode as:

```
        DOWHILE condition p is true
            statement block
        ENDDO
```

The DOWHILE loop is a leading decision loop; that is, the condition is tested before any statements are executed. If the condition in the DOWHILE statement is found to be true, the block of statements following that statement is executed once. The delimiter ENDDO then triggers a return of control to the retesting of the condition. If the condition is still true, the statements are repeated, and so the repetition process continues until the condition is found to be false. Control then passes to the statement that follows the ENDDO statement. It is imperative that at least one statement within the statement block alters the condition and eventually renders it false, because otherwise the logic may result in an endless loop.

Here is a pseudocode example that represents the repetition control structure:

```
Set student_total to zero
DOWHILE student_total < 50
    Read student record
    Print student name, address to report
    add 1 to student_total
ENDDO
```

This example illustrates a number of points:

1   The variable student_total is initialised before the DOWHILE condition is executed.
2   As long as student_total is less than 50 (that is, the DOWHILE condition is true), the statement block will be repeated.
3   Each time the statement block is executed, one instruction within that block will cause the variable student_total to be incremented.
4   After 50 iterations, student_total will equal 50, which causes the DOWHILE condition to become false and the repetition to cease.

It is important to realise that the initialising and subsequent incrementing of the variable tested in the condition is an essential feature of the DOWHILE construct. The repetition control structure is discussed fully in Chapter 5.

Chapter summary

In this chapter, six basic computer operations – to receive information, put out information, perform arithmetic, assign a value to a variable, decide between two alternative actions, and repeat a group of actions – were listed, along with the pseudocode words and keywords to represent them. Typical pseudocode examples were given as illustrations, and the importance of using meaningful names was discussed.

The Structure Theorem was introduced. It states that it is possible to write any computer program by using only three basic control structures: sequence, selection and repetition. Each control structure was defined, and its association with each of the six basic computer operations was indicated. Pseudocode examples for each control structure were provided.

Developing an algorithm

3

Define the problem...

Design the solution...

work through the solution.

Objectives

- To introduce methods of analysing a problem and developing a solution
- To develop simple algorithms using the sequence control structure
- To introduce methods of manually checking the developed solution

Outline

3.1 Defining the problem

Chapter 1 described seven steps in the development of a computer program. The very first step, and one of the most important, is defining the problem. This involves carefully reading and rereading the problem until you understand completely what is required. Quite often, additional information will need to be sought to help resolve any ambiguities or deficiencies in the problem specifications. To help with this initial analysis, the problem should be divided into three separate components:

1 *Input:* a list of the source data provided to the problem.
2 *Output:* a list of the outputs required.
3 *Processing:* a list of actions needed to produce the required outputs.

When reading the problem statement, the input and output components are easily identified, because they use descriptive words such as nouns and adjectives. The processing component is also identified easily. The problem statement usually describes the processing steps as actions, using verbs and adverbs.

When dividing a problem into its three different components, analyse the actual words used in the specification, and divide them into those that are descriptive and those that imply actions. It may help to underline the nouns, adjectives and verbs used in the specification.

In some programming problems, the inputs, processes and outputs may not be clearly defined. In such cases, it is best to concentrate on the outputs required. Doing this will then determine the inputs, and the way will be set for determining the processing steps required to produce the desired output.

At this stage, the processing section should be a list of what actions need to be performed, not how they will be accomplished. Do not attempt to find a solution until the problem has been completely defined. Let's look at a simple example.

EXAMPLE 3.1   Add three numbers

A program is required to read three numbers, add them together and print their total.

Tackle this problem in two stages. First, underline the nouns and adjectives used in the specification. This will establish the input and output components, as well as any objects that are required. With the nouns and adjectives underlined, our example would look like this:

A program is required to read <u>three numbers</u>, add them together and print their <u>total</u>.

By looking at the underlined nouns and adjectives, it is easy to see that the input for this problem is three numbers and the output is the total. It is helpful to write down these first two components in a simple diagram, called a defining diagram.

Input	Processing	Output
number1		total
number2		
number3		

Second, underline (in a different colour) the verbs and adverbs used in the specification. This will establish the actions required. Example 3.1 should now look like this:

A program is required to <u>read</u> three numbers, <u>add</u> them <u>together</u> and <u>print</u> their total.

By looking at the underlined words, it can be seen that the processing verbs are 'read', 'add together' and 'print'. These steps can now be added to our defining diagram to make it complete. When writing down each processing verb, also include the objects or nouns associated with each verb. The defining diagram now becomes:

Input	Processing	Output
number1	Read three numbers	total
number2	Add numbers together	
number3	Print total number	

Now that all the nouns and verbs in the specification have been considered and the defining diagram is complete, the problem has been properly defined. That is, we now understand the input to the problem, the output to be produced, and the processing steps required to convert the input to the output.

When it comes to writing down the processing steps in an algorithm, use words that describe the work to be done in terms of single specific tasks or functions. For example:

```
Read three numbers
add numbers together
Print total number
```

There is a pattern in the words chosen to describe these steps. Each action is described as a single verb followed by a two-word object. Studies have shown that if you follow this convention to describe a processing step, two benefits will result. First, you are using a disciplined approach to defining the problem and, second, the processing is being divided into separate tasks or functions. This simple operation of dividing a problem into separate functions and choosing a proper name for each function will be extremely important later, when considering algorithm modules.

EXAMPLE 3.2 Find average temperature

A program is required to prompt the terminal operator for the maximum and minimum temperature readings on a particular day, accept those readings as integers, and calculate and display to the screen the average temperature, calculated by (maximum temperature + minimum temperature)/2.

First, establish the input and output components by underlining the nouns and adjectives in the problem statement.

A program is required to prompt the terminal operator for the <u>maximum and minimum temperature readings</u> on a particular day, accept those readings as integers, and calculate and display to the screen the <u>average temperature</u>, calculated by (maximum temperature + minimum temperature)/2.

The input components are the maximum and minimum temperature readings, and the output is the average temperature. Using meaningful names, these components can be set up in a defining diagram as follows:

Input	Processing	Output
max_temp min_temp		avg_temp

Now establish the processing steps by underlining the verbs in the problem statement.

A program is required to <u>prompt</u> the terminal operator for the maximum and minimum temperature readings on a particular day, <u>accept</u> those readings as integers, and <u>calculate</u> and <u>display</u> to the screen the average temperature, calculated by (maximum temperature + minimum temperature)/2.

The processing verbs are 'prompt', 'accept', 'calculate' and 'display'. By finding the associated objects of these verbs, the defining diagram can now be completed, as follows:

Input	Processing	Output
max_temp min_temp	Prompt for temperatures Get temperatures Calculate average temperature Display average temperature	avg_temp

EXAMPLE 3.3   Compute mowing time

A program is required to read from the screen the <u>length</u> and <u>width</u> of a rectangular house block, and the <u>length</u> and <u>width</u> of the rectangular house that has been built on the block. The algorithm should then compute and display the <u>mowing time</u> required to cut the grass around the house, at the rate of two square metres per minute.

To establish the input and output components in this problem, the nouns or objects have been underlined. By reading these words, you can see that the input components are the length and width of the block, and the length and width of the house. The output is the mowing time to cut the grass.

The input and output components can be set up in a defining diagram, as follows:

Input	Processing	Output
block_length		mowing_time
block_width		
house_length		
house_width		

Now the verbs and adverbs in the problem statement can be underlined.

A program is required to <u>read</u> from the screen the length and width of a rectangular house block, and the length and width of the rectangular house that has been built on the block. The algorithm should then <u>compute</u> and <u>display</u> the mowing time required to cut the grass around the house, at the rate of two square metres per minute.

The processing steps can now be added to the defining diagram:

Input	Processing	Output
block_length	Prompt for block measurements	mowing_time
block_width	Get block measurements	
house_length	Prompt for house measurements	
house_width	Get house measurements	
	Calculate mowing area	
	Calculate mowing time	

Remember that at this stage you are only concerned with the fact that the mowing time is to be calculated, not how the calculation will be performed. That will come later, when the solution algorithm is established. You must be absolutely confident of what is to be done in the program before you attempt to establish how it is to be done.

3.2 Designing a solution algorithm

Designing a solution algorithm is the most challenging task in the life cycle of a program. Once the problem has been properly defined, you can start to outline your solution. The first attempt at designing a solution algorithm usually does not result in a finished product. Steps may be left out, or some that are included may later be altered or deleted. Pseudocode is useful in this trial-and-error process, since it is relatively easy to add, delete or alter an instruction. Do not hesitate to alter algorithms, or even to discard one and start again, if you are not completely satisfied with it. If the algorithm is not correct, the program will never be.

There is some argument that the work of a programmer ends with the algorithm design. After that, a coder or trainee programmer could take over and code the solution algorithm into a specific programming language. In practice, this usually does not happen. However, it is important that you do not start coding until the necessary steps of defining the problem and designing the solution algorithm have been completed.

Here are solution algorithms for the preceding three examples. All involve sequence control structures only; there are no decisions or loops, so the solution algorithms are relatively simple.

EXAMPLE 3.4   Solution algorithm for Example 3.1

A program is required to read three numbers, add them together and print their total.

A Defining diagram

Input	Processing	Output
number1	Read three numbers	total
number2	Add numbers together	
number3	Print total number	

B Solution algorithm

The defining diagram shows what is required, and a simple calculation will establish how. Using pseudocode and the sequence control structure establish the solution algorithm as follows:

```
Add_three_numbers
    Read number1, number2, number3
    total = number1 + number2 + number3
    Print total
END
```

There are a number of points to consider in this solution algorithm:

1 A name has been given to the algorithm, namely Add_three_numbers. Algorithm names should briefly describe the function of the algorithm, and are usually expressed as a single verb followed by a two-word object.
2 An END statement at the end of the algorithm indicates that the algorithm is complete.
3 All processing steps between the algorithm name and the END statement have been indented for readability.
4 Each processing step in the defining diagram relates directly to one or more statements in the algorithm. For instance, 'Read three numbers' in the defining diagram becomes 'Read number1, number2, number3' in the algorithm; and 'Add numbers together' becomes 'total = number1 + number2 + number3'.

Now that the algorithm is complete, desk check the solution and only then translate it into a programming language. (Desk checking is covered in Section 3.3.)

EXAMPLE 3.5   Solution algorithm for Example 3.2

A program is required to prompt the terminal operator for the maximum and minimum temperature readings on a particular day, accept those readings as integers, and calculate and display to the screen the average temperature, calculated by (maximum temperature + minimum temperature)/2.

A Defining diagram

Input	Processing	Output
max_temp min_temp	Prompt for temperatures Get temperatures Calculate average temperature Display average temperature	avg_temp

B Solution algorithm

Using pseudocode, a simple calculation and the sequence control structure, the algorithm can be expressed as follows:

```
Find_average_temperature
    Prompt operator for max_temp, min_temp
    Get max_temp, min_temp
    avg_temp = (max_temp + min_temp)/2
    Output avg_temp to the screen
END
```

EXAMPLE 3.6   Solution algorithm for Example 3.3

A program is required to read from the screen the length and width of a rectangular house block, and the length and width of the rectangular house that has been built on the block. The algorithm should then compute and display the mowing time required to cut the grass around the house, at the rate of two square metres per minute.

A Defining diagram

Input	Processing	Output
block_length	Prompt for block measurements	mowing_time
block_width	Get block measurements	
house_length	Prompt for house measurements	
house_width	Get house measurements	
	Calculate mowing area	
	Calculate mowing time	

B Solution algorithm

The actions to be carried out in this algorithm are listed sequentially in the processing component of the defining diagram. These steps are expanded in the solution algorithm to include actual calculations, as follows:

```
Calculate_mowing_time
    Prompt operator for block_length, block_width
    Get block_length, block_width
    block_area = block_length * block_width
    Prompt operator for house_length, house_width
    Get house_length, house_width
    house_area = house_length * house_width
    mowing_area = block_area – house_area
    mowing _time = mowing_area/2
    Output mowing_time to screen
END
```

3.3 Checking the solution algorithm

After a solution algorithm has been established, it must be tested for correctness. This step is necessary because most major logic errors occur during the development of the algorithm, and if not detected these errors can be passed on to the program. It is much easier to detect errors in the pseudocode than in the corresponding program code. This is because once programming begins it is usually assumed that the logic of the algorithm is correct. Then, when an error is detected, your attention is focused on the individual lines of code to identify the problem, rather than on the logic expressed in the algorithm. It is often too difficult to step back and analyse the program as a whole. As a result, many frustrating hours can be wasted during testing, which could have been avoided by spending a few minutes desk checking the solution algorithm.

Desk checking involves tracing through the logic of the algorithm with some chosen test data. That is, 'walk' through the logic of the algorithm exactly as a computer would, keeping track of all major variable values on a sheet of paper. This 'playing computer' not only helps to detect errors early, but also helps you to become familiar with the way the program runs. The closer you are to the execution of the program, the easier it is to detect errors.

Selecting test data

When selecting test data to desk check an algorithm, look at the program specification and choose simple test cases that are based on the requirements of the specification, not the algorithm. By doing this, you will still be able to concentrate on *what* the program is supposed to do, not *how*.

To desk check the algorithm, you need only a few simple test cases that will follow the major paths of the algorithm logic. A much more comprehensive test will be performed once the algorithm has been coded into a programming language.

Steps in desk checking an algorithm

There are six simple steps to follow when desk checking an algorithm:

1 Choose simple input test cases that are valid. Two or three test cases are usually sufficient.
2 Establish what the expected result should be for each test case. This is one of the reasons for choosing simple test data in the first place: it is much easier to determine the total of 10, 20 and 30 than 3.75, 2.89 and 5.31!
3 Make a table on a piece of paper of the relevant variable names within the algorithm.
4 Walk the first test case through the algorithm, line by line, keeping a step-by-step record of the contents of each variable in the table as the data passes through the logic.
5 Repeat the walk-through process using the other test data cases, until the algorithm has reached its logical end.
6 Check that the expected result established in Step 2 matches the actual result developed in Step 5.

By desk checking an algorithm, you are attempting to detect errors early. It is a good idea for someone other than the author of the solution algorithm to design the test data for the program, as they are not influenced by the program logic. Desk checking will eliminate most errors, but it still cannot prove that the algorithm is 100% correct!

Now let's desk check each of the algorithms developed in this chapter. Note that the statements in the algorithm have been numbered; however, this is for desk checking purposes only and is not required at any other time.

EXAMPLE 3.7 · Desk check of Example 3.1

A Solution algorithm

```
        Add_three_numbers
1           Read number1, number2, number3
2           total = number1 + number2 + number3
3           Print total
        END
```

B Desk checking

1 Choose two sets of input test data. The three numbers selected will be 10, 20 and 30 for the first test case and 40, 41 and 42 for the second.

	First data set	Second data set
number1	10	40
number2	20	41
number3	30	42

2 Establish the expected result for each test case.

	First data set	Second data set
total	60	123

3 Set up a table of relevant variable names, and pass each test data set through the solution algorithm, statement by statement. Line numbers have been used to identify each statement within the program.

Statement number	number1	number2	number3	total
First pass				
1	10	20	30	
2				60
3				print
Second pass				
1	40	41	42	
2				123
3				print

4 Check that the expected results (60 and 123) match the actual results (the total column in the table).

This desk check, which should take no more than a few minutes, indicates that the algorithm is correct. You can now proceed to code the algorithm into a programming language. Note that if, at the end of a desk check, the actual results do not match the expected results, the solution algorithm probably contains a logic error. In this case, it is necessary to go back to the solution algorithm, fix the error, then desk check the algorithm again. (See Example 3.10.)

EXAMPLE 3.8 Desk check of Example 3.2

A Solution algorithm

```
      Find_average_temperature
1         Prompt operator for max_temp, min_temp
2         Get max_temp, min_temp
3         avg_temp = (max_temp + min_temp)/2
4         Output avg_temp to the screen
      END
```

B Desk checking

1 Choose two sets of input test data. The max_temp and min_temp values will be 30 and 10 for the first case, and 40 and 20 for the second.

	First data set	Second data set
max_temp	30	40
min_temp	10	20

2 Establish the expected result for each test case.

	First data set	Second data set
avg_temp	20	30

3 Set up a table of variable names and then pass each test data set through the solution algorithm, statement by statement, using the algorithm line numbers as indicated.

Statement number	max_temp	min_temp	avg_temp
First pass			
1, 2	30	10	
3			20
4			output
Second pass			
1, 2	40	20	
3			30
4			output

4 Check that the expected results in Step 2 match the actual results in Step 3.

EXAMPLE 3.9   Desk check of Example 3.3

A Solution algorithm

```
      Calculate_mowing_time
1         Prompt operator for block_length, block_width
2         Get block_length, block_width
3         block_area = block_length * block_width
4         Prompt operator for house_length, house_width
5         Get house_length, house_width
6         house_area = house_length * house_width
7         mowing_area = block_area – house_area
8         mowing _time = mowing_area/2
9         Output mowing_time to screen
      END
```

B Desk checking

1 Input data:

	First data set	Second data set
block_length	30	40
block_width	30	20
house_length	20	20
house_width	20	10

2 Expected results:

	First data set	Second data set
mowing_time	250 minutes	300 minutes

3 Set up a table of variable names and then pass each test data set through the solution algorithm, statement by statement.

Statement number	block_ length	block_ width	house_ length	house_ width	block_ area	house_ area	mowing_ area	mowing_ time
First pass								
1, 2	30	30						
3					900			
4, 5			20	20				
6						400		
7							500	
8								250
9								output
Second pass								
1, 2	40	20						
3					800			
4, 5			20	10				
6						200		
7							600	
8								300
9								output

4 Check that the expected results match the actual results. Yes, the expected result for each set of data matches the calculated result.

EXAMPLE 3.10   Desk check of Example 3.3, which now contains a logic error

A Solution algorithm

```
        Calculate_mowing_time
1           Prompt operator for block_length, block_width
2           Get block_length, block_width
3           block_area = block_length * block_width
4           Prompt operator for house_length, house_width
5           Get house_length, house_width
6           house_area = block_length * block_width
7           mowing_area = block_area – house_area
8           mowing_time = mowing_area / 2
9           Output mowing_time to screen
        END
```

B Desk checking

1 Input data:

	First data set	Second data set
block_length	30	40
block_width	30	20
house_length	20	20
house_width	20	10

2 Expected results:

	First data set	Second data set
mowing_time	250 minutes	300 minutes

3 Set up a table of variable names and then pass each test data set through the solution algorithm, statement by statement.

Statement number	block_ length	block_ width	house_ length	house_ width	block_ area	house_ area	mowing_ area	mowing_ time
First pass								
1, 2	30	30						
3					900			
4, 5			20	20				
6						900		
7							0	
8								0
9								output
Second pass								
1, 2	40	20						
3					800			
4, 5			20	10				
6						800		
7							0	
8								0
9								output

4 Check that the expected results match the actual results. Here, you can see that the calculation for house_area in line 6 is incorrect, because when house_area is subtracted from block_area in line 7, the result is zero, which cannot be right. The algorithm needs to be adjusted. The statement

    house_area = block_length * block_width

is changed to

    house_area = house_length * house_width

Another desk check would establish that the algorithm is now correct.

Chapter summary

The first section of this chapter was devoted to methods of analysing and defining a programming problem. You must fully understand a problem before you can attempt to find a solution. The method suggested was to analyse the actual words used in the specification with the aim of dividing the problem into three separate components: input, output and processing. Several examples were explored and the use of a defining diagram was established. It was emphasised that the processing steps should list *what* tasks need to be performed, rather than *how* they are to be accomplished.

The second section was devoted to the establishment of a solution algorithm. After the initial analysis of the problem, you must attempt to find a solution and express this solution as an algorithm. To do this, you must use the defining diagram, the correct pseudocode statements and the three basic control structures. Only algorithms using the sequence control structure were used as examples.

The third section was concerned with checking the algorithm for correctness. A method of playing computer by tracing through the algorithm step by step was introduced, with examples to previous problems given.

Programming problems

In the following problems, you will need to:

- define the problem by constructing a defining diagram
- create a solution algorithm using pseudocode
- desk check the solution algorithm using two valid test cases.

1 Construct an algorithm that will prompt an operator to input three characters, receive those three characters, and display a welcoming message to the screen such as 'Hello xxx! We hope you have a nice day'.
2 You require an algorithm that will receive two integer items from a terminal operator, and display to the screen their sum, difference, product and quotient.
3 You require an algorithm that will receive an integer from the screen, add 5 to it, double it, subtract 7 from it, and display the final number to the screen.
4 You require an algorithm that will read in a tax rate (as a percentage) and the prices of five items. The program is to calculate the total price of the items before tax and then the tax payable on those items. The tax payable is calculated by applying the tax rate percentage to the total price. Print the total price and the tax payable as output.
5 You require an algorithm to read in three values from a customer's bank account: the account balance at the beginning of the month, a total of all withdrawals from the account for the month, and a total of all deposits into the account during the month. A federal tax charge of 1% is applied to all transactions made during the month. The program is to calculate the account balance at the end of the month

by (1) subtracting the total withdrawals from the account balance at the beginning of the month, (2) adding the total deposits to this new balance, (3) calculating the federal tax (1% of total transactions – that is, total withdrawals + total deposits), and (4) subtracting this federal tax from the new balance. After these calculations, print the final end-of-month balance.

6   You require a program to read in the values from an employee's time sheet, and calculate and print the weekly pay for that employee. The values read in are the total number of regular hours worked, the total overtime hours and the hourly wage rate. Weekly pay is calculated as payment for regular hours worked, plus payment for overtime hours worked. Payment for regular hours worked is calculated as (wage rate times regular hours worked); payment for overtime hours worked is calculated as (wage rate times overtime hours worked times 1.5).

Selection control structures

4

Objectives

- To elaborate on the uses of simple selection, multiple selection and nested selection in algorithms
- To introduce the case construct in pseudocode
- To develop algorithms using variations of the selection control structure

Outline

4.1 The selection control structure

The selection control structure was introduced in Chapter 2 as the second construct in the Structure Theorem. This structure represents the decision-making abilities of a computer. That is, you can use the selection control structure in pseudocode to illustrate a choice between two or more actions, depending on whether a condition is true or false. The condition in the IF statement is based on a comparison of two items, and is usually expressed with one of the following relational operators:

<	less than
>	greater than
=	equal to
<=	less than or equal to
>=	greater than or equal to
<>	not equal to

There are a number of variations of the selection structure, as follows.

1 Simple selection (simple IF statement)

Simple selection occurs when a choice is made between two alternative paths, depending on the result of a condition being true or false. The structure is represented in pseudocode using the keywords IF, THEN, ELSE and ENDIF. For example:

```
IF account_balance < $300 THEN
    service_charge = $5.00
ELSE
    service_charge = $2.00
ENDIF
```

Only one of the THEN or ELSE paths will be followed, depending on the result of the condition in the IF clause.

2 Simple selection with null false branch (null ELSE statement)

The null ELSE structure is a variation of the simple IF structure. It is used when a task is performed only when a particular condition is true. If the condition is false, then no processing will take place and the IF statement will be bypassed. For example:

```
IF student_attendance = part_time THEN
    add 1 to part_time_count
ENDIF
```

In this case, the part_time_count field will be altered only if the student's attendance pattern is part-time.

3 Combined selection (combined IF statement)

A combined IF statement is one that contains multiple conditions, each connected with the logical operators AND or OR. If the connector AND is used to combine the conditions then *both* conditions must be true for the combined condition to be true. For example:

```
IF student_attendance = part_time
AND student_gender = female THEN
      add 1 to female_part_time_count
ENDIF
```

In this case, each student record will undergo two tests. Only those students who are female *and* whose attendance is registered as part-time will be selected, and the variable female_part_time_count will be incremented. If either condition is found to be false, the counter will remain unchanged.

If the connector OR is used to combine any two conditions then only one of the conditions needs to be true for the combined condition to be considered true. If neither condition is true, the combined condition is considered false. Changing the AND in the above example to OR dramatically changes the outcome from the processing of the IF statement.

```
IF student_attendance = part_time
OR student_gender = female THEN
      add 1 to female_part_time_count
ENDIF
```

In this example, if either or both conditions are found to be true, the combined condition will be considered true. That is, the counter will be incremented:

1 if the student is part-time, regardless of gender
   or
2 if the student is female, regardless of attendance pattern.

Only those students who are not female and not part-time will be ignored. So, female_part_time_count will contain the total count of female part-time students, male part-time students and female full-time students. As a result, female_part_time_count is no longer a meaningful name for this variable. You must fully understand the processing that takes place when combining conditions with the AND or OR logical operators.

More than two conditions can be linked together with the AND or OR operators. However, if both operators are used in the one IF statement, parentheses must be used to avoid ambiguity. Look at the following example:

```
IF record_code = '23'
OR update_code = delete
AND account_balance = zero THEN
      delete customer record
ENDIF
```

The logic of this statement is confusing. It is uncertain whether the first two conditions should be grouped together and operated on first, or the second two conditions should be grouped together and operated on first. Pseudocode algorithms should never be ambiguous. There are no precedence rules for logical operators in pseudocode, but there are precedence rules in most programming languages. Therefore, parentheses must be used in pseudocode to avoid ambiguity as to the meaning intended, as follows:

```
IF (record_code = '23'
OR update_code = delete)
AND account_balance = zero THEN
    delete customer record
ENDIF
```

The IF statement is now no longer ambiguous, and it is clear what conditions are necessary for the customer record to be deleted. The record will only be deleted if the account balance equals zero and either the record code = 23 or the update code = delete.

The NOT operator

The NOT operator can be used for the logical negation of a condition, as follows:

```
IF NOT (record_code = '23') THEN
    update customer record
ENDIF
```

Here, the IF statement will be executed for all record codes other than code '23', that is, for record codes not equal to '23'.

Note that the AND and OR operators can also be used with the NOT operator, but great care must be taken and parentheses used to avoid ambiguity, as follows:

```
IF NOT (record_code = '23'
    AND update_code = delete) THEN
    update customer record
ENDIF
```

Here, the customer record will only be updated if the record code is not equal to '23' and the update code is not equal to delete.

4   Nested selection (nested IF statement)

Nested selection occurs when the word IF appears more than once within an IF statement. Nested IF statements can be classified as linear or non-linear.

Linear nested IF statements

The linear nested IF statement is used when a field is being tested for various values and a different action is to be taken for each value.

This form of nested IF is called linear, because each ELSE immediately follows the IF condition to which it corresponds. Comparisons are made until a true condition is encountered, and the specified action is executed until the next ELSE statement is reached. Linear nested IF statements should be indented for readability, with each IF, ELSE and corresponding ENDIF aligned. For example:

```
IF record_code = 'A' THEN
    increment counter_A
ELSE
    IF record_code = 'B' THEN
        increment counter_B
    ELSE
        IF record_code = 'C' THEN
            increment counter_C
        ELSE
            increment error_counter
        ENDIF
    ENDIF
ENDIF
```

Note that there are an equal number of IF, ELSE and ENDIF statements, that each ELSE and ENDIF statement is positioned so that it corresponds with its matching IF statement, and that the correct indentation makes it easy to read and understand. A block of nested IF statements like this is sometimes referred to as 'cascading IF statements', as they cascade like a waterfall across the page.

Non-linear nested IF statements

A non-linear nested IF statement occurs when a number of different conditions need to be satisfied before a particular action can occur. It is termed non-linear because the ELSE statement may be separated from the IF statement with which it is paired. Indentation is once again important when expressing this form of selection in pseudocode. Each ELSE and ENDIF statement should be aligned with the IF condition to which it corresponds.

For instance:

```
IF student_attendance = part_time THEN
    IF student_gender = female THEN
        IF student_age > 21 THEN
            add 1 to mature_female_pt_students
        ELSE
            add 1 to young_female_pt_students
        ENDIF
    ELSE
        add 1 to male_pt_students
    ENDIF
ELSE
    add 1 to full_time_students
ENDIF
```

Note that the number of IF conditions is equal to the number of ELSE and ENDIF statements. Using correct indentation helps to see which set of IF, ELSE and ENDIF statements match. However, non-linear nested IF statements may contain logic errors that are difficult to correct, so they should be used sparingly in pseudocode. If possible, replace a series of non-linear nested IF statements with a combined IF statement. This replacement is possible in pseudocode because two consecutive IF statements act like a combined IF statement that uses the AND operator. Take as an example the following non-linear nested IF statement:

```
IF student_attendance = part_time THEN
    IF student_age > 21 THEN
        increment mature_pt_student
    ENDIF
ENDIF
```

This can be written as a combined IF statement:

```
IF student_attendance = part_time
AND student_age > 21 THEN
    increment mature_pt_student
ENDIF
```

The outcome will be the same for both pseudocode expressions, but the format of the latter is preferred, if the logic allows it, simply because it is easier to understand.

4.2 Algorithms using selection

Let us look at some programming examples that use the selection control structure. In each example, the problem will be defined, a solution algorithm will be developed and the algorithm will be manually tested. To help define the problem, the processing verbs in each example have been underlined.

EXAMPLE 4.1   Read three characters

Design an algorithm that will prompt a terminal operator for three characters, accept those characters as input, sort them into ascending sequence and output them to the screen.

A Defining diagram

Input	Processing	Output
char_1	Prompt for characters	char_1
char_2	Accept three characters	char_2
char_3	Sort three characters	char_3
	Output three characters	

B Solution algorithm

The solution algorithm requires a series of IF statements to sort the three characters into ascending sequence.

```
        Read_three_characters
1               Prompt the operator for char_1, char_2, char_3
2               Get char_1, char_2, char_3
3               IF char_1 > char_2 THEN
                    temp = char_1
                    char_1 = char_2
                    char_2 = temp
                ENDIF
4               IF char_2 > char_3 THEN
                    temp = char_2
                    char_2 = char_3
                    char_3 = temp
                ENDIF
5               IF char_1 > char_2 THEN
                    temp = char_1
                    char_1 = char_2
                    char_2 = temp
                ENDIF
6               Output to the screen char_1, char_2, char_3
        END
```

In this solution, most of the logic of the algorithm is concerned with the sorting of the three characters into ascending sequence. This sorting is carried out with the use of pseudocode that 'swaps' two items, as follows:

```
        temp = char_1
        char_1 = char_2
        char_2 = temp
```

Here, the values in the variables char_1 and char_2 are 'swapped', with the use of the temporary variable, temp. Pseudocode such as this must be written carefully to ensure that items are not lost in the shuffle.

To make the algorithm easier to read, this sorting logic can be performed using modules, as demonstrated in Chapter 8.

C Desk checking

Two sets of valid characters will be used to check the algorithm; the characters k, b and g as the first set and z, s and a as the second.

1 Input data

	First data set	Second data set
char_1	k	z
char_2	b	s
char_3	g	a

2 Expected results

	First data set	Second data set
char_1	b	a
char_2	g	s
char_3	k	z

3 Desk check table

Line numbers have been used to identify each statement within the program. Note that when desk checking the logic each IF statement is treated as a single statement.

Statement number	char_1	char_2	char_3	temp
First pass				
1, 2	k	b	g	
3	b	k		k
4		g	k	k
5				
6	output	output	output	
Second pass				
1, 2	z	s	a	
3	s	z		z
4		a	z	z
5	a	s		s
6	output	output	output	

EXAMPLE 4.2   Process customer record

A program is required to <u>read</u> a customer's name, a purchase amount and a tax code. The tax code has been validated and will be one of the following:

0   tax exempt (0%)
1   state sales tax only (3%)
2   federal and state sales tax (5%)
3   special sales tax (7%)

The program must then <u>compute</u> the sales tax and the total amount due, and <u>print</u> the customer's name, purchase amount, sales tax and total amount due.

A Defining diagram

Input	Processing	Output
cust_name	Read customer details	cust_name
purch_amt	Calculate sales tax	purch_amt
tax_code	Calculate total amount	sales_tax
	Print customer details	total_amt

B Solution algorithm

The solution algorithm requires a linear nested IF statement to calculate the sales tax.

```
     Process_customer_record
1        Read cust_name, purch_amt, tax_code
2        IF tax_code = 0 THEN
             sales_tax = 0
         ELSE
             IF tax_code = 1 THEN
                 sales_tax = purch_amt * 0.03
             ELSE
                 IF tax_code = 2 THEN
                     sales_tax = purch_amt * 0.05
                 ELSE
                     sales_tax = purch_amt * 0.07
                 ENDIF
             ENDIF
         ENDIF
3        total_amt = purch_amt + sales_tax
4        Print cust_name, purch_amt, sales_tax, total_amt
     END
```

C Desk checking

Two sets of valid input data for purchase amount and tax code will be used to check the algorithm.

1 Input data

	First data set	Second data set
purch_amt	$10.00	$20.00
tax_code	0	2

2 Expected results

	First data set	Second data set
sales_tax	0	$1.00
total_amt	$10.00	$21.00

Note that when desk checking the logic, the whole linear nested IF statement (13 lines of pseudocode) is counted as a single pseudocode statement.

3 Desk check table

Statement number	purch_amt	tax_code	sales_tax	total_amt
First pass				
1	$10.00	0		
2			0	
3				$10.00
4	print		print	print
Second pass				
1	$20.00	2		
2			$1.00	
3				$21.00
4	print		print	print

As the expected result for the two test cases matches the calculated result, the algorithm can be considered correct.

EXAMPLE 4.3   Calculate employee's pay

A program is required by a company to read an employee's number, pay rate and the number of hours worked in a week. The program is then to validate the pay rate field and the hours worked field and, if valid, compute the employee's weekly pay and then print it and the input data.

Validation: According to the company's rules, the maximum hours an employee can work per week is 60 hours, and the maximum hourly rate is $25.00 per hour. If the hours worked field or the hourly rate field is out of range, the input data and an appropriate message are to be printed and the employee's weekly pay is not to be calculated.

Weekly pay calculation: Weekly pay is calculated as hours worked times pay rate. If more than 35 hours are worked, payment for the overtime hours worked is calculated at time-and-a-half.

A Defining diagram

Input	Processing	Output
emp_no	Read employee details	emp_no
pay_rate	Validate input fields	pay_rate
hrs_worked	Calculate employee pay	hrs_worked
	Print employee details	emp_weekly_pay
		error_message

B Solution algorithm

The solution to this problem will require a series of simple IF and nested IF statements. First, the variables 'pay_rate' and 'hrs_worked' must be validated, and if either is found to be out of range, an appropriate message is to be placed into a variable called 'error_message'.

The employee's weekly pay is only to be calculated if the input variables 'pay_rate' and 'hrs_worked' are valid, so another variable, 'valid_input_fields', will be used to indicate to the program whether or not these input fields are valid.

Boolean variables

The variable valid_input_fields is a Boolean variable – that is, it may contain only one of two possible values (true or false). When using the IF statement with a Boolean variable, the IF statement can be simplified in pseudocode. For example, the following pseudocode

```
IF valid_input_fields = true THEN
    statement
ENDIF
```

can be simplified to imply '= true', and so can be written as:

```
IF valid_input_fields THEN
    statement
ENDIF
```

> Similarly, if we want to test if valid_input_fields is false, we can say in pseudocode:
>
> ```
> IF NOT valid_input_fields THEN
>     statement
> ENDIF
> ```

The variable valid_input_fields acts as an internal switch or flag to the program. It will initially be set to true, and will be assigned the value false if one of the input fields is found to be invalid. The employee's weekly pay will be calculated only if valid_input_fields is true.

```
        Compute_employee_pay
1           Set valid_input_fields to true
2           Set error_message to blank
3           Read emp_no, pay_rate, hrs_worked
4           IF pay_rate > $25 THEN
                error_message = 'Pay rate exceeds $25.00'
                Print emp_no, pay_rate, hrs_worked, error_message
                valid_input_fields = false
            ENDIF
5           IF hrs_worked > 60 THEN
                error_message = 'Hours worked exceeds 60'
                Print emp_no, pay_rate, hrs_worked, error_message
                valid_input_fields = false
            ENDIF
6           IF valid_input_fields THEN
                IF hrs_worked <= 35 THEN
                    emp_weekly_pay = pay_rate * hrs_worked
                ELSE
                    overtime_hrs = hrs_worked – 35
                    overtime_pay = overtime_hrs * pay_rate * 1.5
                    emp_weekly_pay = (pay_rate * 35) + overtime_pay
                ENDIF
                Print emp_no, pay_rate, hrs_worked, emp_weekly_pay
            ENDIF
        END
```

In this solution, there are two separate functions to be performed in the algorithm: the validation of the input data, and the calculation and printing of the employee's weekly pay. These two tasks could have been separated into modules before the algorithm was developed in pseudocode (see Chapter 8).

C Desk checking

Two sets of valid input data for pay rate and hours worked will be used to check this algorithm.

1 Input data

	First data set	Second data set
pay_rate	$10.00	$40.00
hrs_worked	40	35

2 Expected results

	First data set	Second data set
pay_rate	$10.00	$40.00
hrs_worked	40	35
emp_weekly_pay	$425.00	–
error_message	blank	Pay rate exceeds $25.00

3 Desk check table

Statement number	pay_rate	hrs_ worked	overtime_ hrs	overtime_ pay	emp_ weekly_ pay	valid_ input_ fields	error_ message	Print
First pass								
1						true		
2							blank	
3	$10.00	40						
4								
5								
6			5	75.00	425.00			Print fields
Second pass								
1						true		
2							blank	
3	$40.00	35						
4						false	Pay rate exceeds $25.00	Print message
5								
6								

4.3 The case structure

The case control structure in pseudocode is another way of expressing a linear nested IF statement. It is used in pseudocode for two reasons: it can be translated into many high-level languages, and it makes the pseudocode easier to write and understand. Nested IFs often look cumbersome in pseudocode and depend on correct structure and indentation for readability. Let us look at the example used earlier in this chapter:

```
IF record_code = 'A' THEN
    increment counter_A
ELSE
    IF record_code = 'B' THEN
        increment counter_B
    ELSE
        IF record_code = 'C' THEN
            increment counter_C
        ELSE
            increment error_counter
        ENDIF
    ENDIF
ENDIF
```

This linear nested IF structure can be replaced with a case control structure. Case is not really an additional control structure. It simplifies the basic selection control structure and extends it from a choice between two values to a choice from multiple values. In one case structure, several alternative logical paths can be represented. In pseudocode, the keywords CASE OF and ENDCASE serve to identify the structure, with the multiple values indented, as follows:

```
CASE OF single variable
    value_1 : statement block_1
    value_2 : statement block_2

        .
        .
        .

    value_n : statement block_n
    value_other : statement block_other
ENDCASE
```

The path followed in the case structure depends on the value of the variable specified in the CASE OF clause. If the variable contains value_1, statement block_1 is executed; if it contains value_2, statement block_2 is executed, and so on. The value_other is included in the event that the variable contains none of the listed values. We can now rewrite the above linear nested IF statement with a case statement, as follows:

```
CASE OF record_code
     'A'    : increment counter_A
     'B'    : increment counter_B
     'C'    : increment counter_C
     other  : increment error_counter
ENDCASE
```

In both forms of pseudocode, the processing logic is exactly the same. However, the case solution is much more readable.

Let us now look again at Example 4.2. The solution algorithm for this example was earlier expressed as a linear nested IF statement, but it could equally have been expressed as a CASE statement.

EXAMPLE 4.4   Process customer record

A program is required to <u>read</u> a customer's name, a purchase amount and a tax code. The tax code has been validated and will be one of the following:

0   tax exempt (0%)
1   state sales tax only (3%)
2   federal and state sales tax (5%)
3   special sales tax (7%)

The program must then compute the sales tax and the total amount due, and print the customer's name, purchase amount, sales tax and total amount due.

A Defining diagram

Input	Processing	Output
cust_name	Read customer details	cust_name
purch_amt	Calculate sales tax	purch_amt
tax_code	Calculate total amount	sales_tax
	Print customer details	total_amt

B Solution algorithm

The solution algorithm will be expressed using a CASE statement.

```
        Process_customer_record
1           Read cust_name, purch_amt, tax_code
2           CASE OF tax_code
                0 : sales_tax = 0
                1 : sales_tax = purch_amt * 0.03
                2 : sales_tax = purch_amt * 0.05
                3 : sales_tax = purch_amt * 0.07
            ENDCASE
3           total_amt = purch_amt + sales_tax
4           Print cust_name, purch_amt, sales_tax, total_amt
        END
```

C Desk checking

Two sets of valid input data for purchase amount and tax code will be used to check the algorithm. Note that the case structure serves as a single pseudo-code statement.

1 Input data

	First data set	Second data set
purch_amt	$10.00	$20.00
tax_code	0	2

2 Expected results

	First data set	Second data set
sales_tax	0	$1.00
total_amt	$10.00	$21.00

3 Desk check table

Statement number	purch_amt	tax_code	sales_tax	total_amt
First pass				
1	$10.00	0		
2			0	
3				$10.00
4	print		print	print
Second pass				
1	$20.00	2		
2			$1.00	
3				$21.00
4	print		print	print

As the expected result matches the actual result, the algorithm is considered correct.

Chapter summary

This chapter covered the selection control structure in detail. Descriptions and pseudo-code examples were given for simple selection, null ELSE, combined IF and nested IF statements. Several solution algorithms that used the selection structure were developed.

The case structure was introduced as a means of expressing a linear nested IF statement in a simpler and more concise form. Case is available in many high-level languages, and so is a useful construct in pseudocode.

Programming problems

Construct a solution algorithm for the following programming problems. Your solution should contain:

- a defining diagram
- a pseudocode algorithm
- a desk check of the algorithm.

1 Design an algorithm that will receive two integer items from a terminal operator, and display to the screen their sum, difference, product and quotient. Note that the quotient calculation (first integer divided by second integer) is only to be performed if the second integer does not equal zero.

2 Design an algorithm that will read two numbers and an integer code from the screen. The value of the integer code should be 1, 2, 3 or 4. If the value of the code is 1, compute the sum of the two numbers. If the code is 2, compute the difference (first minus second). If the code is 3, compute the product of the two numbers. If the code is 4, and the second number is not zero, compute the quotient (first divided by second). If the code is not equal to 1, 2, 3 or 4, display an error message. The program is then to display the two numbers, the integer code and the computed result to the screen.

3 Design an algorithm that will prompt an operator for a student's serial number and the student's exam score out of 100. Your program is then to match the exam score to a letter grade and print the grade to the screen. Calculate the letter grade as follows:

Exam score	Assigned grade
90 and above	A
80–89	B
70–79	C
60–69	D
below 60	F

4 Design an algorithm that will receive the weight of a parcel and determine the delivery charge for that parcel. Calculate the charges as follows:

Parcel weight (kg)	Cost per kg ($)
<2.5 kg	$3.50 per kg
2.5–5 kg	$2.85 per kg
>5 kg	$2.45 per kg

5 Design an algorithm that will prompt a terminal operator for the price of an article and a pricing code. Your program is then to calculate a discount rate according to the pricing code and print to the screen the original price of the article, the discount amount and the new discounted price. Calculate the pricing code and accompanying discount amount as follows:

Pricing code	Discount rate
H	50%
F	40%
T	33%
Q	25%
Z	0%

If the pricing code is Z, the words 'No discount' are to be printed on the screen. If the pricing code is not H, F, T, Q or Z, the words 'Invalid pricing code' are to be printed.

6 An architect's fee is calculated as a percentage of the cost of a building. The fee is made up as follows:
8% of the first $5000.00 of the cost of a building and
3% on the remainder if the remainder is less than or equal to $80000.00 or
2.5% on the remainder if the remainder is more than $80000.00.

Design an algorithm that will accept the cost of a building and calculate and display the architect's fee.

7 A home mortgage authority requires a deposit on a home loan according to the following schedule:

Loan ($)	Deposit
less than $25 000	5% of loan value
$25 000–$49 999	$1250 + 10% of loan over $25 000
$50 000–$100 000	$5000 + 25% of loan over $50 000

Loans in excess of $100000 are not allowed. Design an algorithm that will read a loan amount and compute and print the required deposit.

8 Design an algorithm that will receive a date in the format dd/mm/yyyy (for example, 21/07/2006) and validate it as follows:

   i   the month must be in the range 1 to 12, and

   ii the day must be in the range of 1 to 31 and acceptable for the corresponding month. (Don't forget a leap year check for February.)

9 The tax payable on taxable incomes for employees in a certain country is set out in the following table:

Taxable income	Tax payable
From $1.00 to $4461.99	Nil
From $4462.00 to $17 893.99	Nil plus 30 cents for each $ in excess of $4462.00
From $17 894.00 to $29 499.99	$4119.00 plus 35 cents for each $ in excess of $17 894.00
From $29 500.00 to $45 787.99	$8656.00 plus 46 cents for each $ in excess of $29 500.00
$45 788.00 and over	$11 179.00 plus 60 cents for each $ in excess of $45 788.00

Design an algorithm that will read as input the taxable income amount and calculate and print the tax payable on that amount.

10 A transaction record on a sales commission file contains the retail price of an item sold, a transaction code that indicates the sales commission category to which an item can belong, and the employee number of the person who sold the item. The transaction code can contain the values S, M or L, which indicate that the percentage commission will be 5%, 7% or 10% respectively. Construct an algorithm that will read a record on the file, calculate the commission owing for that record, and print the retail price, commission and employee number.

Repetition control structures

5

DESK CHECKING...

DOWHILE
you've got
nothing better
to do...

Objectives

- To develop algorithms that use the DOWHILE and REPEAT... UNTIL control structures
- To introduce a pseudocode structure for counted repetition loops
- To develop algorithms using variations of the repetition construct

Outline

5.1 Repetition using the DOWHILE structure

The solution algorithms developed so far have one characteristic in common: they show the program logic required to process just one set of input values. However, most programs require the same logic to be repeated for several sets of data. The most efficient way to deal with this situation is to establish a looping structure in the algorithm that will cause the processing logic to be repeated a number of times.

There are three different ways in which a set of instructions can be repeated, and each way is determined by where the decision to repeat is placed:

- at the beginning of the loop (leading decision loop)
- at the end of the loop (trailing decision loop)
- a counted number of times (counted loop).

Leading decision loop

In Chapter 2, the DOWHILE construct was introduced as the pseudocode representation of a repetitive loop. Its format is:

```
DOWHILE condition p is true
    statement block
ENDDO
```

The DOWHILE construct is a leading decision loop – the condition is tested before any statements are executed. In the above DOWHILE loop, the following processing takes place:

1 The logical condition p is tested.
2 If condition p is found to be true, the statements within the statement block are executed once. The delimiter ENDDO then triggers a return of control to the retesting of condition p.
3 If condition p is still true, the statements are executed again, and so the repetition process continues until the condition is found to be false.
4 If condition p is found to be false, control passes to the next statement after the delimiter ENDDO and no further processing takes place within the loop.

There are two important considerations of which you must be aware before designing a DOWHILE loop:

- The testing of the condition is at the beginning of the loop. This means that it may be necessary to perform some initial processing to adequately set up the condition before it can be tested.
- The only way to terminate the loop is to render the DOWHILE condition false. This means some process must be set up within the statement block that will eventually change the condition so that the condition becomes false. Failure to do this results in an endless loop.

Using DOWHILE to repeat a set of instructions a known number of times

When a set of instructions is to be repeated a specific number of times, a counter can be used in pseudocode, which is initialised before the DOWHILE statement and incremented just before the ENDDO statement. Let's look at an example.

EXAMPLE 5.1   Fahrenheit–Celsius conversion

Every day, a weather station receives 15 temperatures expressed in degrees Fahrenheit. A program is to be written that will accept each Fahrenheit temperature, convert it to Celsius and display the converted temperature to the screen. After 15 temperatures have been processed, the words 'All temperatures processed' are to be displayed on the screen.

A Defining diagram

Input	Processing	Output
f_temp	Get Fahrenheit temperatures	c_temp
(15 temperatures)	Convert temperatures	(15 temperatures)
	Display Celsius temperatures	
	Display screen message	

Having defined the input, output and processing, you are ready to outline a solution to the problem. This can be done by writing down the control structures needed and any extra variables that are to be used in the solution algorithm. In this example, you need:

- a DOWHILE structure to repeat the necessary processing
- a counter, called temperature_count, initialised to zero, that will control the 15 repetitions.

B Solution algorithm

```
        Fahrenheit_Celsius_conversion
1           Set temperature_count to zero
2           DOWHILE temperature_count < 15
3               Prompt operator for f_temp
4               Get f_temp
5               compute c_temp = (f_temp – 32) * 5/9
6               Display c_temp
7               add 1 to temperature_count
            ENDDO
8           Display 'All temperatures processed' to the screen
        END
```

This solution algorithm illustrates a number of points:

1 The temperature_count variable is initialised before the DOWHILE condition is executed.
2 As long as temperature_count is less than 15 (that is, the DOWHILE condition is true), the statements between DOWHILE and ENDDO will be executed.
3 The variable temperature_count is incremented once within the loop, just before the ENDDO delimiter (that is, just before it is tested again in the DOWHILE condition).
4 After 15 iterations, temperature_count will equal 15, which causes the DOWHILE condition to become false and control to be passed to the statement after ENDDO.

C Desk checking

Although the program will require 15 records to process properly, at this stage it is only necessary to check the algorithm with two valid sets of data.

1 Input data

	First data set	Second data set
f_temp	32	50

2 Expected results

	First data set	Second data set
c_temp	0	10

3 Desk check table

Statement number	temperature_count	DOWHILE condition	f_temp	c_temp
1	0			
2		true		
3, 4			32	
5				0
6				display
7	1			
2		true		
3, 4			50	
5				10
6				display
7	2			

Using DOWHILE to repeat a set of instructions an unknown number of times

1 When a trailer record or sentinel exists

When there are an unknown number of items to process, a counter cannot be used, so another way of controlling the repetition must be found. Often, a trailer record or sentinel signifies the end of the data. This sentinel is a special record or value placed at the end of valid data to signify the end of that data. It must contain a value that is clearly distinguishable from the other data to be processed. It is referred to as a sentinel because it indicates that no more data follows. Let's look at an example.

EXAMPLE 5.2   Print examination scores

A program is required to read and print a series of names and exam scores for students enrolled in a mathematics course. The class average is to be calculated and printed at the end of the report. Scores can range from 0 to 100. The last record contains a blank name and a score of 999 and is not to be included in the calculations.

A Defining diagram

Input	Processing	Output
name	Read student details	name
exam_score	Print student details	exam_score
	Calculate average score	average_score
	Print average score	

You will need to consider the following when establishing a solution algorithm:

- a DOWHILE structure to control the reading of exam scores, until it reaches a score of 999
- an accumulator for total scores, namely total_score
- an accumulator for the total students, namely total_students.

B Solution algorithm

```
       Print_examination_scores
1          Set total_score to zero
2          Set total_students to zero
3          Read name, exam_score
4          DOWHILE exam_score not = 999
5              add 1 to total_students
6              Print name, exam_score
7              add exam_score to total_score
8              Read name, exam_score
           ENDDO
9          IF total_students not = zero THEN
               average_score = total_score/total_students
               Print average_score
           ENDIF
       END
```

In this example, the DOWHILE condition tests for the existence of the trailer record or sentinel (record 999). However, this condition cannot be tested until at least one exam mark has been read. Hence, the initial processing that sets up the condition is a Read statement immediately before the DOWHILE clause (Read name, exam_score). This is known as a priming read.

The algorithm will require another Read statement, this time within the body of the loop. Its position is also important. The trailer record or sentinel must not be included in the calculation of the average score, so each time an exam score is read it must be tested for a 999 value before further processing can take place. For this reason, the Read statement is placed at the end of the loop, immediately before ENDDO, so that its value can be tested when control returns to the DOWHILE condition. As soon as the trailer record has been read, control will pass from the loop to the next statement after ENDDO – the calculation of average_score.

C Desk checking

Two valid records and a trailer record should be sufficient to desk check this algorithm.

1 Input data

	First record	Second record	Third record
score	50	100	999

2 Expected results

First name, and score of 50
Second name, and score of 100
Average score 75

3 Desk check table

Statement number	total_score	total_ students	exam_score	DOWHILE condition	average_ score
1, 2	0	0			
3			50		
4				true	
5		1			
6			print		
7	50				
8			100		
4				true	
5		2			
6			print		
7	150				
8			999		
4				false	
9					75
					print

2   When a trailer record or sentinel does not exist

When there is no trailer record or sentinel to signify the end of the data, it is necessary to check for an end-of-file marker (EOF). This EOF marker is added when the file is created, as the last character in the file. The check for EOF is positioned in the DOWHILE clause, using one of the following equivalent expressions:

DOWHILE more data
DOWHILE more records
DOWHILE records exist
DOWHILE NOT EOF

In this case, all statements between the words DOWHILE and ENDDO will be repeated until an attempt is made to read a record but no more records exist. When this occurs, a signal is sent to the program to indicate that there are no more records and so the 'DOWHILE more records' condition is rendered false. Let's look at an example.

EXAMPLE 5.3   Process student enrolments

A program is required that will read a file of student records, and select and print only the records of those students enrolled in a course unit named Programming I. Each student record contains student number, name, address, postcode, gender and course unit number. The course unit number for Programming I is 18500. Three totals are to be printed at the end of the report: total females enrolled in the course, total males enrolled in the course, and total students enrolled in the course.

A Defining diagram

Input	Processing	Output
student_record	Read student records	selected student records
• student_no	Select student records	total_females_enrolled
• name	Print selected records	total_males_enrolled
• address	Compute total females enrolled	total_students_enrolled
• postcode	Compute total males enrolled	
• gender	Compute total students enrolled	
• course_unit	Print totals	

You will need to consider the following requirements when establishing a solution algorithm:

- a DOWHILE structure to perform the repetition
- IF statements to select the required students
- accumulators for the three total fields.

B Solution algorithm

```
      Process_student_enrolments
1         Set total_females_enrolled to zero
2         Set total_males_enrolled to zero
3         Set total_students_enrolled to zero
4         Read student record
5         DOWHILE records exist
6             IF course_unit = 18500 THEN
                  print student details
                  increment total_students_enrolled
                  IF student_gender = female THEN
                      increment total_females_enrolled
                  ELSE
                      increment total_males_enrolled
                  ENDIF
              ENDIF
7             Read student record
          ENDDO
8         Print total_females_enrolled
9         Print total_males_enrolled
10        Print total_students_enrolled
      END
```

C Desk checking

Three valid student records should be sufficient to desk check this algorithm. Since student_no, name, address and postcode are not operated upon in this algorithm, they do not need to be provided as input test data.

1 Input data

	First record	Second record	Third record
course_unit	20000	18500	18500
gender	F	F	M

2 Expected results

Student number, name, address, postcode, F (2nd student)
Student number, name, address, postcode, M (3rd student)
Total females enrolled   1
Total males enrolled   1
Total students enrolled   2

3 Desk check table

Statement number	course_ unit	gender	DOWHILE condition	total_ females_ enrolled	total_ males_ enrolled	total_ students_ enrolled
1, 2, 3				0	0	0
4	20000	F				
5			true			
6						
7	18500	F				
5			true			
6	print	print		1		1
7	18500	M				
5			true			
6	print	print			1	2
7	EOF					
5			false			
8, 9, 10				print	print	print

The priming Read before the DOWHILE condition, together with the subsequent Read within the loop, immediately before the ENDDO statement, form the basic framework for DOWHILE repetitions in pseudocode. In general, all algorithms using a DOWHILE construct to process a sequential file should have the same basic pattern, as follows:

```
Process_sequential_file
    Initial processing
    Read first record
    DOWHILE more records exist
        Process this record
        Read next record
    ENDDO
    Final processing
END
```

5.2 Repetition using the REPEAT...UNTIL structure

Trailing decision loop

The REPEAT...UNTIL structure is similar to the DOWHILE structure, in that a group of statements is repeated in accordance with a specified condition. However, where the DOWHILE structure tests the condition at the beginning of the loop, a REPEAT...UNTIL structure tests the condition at the end of the loop. This means that the statements within the loop will be executed once before the condition is tested. If the condition is false, the statements will be repeated UNTIL the condition becomes true.

The format of the REPEAT...UNTIL structure is:

```
REPEAT
    statement
    statement
        .
        .
        .
    UNTIL condition is true
```

REPEAT...UNTIL is a trailing decision loop; the statements are executed once before the condition is tested. There are two considerations of which you need to be aware before using REPEAT...UNTIL.

First, REPEAT...UNTIL loops are executed when the condition is false; it is only when the condition becomes true that repetition ceases. Thus, the logic of the condition clause of the REPEAT...UNTIL structure is the opposite of DOWHILE. For instance, 'DOWHILE more records' is equivalent to 'REPEAT... UNTIL no more records', and 'DOWHILE number NOT = 99' is equivalent to 'REPEAT...UNTIL number = 99'.

Second, the statements within a REPEAT...UNTIL structure will always be executed at least once. As a result, there is no need for a priming Read when using REPEAT...UNTIL. One Read statement at the beginning of the loop is sufficient; however, an extra IF statement immediately after the Read statement must be included, to prevent the processing of the trailer record.

Let us now compare an algorithm that uses a DOWHILE structure with the same problem using a REPEAT...UNTIL structure. Consider the following DOWHILE loop:

```
Process_student_records
    Set student_count to zero
    Read student record
    DOWHILE student_number NOT = 999
        Write student record
        increment student_count
        Read student record
    ENDDO
    Print student_count
END
```

This can be rewritten as a trailing decision loop, using the REPEAT...UNTIL structure as follows:

```
Process_student_records
    Set student_count to zero
    REPEAT
        Read student record
        IF student number NOT = 999 THEN
            Write student record
            increment student_count
        ENDIF
    UNTIL student number = 999
    Print student_count
END
```

Let us look at an example.

EXAMPLE 5.4   Process inventory items

A program is required to read a series of inventory records that contain an item number, an item description and a stock figure. The last record in the file has an item number of zero. The program is to produce a low stock items report, by printing only those records that have a stock figure of less than 20 items. A heading is to be printed at the top of the report and a total low stock item count printed at the end.

A Defining diagram

Input	Processing	Output
inventory record	Read inventory records	heading
• item_number	Select low stock items	selected records
• item_description	Print low stock records	• item_number
• stock_figure	Print total low stock items	• item_description
		• stock_figure
		total_low_stock_items

You will need to consider the following requirements when establishing a solution algorithm:

- a REPEAT...UNTIL to perform the repetition
- an IF statement to select stock figures of less than 20
- an accumulator for total_low_stock_items
- an extra IF, within the REPEAT loop, to ensure the trailer record is not processed.

B Solution algorithm using REPEAT...UNTIL

```
      Process_inventory_records
1         Set total_low_stock_items to zero
2         Print 'Low Stock Items' heading
          REPEAT
3             Read inventory record
4             IF item_number > zero THEN
                  IF stock_figure < 20 THEN
                      Print item_number, item_description, stock_figure
                      increment total_low_stock_items
                  ENDIF
              ENDIF
5         UNTIL item_number = zero
6         Print total_low_stock_items
      END
```

The solution algorithm has a simple structure, with a single Read statement at the beginning of the REPEAT...UNTIL loop and an extra IF statement within the loop to ensure the trailer record is not incorrectly incremented into the total_low_stock_items accumulator.

C Desk checking

Two valid records and a trailer record (item number equal to zero) will be used to test the algorithm:

1 Input data

	First record	Second record	Third record
item_number	123	124	0
stock_figure	8	25	

2 Expected results
Low Stock Items
123 8   (first record)
Total Low Stock Items = 1

3 Desk check table

Statement number	item_number	stock_figure	REPEAT UNTIL	total_low_ stock_items	heading
1				0	
2					print
3	123	8			
4	print	print		1	
5			false		
3	124	25			
4					
5			false		
3	0				
4					
5			true		
6				print	

5.3 Counted repetition

Counted loop

Counted repetition occurs when the exact number of loop iterations is known in advance. The execution of the loop is controlled by a loop index, and instead of using DOWHILE, or REPEAT…UNTIL, the simple keyword DO is used as follows:

```
DO loop_index = initial_value to final_value
    statement block
ENDDO
```

The DO loop does more than just repeat the statement block. It will:

1 initialise the loop_index to the required initial_value
2 increment the loop_index by 1 for each pass through the loop
3 test the value of loop_index at the beginning of each loop to ensure that it is within the stated range of values
4 terminate the loop when the loop_index has exceeded the specified final_ value.

In other words, a counted repetition construct will perform the initialising, incrementing and testing of the loop counter automatically. It will also terminate the loop once the required number of repetitions has been executed.

Let us look again at Example 5.1, which processes 15 temperatures at a weather station each day. The solution algorithm can be rewritten to use a DO loop.

EXAMPLE 5.5   Fahrenheit–Celsius conversion

Every day, a weather station receives 15 temperatures expressed in degrees Fahrenheit. A program is to be written that will <u>accept</u> each Fahrenheit temperature, <u>convert</u> it to Celsius and <u>display</u> the converted temperature to the screen. After 15 temperatures have been processed, the words 'All temperatures processed' are to be <u>displayed</u> on the screen.

A Defining diagram

Input	Processing	Output
f_temp	Get Fahrenheit temperatures	c_temp
(15 temperatures)	Convert temperatures	(15 temperatures)
	Display Celsius temperatures	
	Display screen message	

B Solution algorithm

The solution will require a DO loop and a loop counter (temperature_count) to process the repetition.

```
      Fahrenheit_Celsius_conversion
1         DO temperature_count = 1 to 15
2             Prompt operator for f_temp
3             Get f_temp
4             compute c_temp = (f_temp – 32) * 5/9
5             Display c_temp
          ENDDO
6         Display 'All temperatures processed' to the screen
      END
```

Note that the DO loop controls all the repetition:

- It initialises temperature_count to 1.
- It increments temperature_count by 1 for each pass through the loop.
- It tests temperature_count at the beginning of each pass to ensure that it is within the range 1 to 15.
- It automatically terminates the loop once temperature_count has exceeded 15.

C Desk checking

Two valid records should be sufficient to test the algorithm for correctness. It is not necessary to check the DO loop construct for all 15 records.

1 Input data

	First data set	Second data set
f_temp	32	50

2 Expected results

	First data set	Second data set
c_temp	0	10

3 Desk check table

Statement number	temperature_count	f_temp	c_temp
1	1		
2, 3		32	
4			0
5			display
1	2		
2, 3		50	
4			10
5			display

Desk checking the algorithm with the two input test cases indicates that the expected results have been achieved.

A requirement of counted repetition loops is that the exact number of input data items or records needs to be known before the algorithm can be written. Counted repetition loops are used extensively with arrays or tables, as seen in Chapter 7.

Chapter summary

This chapter covered the repetition control structure in detail. Descriptions and pseudocode examples were given for leading decision loops (DOWHILE), trailing decision loops (REPEAT...UNTIL) and counted loops (DO). Several solution algorithms that used each of the three control structures were defined, developed and desk checked.

We saw that most of the solution algorithms that used the DOWHILE structure had the same general pattern. This pattern consisted of:

1 some initial processing before the loop
2 some processing for each record within the loop
3 some final processing once the loop has been exited.

Expressed as a solution algorithm, this basic pattern was developed as a general solution:

```
Process_sequential_file
    Initial processing
    Read first record
    DOWHILE more records exist
        Process this record
        Read next record
    ENDDO
    Final processing
END
```

Programming problems

Construct a solution algorithm for the following programming problems. Your solution should contain:
* a defining diagram
* a pseudocode algorithm
* a desk check of the algorithm.

1 Design an algorithm that will output the seven times table, as follows:
  7 × 1 = 7
  7 × 2 = 14
  7 × 3 = 21 . . .

2 Design an algorithm that will display to the screen the first 20 numbers, with their squares and cubes, as follows:

Number	Square	Cube
1	1	1
2	4	8
3	9	27 . . .

3 Design an algorithm that will prompt for, receive and total a collection of payroll amounts entered at the terminal until a sentinel amount of 999 is entered. After the sentinel has been entered, display the total payroll amount to the screen.

4 Design an algorithm that will read a series of integers at the terminal. The first integer is special, as it indicates how many more integers will follow. Your algorithm is to calculate the sum and average of the integers, excluding the first integer, and display these values to the screen.

5 Design an algorithm that will prompt for and receive the time expressed in 2400 format (e.g. 2305 hours), convert it to 12-hour format (e.g. 11.05 pm) and display the new time to the screen. Your program is to repeat the processing until a sentinel time of 9999 is entered.

6 Design a program that will read a file of product records, each containing the item number, the item name, the quantity sold this year and the quantity sold last year. The program is to produce a product list showing the item number, the item name, and the increase or decrease in the quantity sold this year for each item.

7 The first record of a set of records contains a bank account number and an opening balance. Each of the remaining records in the set contains the amount of a cheque drawn on that bank account. The trailer record contains a zero amount. Design a program that will read and print the bank account number and opening balance on a statement of account report. The following cheque amounts are to be read and printed on the report, each with a new running balance. Print a closing balance at the end of the report.

8 Design a program that will read a file of employee records containing employee number, employee name, hourly pay rate, regular hours worked and overtime hours worked. The company pays its employees weekly, according to the following rules:

regular pay = regular hours worked × hourly rate of pay
overtime pay = overtime hours worked × hourly rate of pay × 1.5
total pay = regular pay + overtime pay

Your program is to read the input data on each employee's record and compute and print the employee's total pay on the weekly payroll report. All input data and calculated amounts are to appear on the report. A total payroll amount is to appear at the end of the report.

9 Design an algorithm that will process the weekly employee time cards for all the employees of an organisation. Each employee time card will have three data items: an employee number, an hourly wage rate and the number of hours worked during a given week. Each employee is to be paid time-and-a-half for all hours worked over 35. A tax amount of 15% of gross salary is to be deducted. The output to the screen should display the employee's number and net pay. At the end of the run, display the total payroll amount and the average amount paid.

10 As a form of quality control, the Pancake Kitchen has recorded, on a Pancake file, two measurements for each of its pancakes made in a certain month: the thickness in mm (millimetres) and the diameter in cm (centimetres). Each record on the file contains the two measurements for a pancake, thickness followed by diameter. The last record in the file contains values of 99 for each measurement. Design a program that will read the Pancake file, calculate the minimum, the maximum and the average for both dimensions, and print these values on a report.

Pseudocode algorithms using sequence, selection and repetition

6

what a complicated chapter

Yeah! I thought this book was supposed to be SIMPLE !

Objectives

* To develop solution algorithms to eight typical programming problems using sequence, selection and repetition constructs

Outline

6.1 Eight solution algorithms

This chapter develops solution algorithms to eight programming problems of increasing complexity. All the algorithms will use a combination of sequence, selection and repetition constructs. The algorithms have been designed to be interactive or to process sequential files. Reading these algorithms will consolidate the groundwork developed in the previous chapters.

Each programming problem will be defined, the control structures required will be determined and a solution algorithm will be devised.

1 Defining the problem

It is important to divide the problem into its three components: input, output and processing. The processing component should list the tasks to be performed, that is, *what* needs to be done, not *how*. The verbs in each problem have been underlined to help identify the actions to be performed.

2 The control structures required

Once the problem has been defined, write down the control structures (sequence, selection and repetition) that may be needed, as well as any extra variables that the solution may require.

3 The solution algorithm

Having defined the problem and determined the required control structures, devise a solution algorithm and represent it using pseudocode. Each solution algorithm presented in this chapter is only one solution to the particular problem; other solutions could be equally correct.

4 Desk checking

Desk check each of the algorithms with two or more test cases.

EXAMPLE 6.1   Process number pairs

Design an algorithm that will prompt for and receive pairs of numbers from an operator at a terminal and display their sum, product and average on the screen. If the calculated sum is over 200, an asterisk is to be displayed beside the sum. The program is to terminate when a pair of zero values is entered.

A Defining diagram

Input	Processing	Output
number1	Prompt for numbers	sum
number2	Get numbers	product
	Calculate sum	average
	Calculate product	'*'
	Calculate average	
	Display sum, product, average	
	Display '*'	

B Control structures required

1 A DOWHILE loop to control the repetition
2 An IF statement to determine if an asterisk is to be displayed

C Solution algorithm

Note the use of the NOT operand with the AND logical operator.

```
Process_number_pairs
    Set sum to zero
    Prompt for number1, number2
    Get number1, number2
    DOWHILE NOT (number1 = 0 AND number2 = 0)
        sum = number1 + number2
        product = number1 * number2
        average = sum / 2
        IF sum > 200 THEN
            Display sum, '*', product, average
        ELSE
            Display sum, product, average
        ENDIF
        Prompt for number1, number2
        Get number1, number2
    ENDDO
END
```

EXAMPLE 6.2   Print student records

A file of student records consists of 'S' records and 'U' records. An 'S' record contains the student's number, name, age, gender, address and attendance pattern – full-time (F/T) or part-time (P/T). A 'U' record contains the number and name of the unit or units in which the student has enrolled. There may be more than one 'U' record for each 'S' record. Design a solution algorithm that will <u>read</u> the file of student records and <u>print</u> only the student's number, name and address on a 'STUDENT LIST'.

A Defining diagram

Input	Processing	Output
'S' records	Print heading	Heading line
• number	Read student records	selected student records
• name	Select 'S' records	• number
• address	Print selected records	• name
• age		• address
• gender		
• attendance_pattern		
'U' records		

B Control structures required

1 A DOWHILE loop to control the repetition
2 An IF statement to select 'S' records

C Solution algorithm

```
Print_student_records
    Print 'STUDENT LIST' heading
    Read student record
    DOWHILE more records exist
        IF student record = 'S' record THEN
            Print student_number, name, address
        ENDIF
        Read student record
    ENDDO
END
```

EXAMPLE 6.3   Print selected students

Design a solution algorithm that will <u>read</u> the same student file as in Example 6.2, and <u>produce</u> a report of all female students who are enrolled part-time. The report is to be headed 'FEMALE PART-TIME STUDENTS' and is to <u>show</u> the student's number, name, address and age.

A Defining diagram

Input	Processing	Output
'S' records	Print heading	Heading line
• number	Read student records	selected student records
• name	Select female P/T students	• number
• address	Print selected records	• name
• age		• address
• gender		• age
• attendance_pattern		
'U' records		

B Control structures required

1   A DOWHILE loop to control the repetition
2   An IF statement or statements to select 'S', female and part-time (P/T) students

C Solution algorithm

Several algorithms for this problem will be presented, and all are equally correct. The algorithms only differ in the way the IF statement is expressed. It is interesting to compare the three different solutions.

Solution 1 uses a non-linear nested IF:

```
Produce_part_time_female_list
    Print 'FEMALE PART-TIME STUDENTS' heading
    Read student record
    DOWHILE more records
        IF student record = 'S' record THEN
            IF attendance_pattern = P/T THEN
                IF gender = female THEN
                    Print student_number, name, address, age
                ENDIF
            ENDIF
        ENDIF
        Read student record
    ENDDO
END
```

Solution 2 uses a nested and compound IF statement:

```
Produce_part_time_female_list
    Print 'FEMALE PART-TIME STUDENTS' heading
    Read student record
    DOWHILE more records
        IF student record = 'S' record THEN
            IF (attendance_pattern = P/T
            AND gender = female) THEN
                Print student_number, name, address, age
            ENDIF
        ENDIF
        Read student record
    ENDDO
END
```

Solution 3 also uses a compound IF statement:

```
Produce_part_time_female_list
    Print 'FEMALE PART-TIME STUDENTS' heading
    Read student record
    DOWHILE more records
        IF student record = 'S' record
        AND attendance_pattern = P/T
        AND gender = female THEN
            Print student_number, name, address, age
        ENDIF
        Read student record
    ENDDO
END
```

EXAMPLE 6.4   Print and total selected students

Design a solution algorithm that will read the same student file as in Example 6.3 and produce the same 'FEMALE PART-TIME STUDENTS' report. In addition, at the end of the report you are to print the number of students who have been selected and listed, and the total number of students on the file.

A Defining diagram

Input	Processing	Output
'S' records	Print heading	Heading line
• number	Read student records	selected student records
• name	Select female P/T students	• number
• address	Print selected records	• name
• age	Compute total students	• address
• gender	Compute total selected students	• age
• attendance_pattern	Print totals	total_students
'U' records		total_selected_students

B Control structures required

1 A DOWHILE loop to control the repetition
2 IF statements to select 'S', female and P/T students
3 Accumulators for total_selected_students and total_students

C Solution algorithm

```
Produce_part_time_female_list
    Print 'FEMALE PART-TIME STUDENTS' heading
    Set total_students to zero
    Set total_selected_students to zero
    Read student record
    DOWHILE records exist
        IF student record = 'S' record THEN
            increment total_students
            IF (attendance_pattern = P/T
            AND gender = female) THEN
                increment total_selected_students
                Print student_number, name, address, age
            ENDIF
        ENDIF
        Read student record
    ENDDO
    Print total_students
    Print total_selected_students
END
```

Note the positions where the total accumulators are incremented. If these statements are not placed accurately within their respective IF statements, the algorithm could produce erroneous results.

EXAMPLE 6.5 Print student report

Design an algorithm that will read the same student file as in Example 6.4 and, for each student, print the name, number and attendance pattern from the 'S' records (student records) and the unit number and unit name from the 'U' records (enrolled units records) as follows:

```
STUDENT REPORT

Student name          ...........................................
Student number        ...........................................
Attendance            ...........................................
Enrolled units        ...........................................   ...........................................
                      ...........................................   ...........................................
                      ...........................................   ...........................................
```

At the end of the report, print the total number of students enrolled.

A Defining diagram

Input	Processing	Output
'S' records	Print heading	Heading line
• number	Read student records	detail lines
• name	Print 'S' record details	• name
• attendance_pattern	Print 'U' record details	• number
'U' records	Compute total students	• attendance_pattern
• unit_number	Print total students	• unit_number
• unit_name		• unit_name
		total_students

B Control structures required

1 A DOWHILE loop to control the repetition
2 An IF statement to select 'S' or 'U' records
3 An accumulator for total_students

C Solution algorithm

```
Print_student_report
    Print 'STUDENT REPORT' heading
    Set total_students to zero
    Read student record
    DOWHILE records exist
        IF student record = 'S' THEN
            add 1 to total_students
            Print 'Student name', name
            Print 'Student number', number
            Print 'Attendance', attendance_pattern
            Print 'Enrolled units'
        ELSE
            IF student record = 'U' THEN
                Print unit_number, unit_name
            ELSE
                Print 'student record error'
            ENDIF
        ENDIF
        Read student record
    ENDDO
    Print 'Total students', total_students
END
```

EXAMPLE 6.6   Produce sales report

Design a program that will <u>read</u> a file of sales records and <u>produce</u> a sales report. Each record in the file contains a customer's number and name, a sales amount and a tax code. The tax code is to be applied to the sales amount to determine the sales tax due for that sale, as follows:

Tax code	Sales tax
0	tax exempt
1	3%
2	5%

The report is to print a heading 'SALES REPORT', and detail lines listing the customer number, name, sales amount, sales tax and the total amount owing.

A Defining diagram

Input	Processing	Output
sales record	Print heading	Heading line
• customer_number	Read sales records	detail lines
• name	Calculate sales tax	• customer_number
• sales_amt	Calculate total amount	• name
• tax_code	Print customer details	• sales_amt
		• sales_tax
		• total_amount

B Control structures required

1 A DOWHILE loop to control the repetition
2 A case statement to calculate the sales_tax

Assume that the tax_code field has been validated and will only contain a value of 0, 1 or 2.

C Solution algorithm

```
Produce_sales_report
    Print 'SALES REPORT' heading
    Read sales record
    DOWHILE not EOF
        CASE of tax_code
            0 : sales_tax = 0
            1 : sales_tax = sales_amt * 0.03
            2 : sales_tax = sales_amt * 0.05
        ENDCASE
        total_amt = sales_amt + sales_tax
        Print customer_number, name, sales_amt, sales_tax, total_amt
        Read sales record
    ENDDO
END
```

EXAMPLE 6.7 Student test results

Design a solution algorithm that will <u>read</u> a file of student test results and <u>produce</u> a student test grades report. Each test record contains the student number, name and test score (out of 50). The program is to <u>calculate</u> for each student the test score as a percentage and to <u>print</u> the student's number, name, test score (out of 50) and letter grade on the report. The letter grade is determined as follows:

> A = 90–100%
> B = 80–89%
> C = 70–79%
> D = 60–69%
> F = 0–59%

A Defining diagram

Input	Processing	Output
Student test records	Print heading	Heading line
• student_number	Read student records	student details
• name	Calculate test percentage	• student_number
• test_score	Calculate letter grade	• name
	Print student details	• test_score
		• grade

B Control structures required

1 A DOWHILE loop to control the repetition
2 A formula to calculate the percentage
3 A linear nested IF statement to calculate the grade

(The case construct cannot be used here, as CASE is not designed to cater for a range of values such as, 0–59%.)

C Solution algorithm

```
Print_student_results
    Print 'STUDENT TEST GRADES' heading
    Read student record
    DOWHILE not EOF
        percentage = test_score * 2
        IF percentage >= 90 THEN
            grade = 'A'
        ELSE
            IF percentage >= 80 THEN
                grade = 'B'
            ELSE
                IF percentage >= 70 THEN
                    grade = 'C'
                ELSE
                    IF percentage >= 60 THEN
                        grade = 'D'
                    ELSE
                        grade = 'F'
                    ENDIF
                ENDIF
            ENDIF
        ENDIF
        Print student_number, name, test_score, grade
        Read student record
    ENDDO
END
```

Note that the linear nested IF has been worded so that all alternatives have been considered.

EXAMPLE 6.8   Gas supply billing

The Domestic Gas Supply Company records its customers' gas usage figures on a customer usage file. Each record on the file contains the customer's number, name and address, and their gas usage expressed in cubic metres. Design a solution algorithm that will read the customer usage file, calculate the amount owing for gas usage for each customer, and print a report listing each customer's number, name, address, gas usage and the amount owing.

The company bills its customers according to the following rate: if the customer's usage is 60 cubic metres or less, a rate of $2.00 per cubic metre is applied; if the customer's usage is more than 60 cubic metres, then a rate of $1.75 per cubic metre is applied for the first 60 cubic metres and $1.50 per cubic metre for the remaining usage.

At the end of the report, print the total number of customers and the total amount owing to the company.

A Defining diagram

Input	Processing	Output
customer usage records • customer_number • name • address • gas_usage	Print heading Read usage records Calculate amount owing Print customer details Compute total customers Compute total amount owing Print totals	Heading line customer details • customer_number • name • address • gas_usage • amount_owing total_customers total_amount_owing

B Control structures required

1 A DOWHILE loop to control the repetition
2 An IF statement to calculate the amount_owing
3 Accumulators for total_customers and total_amount_owing

C Solution algorithm

```
Bill_gas_customers
    Print 'CUSTOMER USAGE FIGURES' heading
    Set total_customers to zero
    Set total_amount_owing to zero
    Read customer record
    DOWHILE more records
        IF usage <= 60 THEN
            amount_owing = usage * $2.00
        ELSE
            amount_owing = (60 * $1.75) + ((usage – 60) * $1.50)
        ENDIF
        Print customer_number, name, address, gas_usage, amount_owing
        Add amount_owing to total_amount_owing
        Add 1 to total_customers
        Read customer record
    ENDDO
    Print total_customers
    Print total_amount_owing
END
```

Chapter summary

This chapter developed solution algorithms to eight typical programming problems. The approach to all eight problems followed the same pattern:

1 A defining diagram was used to define the problem.
2 The control structures required were written down, along with any extra variables required.
3 The solution algorithm was produced using pseudocode and the three basic control structures: sequence, selection and repetition.

It was noted that the solution algorithms followed the same basic pattern, although the statements within the pattern were different. This pattern was first introduced in Chapter 5, as follows:

```
Process_sequential_file
    Initial processing
    Read first record
    DOWHILE more records exist
        Process this record
        Read next record
    ENDDO
    Final processing
END
```

Programming problems

Construct a solution algorithm for the following programming problems. Your solution should contain:

* a defining diagram
* a list of control structures required
* a pseudocode algorithm
* a desk check of the algorithm.

1 Design an algorithm that will prompt for and receive a person's age in years and months and calculate and display the age in months. If the calculated months figure is more than 500, three asterisks should also appear beside the month figure. Your program is to continue processing until a sentinel of 9999 is entered.
2 Design an algorithm that will prompt for and receive the measurement for the diameter of a circle, and calculate and display the area and circumference of that circle. Your program is to continue processing until a sentinel of 999 is entered.
3 A file of student records contains name, sex (M or F), age (in years) and marital status (single or married) for each student. Design an algorithm that will read through the file and calculate the numbers of married men, single men, married women

and single women. Print these numbers on a student summary report. If any single men are over 30 years of age, print their names and ages on a separate eligible bachelors report.

4   Design an algorithm that will read a file of employee records and produce a weekly report of gross earnings for those employees. Gross earnings are earnings before tax and other deductions have been deducted. Each input record contains the employee number, the hours worked and the hourly rate of pay. Each employee's gross pay is calculated as the product of the hours worked and the rate of pay. At the end of the report, print the total gross earnings for that week.

5   Design an algorithm that will read the same file as in Problem 4, and produce a weekly report of the net earnings for those employees. Net earnings are gross earnings minus deductions. Each employee has two deductions from their gross earnings each week: tax payable (15% of gross earnings) and medical levy (1% of gross earnings). Your report is to print the gross earnings, tax payable, medical levy and net earnings for each employee. At the end of the report, print the total gross earnings, total tax, total medical levy and total net earnings.

6   A parts inventory record contains the following fields:
    • record code (only code 11 is valid)
    • part number (six characters; two alpha and four numeric, for example AA1234)
    • part description
    • inventory balance.
    Design an algorithm that will read the file of parts inventory records, validate the record code and part number on each record, and print the details of all valid inventory records that have an inventory balance equal to zero.

7   Design a program that will read the same parts inventory file described in Problem 6, validate the record code and part number on each record, and print the details of all valid records whose part numbers fall within the values AA3000 and AA3999 inclusive. Also print a count of these selected records at the end of the parts listing.

8   Design a program that will produce the same report as in Problem 7, but will also print at the end of the parts listing a count of all the records with part numbers between AA3000 and AA3999, as well as a count of all records with part numbers that begin with AA.

9   An electricity supply authority records on an electricity usage file the amount of electricity that each customer uses. This file consists of:
    a   a header record (first record), which provides the total kilowatt hours used during the month by all customers
    b   a number of detail records, each containing the customer number, customer name and electricity usage (in kilowatt hours) for the month.
    Design a solution algorithm that will read the electricity usage file and produce an electricity usage report showing the customer number, customer name, electricity usage and the amount owing. The amount owing is calculated at 11 cents for each kilowatt hour used, up to 200 hours, and 8 cents for each kilowatt hour used over 200 hours. The total electricity usage in kilowatt hours is also to be accumulated.

At the end of the program, compare the total electricity usage accumulated in the program with the value provided in the header record, and print an appropriate message if the totals are not equal.

10 Design an algorithm that will read a file of customer records showing the total amount owing on his or her credit card, and produce a report showing the customer's minimum amount due. Each customer record contains the customer's number, name, address and postcode, and total amount owing. The minimum amount due is calculated on the total amount owing, as follows:

If the total amount owing is less than $5.00, the total amount owing becomes the minimum amount due. If the total amount owing is greater than $5.00, the minimum amount due is calculated to be one-quarter of the total amount owing, provided this resulting amount is not less than $5.00. If the resulting amount is less than $5.00, the minimum amount due is $5.00.

Array processing

Array of sunshine

Objectives

- To introduce arrays and the uses of arrays
- To develop pseudocode algorithms for common operations on arrays
- To illustrate the manipulation of single- and two-dimensional arrays

Outline

7.1 Array processing

Arrays are one of the most powerful programming tools available. They provide the programmer with a way of organising a collection of homogeneous data items (that is, items that have the same type and the same length) into a single data structure. An array, then, is a data structure that is made up of a number of variables all of which have the same data type, for example all the exam scores for a class of 30 mathematics students. By using an array, a single variable name such as 'scores' can be associated with all 30 exam scores.

The individual data items that make up the array are referred to as the elements of the array. Elements in the array are distinguished from one another by the use of an index or subscript, enclosed in parentheses, following the array name, for example 'scores (3)'.

The subscript indicates the position of an element within the array; so, scores (3) refers to the third exam score, or the third element of the array scores, and scores (23) refers to the 23rd exam score.

The subscript or index may be a number or a variable, and may then be used to access any item within the valid bounds of an array, for example:

scores (6), or
scores (index)

Arrays are an internal data structure; they are required only for the duration of the program in which they are defined. They are a very convenient mechanism for storing and manipulating a collection of similar data items in a program, and you should be familiar with the operations most commonly performed on them. Arrays are sometimes referred to as tables.

Operations on arrays

The most typical operations performed on arrays are:

- loading a set of initial values into the elements of an array
- processing the elements of an array
- searching an array, using a linear or binary search, for a particular element
- writing the contents of an array to a report.

Usually, the elements of an array are processed in sequence, starting with the first element. This can be accomplished easily in pseudocode with either a DO loop or a DOWHILE loop.

Simple algorithms that manipulate arrays

The following algorithms involve the simple manipulation of arrays. Each algorithm is written using a DO loop. In each algorithm, the array is named 'array', the subscript is named 'index' and the contents of the array and the number of elements have been established. The number of elements in the array is stored in the variable number_of_elements.

EXAMPLE 7.1 Find the sum of the elements of an array

In this example, each element of the array is accumulated into a variable called sum. When all elements have been added, the variable sum is printed.

```
Find_sum_of_elements
    Set sum to zero
    DO index = 1 to number_of_elements
        sum = sum + array (index)
    ENDDO
    Print sum
END
```

EXAMPLE 7.2 Find the mean (average) of the elements of an array

In this example, each element of the array is accumulated into a variable called sum. When all elements have been added, the average of the elements is found and printed.

```
Find_element_average
    Set sum to zero
    DO index = 1 to number_of_elements
        sum = sum + array (index)
    ENDDO
    average = sum / number_of_elements
    Print average
END
```

EXAMPLE 7.3 Find the largest of the elements of an array

In this example, the elements of an array are searched to determine which element is the largest. The algorithm starts by putting the first element of the array into the variable largest_element, and then looks at the other elements of the array to see if a larger value exists. The largest value is then printed.

```
Find_largest_element
    Set largest_element to array (1)
    DO index = 2 to number_of_elements
        IF array (index) > largest_element THEN
            largest_element = array (index)
        ENDIF
    ENDDO
    Print largest_element
END
```

EXAMPLE 7.4 Find the smallest of the elements of an array

In this example, the elements of an array are searched to determine the smallest element. The algorithm starts by putting the first element of the array into the variable smallest_element, and then looks at the other elements of the array to see if a smaller value exists. The smallest value is then printed.

```
Find_smallest_element
    Set smallest_element to array (1)
    DO index = 2 to number_of_elements
        IF array (index) < smallest_element THEN
            smallest_element = array (index)
        ENDIF
    ENDDO
    Print smallest_element
END
```

EXAMPLE 7.5 Find the range of the elements of an array

In this example, the elements of an array are searched to determine the smallest and the largest elements. The algorithm starts by putting the first element of the array into the variables smallest_element and largest_element, and then looks at the other elements to see if a smaller or larger value exists. The two values are then printed.

```
Find_range_of_elements
    Set smallest_element to array (1)
    Set largest_element to array (1)
    DO index = 2 to number_of_elements
        IF array (index) < smallest_element THEN
            smallest_element = array (index)
        ELSE
            IF array (index) > largest_element THEN
                largest_element = array (index)
            ENDIF
        ENDIF
    ENDDO
    Print the range as smallest_element followed by largest_element
END
```

7.2 Initialising the elements of an array

Because an array is an internal data structure, initial values must be placed into the array before any information can be retrieved from it. These initial values can be assigned to the elements of the array as constants, or they can be read into the array from a file.

Loading constant values into an array

This method should only be used when the data in the array is unlikely to be changed – for example, the names of the 12 months of the year. To initialise such an array, establish an array called month_table, which contains 12 elements all of the same size. Then assign the elements of the array with the names of the months, one by one, as follows:

```
Initialise_month_table
    month_table(1) = 'January  '
    month_table(2) = 'February '
        :
        :
        :
    month_table(12) = 'December '
END
```

Note that each element of the array must be the size of the largest element – in this case September – so, the shorter month names must be padded with blanks (spaces).

Loading initial values into an array from an input file

Defining array elements as constants in a program is not recommended if the values change frequently, as the program will need to be changed every time an array element changes. A common procedure is to read the input values into the elements of an array from an input file.

The reading of a series of values from a file into an array can be represented by a simple DOWHILE loop. The loop should terminate when either the array is full or the input file has reached end of file. Both of these conditions can be catered for in the condition clause of the DOWHILE loop.

In the following pseudocode algorithm, values are read from an input file and assigned to the elements of an array, starting with the first element, until there are no more input values or the array is full. The array name is 'array', the subscript is 'index', and the maximum number of elements that the array can hold is max_num_elements.

```
Read_values_into_array
    Set max_num_elements to required value
    Set index to zero
    Read first input value
    DOWHILE (input values exist) AND (index < max_num_elements)
        index = index + 1
        array (index) = input value
        Read next input value
    ENDDO
    IF (input values exist) AND index = max_num_elements THEN
        Print 'Array size too small'
    ENDIF
END
```

Note that the processing will terminate when either the input file has reached EOF or the array is full. An error message will be printed if there are more input data items than there are elements in the array.

Arrays of variable size

In some programs, the number of entries in an array can vary. In this case, a sentinel value (for example, 9999) is used to mark the last element of the array, both in the initialising file of data items and in the array itself. The sentinel record will indicate the end of input records during initial processing and the last element of the array during further processing. The algorithm for loading values into an array of variable size must include a check to ensure that no attempt is made to load more entries into the array than there are elements, as in the following example:

```
Read_values_into_variable_array
    Set max_num_elements to required value
    Set index to zero
    Read first input value
    DOWHILE (input value NOT = 9999) AND (index < max_num_elements)
        index = index + 1
        array (index) = input value
        Read next input value
    ENDDO
    IF index < max_num_elements THEN
        index = index + 1
        array (index) = 9999
    ELSE
        Print 'Array size too small'
    ENDIF
END
```

Note that the processing will terminate when either the sentinel record has been read or the array is full. An error message will be printed if there are more input data items than there are elements in the array.

Paired arrays

Many arrays in business applications are paired; that is, there are two arrays that have the same number of elements. The arrays are paired because the elements in the first array correspond to the elements in the same position in the second array. For example, a sales number array can be paired with a sales name array. Both arrays would have the same number of elements, with corresponding sales numbers and sales names. When you have determined where in the sales number array a particular salesperson's number appears, retrieve the salesperson's name from the corresponding position in the sales name array. In this way, the salesperson's number and name can appear on the same report, without any extra keying.

In the following example, an algorithm has been designed to read a file of product codes and corresponding selling prices for a particular company and to load them into two corresponding arrays, named product_codes and selling_prices. In the algorithm, the subscript is 'index', and the field max_num_elements contains the total number of elements in each array.

```
Read_values_into_paired_arrays
    Set max_num_elements to required value
    Set index to zero
    Read first input record
    DOWHILE (NOT EOF input record) AND (index < max_num_elements)
        index = index + 1
        product_codes (index) = input product_code
        selling_prices (index) = input selling_price
        Read next record
    ENDDO
    IF (NOT EOF input record) AND index = max_num_elements THEN
        Print 'Array size too small'
    ENDIF
END
```

7.3 Searching an array

A common operation on arrays is to search the elements of an array for a particular data item. The reasons for searching an array may be:

- to edit an input value – that is, to check that it is a valid element of an array
- to retrieve information from an array
- to retrieve information from a corresponding element in a paired array.

When searching an array, it is an advantage to have the array sorted into ascending sequence, so that, when a match is found, the rest of the array does not have to be searched. If you find an array element that is equal to an input entry, a match has been found and the search can be stopped. Also, if you find an array element that is greater than an input entry, no match has been found and the search can be stopped. Note that if the larger entries of an array are searched more often than the smaller entries, it may be an advantage to sort the array into descending sequence.

An array can be searched using either a linear search or a binary search.

A linear search of an array

A linear search involves looking at each of the elements of the array, one by one, starting with the first element. Continue the search until either you find the element being looked for or you reach the end of the array. A linear search is often used to validate data items.

The pseudocode algorithm for a linear search of an array will require a program flag named element_found. This flag, initially set to false, will be set to true once the value being looked for is found, that is, when the current element of the array is equal to the data item being looked for. In the following algorithm, the data item being searched for is stored in the variable input_value, and the variable max_num_elements contains the total number of elements in the array.

```
Linear_search_of_an_array
    Set max_num_elements to required value
    Set element_found to false
    Set index to 1
    DOWHILE (NOT element_found) AND (index <= max_num_elements)
        IF array (index) = input_value THEN
            Set element_found to true
        ELSE
            index = index + 1
        ENDIF
    ENDDO
    IF element_found THEN
        Print array (index)
    ELSE
        Print 'value not found', input_value
    ENDIF
END
```

A binary search of an array

When the number of elements in an array exceeds 25, and the elements are sorted into ascending sequence, a more efficient method of searching the array is a binary search.

A binary search locates the middle element of the array first, and determines if the element being searched for is in the first or second half of the table. The search then points to the middle element of the relevant half table, and the comparison is repeated. This technique of continually halving the number of elements under consideration is continued until the data item being searched for is found, or its absence is detected.

In the following algorithm, a program flag named element_found is used to indicate whether the data item being looked for has been found. The variable low_element indicates the bottom position of the section of the table being searched, and high_element indicates the top position. The maximum number of elements that the array can hold is placed in the variable max_num_elements.

The binary search will continue until the data item has been found, or there can be no more halving operations (that is, low_element is not less than high_element).

```
Binary_search_of_an_array
    Set element_found to false
    Set low_element to 1
    Set high_element to max_num_elements
    DOWHILE (NOT element_found) AND (low_element <= high_element)
        index = (low_element + high_element) / 2
        IF input_value = array (index) THEN
            Set element_found to true
        ELSE
            IF input_value < array (index) THEN
                high_element = index − 1
            ELSE
                low_element = index + 1
            ENDIF
        ENDIF
    ENDDO
    IF element_found THEN
        Print array (index)
    ELSE
        Print 'value not found', input_value
    ENDIF
END
```

7.4 Writing out the contents of an array

The elements of an array can be used as accumulators of data, to be written to a report. Writing out the contents of an array involves starting with the first element of the array and continuing until all elements have been written. This can be represented by a simple DO loop.

In the following pseudocode algorithm, the name of the array is 'array' and the subscript is 'index'. The number of elements in the array is represented by number_of_elements.

```
Write_values_of_array
    DO index = 1 to number_of_elements
        Print array (index)
    ENDDO
END
```

7.5 Programming examples using arrays

EXAMPLE 7.6   Process exam scores

Design a program that will <u>prompt</u> for and <u>receive</u> 18 examination scores from a mathematics test, <u>calculate</u> the class average, and <u>display</u> all the scores and the average score to the score screen.

A Defining diagram

Input	Processing	Output
18 exam scores	Prompt for scores Get scores Calculate average score Display scores Display average score	18 exam scores average_score

B Control structures required

1 An array to store the exam scores – 'scores'
2 An index to identify each element in the array
3 A DO loop to accept the scores
4 Another DO loop to display the scores to the screen

C Solution algorithm

```
Process_exam_scores
    Set total_score to zero
    DO index = 1 to 18
        Prompt operator for score
        Get score
        scores (index) = score
        total_score = total_score + scores (index)
    ENDDO
    Compute average_score = total_score / 18
    DO index = 1 to 18
        Display scores (index)
    ENDDO
    Display average_score
END
```

EXAMPLE 7.7   Process integer array

Design an algorithm that will <u>read</u> an array of 100 integer values, <u>calculate</u> the average integer value, and <u>count</u> the number of integers in the array that are greater than the average integer value. The algorithm is to <u>display</u> the average integer value and the count of integers greater than the average.

A Defining diagram

Input	Processing	Output
100 integer values	Read integer values Compute integer average Compute integer count Display integer average Display integer count	integer_average integer_count

B Control structures required

1 An array of integer values – 'numbers'
2 A DO loop to calculate the average of the integers
3 A DO loop to count the number of integers greater than the average

C Solution algorithm

```
Process_integer_array
    Set integer_total to zero
    Set integer_count to zero
    DO index = 1 to 100
        integer_total = integer_total + numbers (index)
    ENDDO
    integer_average = integer_total / 100
    DO index = 1 to 100
        IF numbers (index) > integer_average THEN
            add 1 to integer_count
        ENDIF
    ENDDO
    Display integer_average, integer_count
END
```

EXAMPLE 7.8   Validate sales number

Design an algorithm that will <u>read</u> a file of sales transactions and <u>validate</u> the sales numbers on each record. As each sales record is read, the sales number on the record is to be verified against an array of 35 sales numbers. Any sales number not found in the array is to be <u>flagged</u> as an error.

A Defining diagram

Input	Processing	Output
sales records • sales_number	Read sales records Validate sales numbers Print error message	error_message

B Control structures required

1   A previously initialised array of sales numbers – 'sales_numbers'
2   A DOWHILE loop to read the sales file
3   A DOWHILE loop to perform a linear search of the array for the sales number
4   A variable element_found that will stop the search when the sales number is found

C Solution algorithm

```
Validate_sales_numbers
    Set max_num_elements to 35
    Read sales record
    DOWHILE sales records exist
        Set element_found to false
        Set index to 1
        DOWHILE (NOT element_found) AND (index <= max_num_elements)
            IF sales_numbers (index) = input sales number THEN
                Set element_found to true
            ELSE
                index = index + 1
            ENDIF
        ENDDO
        IF NOT element_found THEN
            Print 'invalid sales number', input sales number
        ENDIF
        Read sales record
    ENDDO
END
```

EXAMPLE 7.9   Calculate freight charge

Design an algorithm that will <u>read</u> an input weight for an item to be shipped, <u>search</u> an array of shipping weights and <u>retrieve</u> a corresponding freight charge. In this algorithm, two paired arrays, each containing six elements, have been established and initialised. The array 'shipping_weights' contains a range of shipping weights in grams, and the array 'freight_charges' contains a corresponding array of freight charges in dollars, as follows:

Shipping weights (grams)	Freight charges
1–100	3.00
101–500	5.00
501–1000	7.50
1001–3000	12.00
3001–5000	16.00
5001–9999	35.00

A Defining diagram

Input	Processing	Output
entry weight	Prompt for entry weight Get entry weight Search shipping weights array Compute freight charge Display freight charge	freight_charge error_message

B Control structures required

1 Two arrays – 'shipping_weights' and 'freight_charges' – already initialised
2 A DOWHILE loop to search the shipping_weights array and hence retrieve the freight charge
3 A variable element_found that will stop the search when the entry weight is found

C Solution algorithm

```
Calculate_freight_charge
    Set max_num_elements to 6
    Set index to 1
    Set element_found to false
    Prompt for entry weight
    Get entry weight
    DOWHILE (NOT element_found) AND (index <= max_num_elements)
        IF shipping_weights (index) < entry weight THEN
            add 1 to index
        ELSE
            Set element_found to true
        ENDIF
    ENDDO
    IF element_found THEN
        freight_charge = freight_charges (index)
        Display 'Freight charge is', freight_charge
    ELSE
        Display 'invalid shipping weight', entry weight
    ENDIF
END
```

7.6 Two-dimensional arrays

So far, all algorithms in this chapter have manipulated one-dimensional arrays; that is, only one subscript is needed to locate an element in an array. In some business applications, for example, there is a need for multidimensional arrays, in which two or more subscripts are required to locate an element in an array. The following freight charge array is an example of a two-dimensional array, and is an extension of Example 7.9 above. It is a two-dimensional array because the calculation of the freight charge to ship an article depends on two values: the shipping weight of the article, and the geographical area or zone to which it is to be shipped, namely zone 1, 2, 3 or 4.

The range of shipping weights, in grams, is provided in the same one-dimensional array as in Example 7.9, as follows:

Shipping weights (grams)
1–100
101–500
501–1000
1001–3000
3001–5000
5001–9999

Freight charges ($) (by shipping zone)			
1	2	3	4
2.50	3.50	4.00	5.00
3.50	4.00	5.00	6.50
4.50	6.50	7.50	10.00
10.00	11.00	12.00	13.50
13.50	16.00	20.00	27.50
32.00	34.00	35.00	38.00

In the freight charges array, any one of four freight charges may apply to a particular shipping weight, depending on the zone to which the shipment is to be delivered. Thus, the array is set out as having rows and columns, where the six rows represent the six shipping weight ranges, and the four columns represent the four geographical zones.

The number of elements in a two-dimensional array is calculated as the product of the number of rows and the number of columns – in this case, $6 \times 4 = 24$.

An element of a two-dimensional array is specified using the name of the array, followed by two subscripts, enclosed in parentheses and separated by a comma. The row subscript is specified first, followed by the column subscript. Thus, an element of the above freight charges array would be specified as freight_charges (row_index, column_index). So, freight_charges (5, 3) refers to the freight charge listed in the array where the fifth row and the third column intersect – that is, a charge of $20.00.

Loading a two-dimensional array

A two-dimensional array is loaded in columns within row order; all the columns for row one are loaded before moving to row two and loading the columns for that row, and so on.

In the following pseudocode algorithm, values are read from an input file of freight charges and assigned to a two-dimensional freight_charges array. The array has six rows, representing the six shipping weight ranges, and four columns, representing the four geographical shipping zones, as in the above example.

The reading of a series of values from a file into a two-dimensional array can be represented by a DO loop within a DOWHILE loop.

```
Read_values_into_array
    Set max_num_elements to 24
    Set row_index to zero
    Read input file
    DOWHILE (input values exist) AND (row_index < 6)
        row_index = row_index + 1
        DO column_index = 1 to 4
            freight_charges (row_index, column_index) = input value
            Read input file
        ENDDO
    ENDDO
    IF (input values exist) AND row_index = 6 THEN
        Print 'Array size too small'
    ENDIF
END
```

Searching a two-dimensional array

Search method 1

In the following pseudocode algorithm, the freight charges for an article are to be calculated by searching a previously initialised two-dimensional array. The input values for the algorithm are the shipping weight of the article, and the geographical zone to which it is to be shipped.

First, the one-dimensional shipping_weights array is searched for the correct weight category (row_index) and then the two-dimensional freight_charges array is looked up using that weight category (row_index) and geographical zone (column_index).

```
Calculate_Freight_Charges
    Set row_index to 1
    Set element_found to false
    Prompt for shipping_weight, zone
    Get shipping_weight, zone
    DOWHILE (NOT element_found) AND (row_index <= 6)
        IF shipping_weights (row_index) < input shipping_weight THEN
            add 1 to row_index
        ELSE
            Set element_found to true
        ENDIF
    ENDDO
    IF element_found THEN
        IF zone = (1 or 2 or 3 or 4) THEN
            freight_charge = freight_charges (row_index, zone)
            Display 'Freight charge is', freight_charge
        ELSE
            Display 'invalid zone', zone
        ENDIF
    ELSE
        Display 'invalid shipping weight', input shipping_weight
    ENDIF
END
```

Search method 2

In the following algorithm, an input employee number is validated against a two-dimensional array of employee numbers, which has 10 rows and five columns. The array is searched sequentially, by columns within rows, using two DOWHILE loops until a match is found. If no match is found, an error message is printed.

```
Search_employee_numbers
    Set row_index to 1
    Set employee_found to false
    Read input employee_number
    DOWHILE (NOT employee_found) AND (row_index <=10)
        Set column_index to 1
        DOWHILE (NOT employee_found) AND (column_index <= 5)
            IF employee_number (row_index, column_index) = input
                employee_number THEN
                Set employee_found to true
            ENDIF
            column_index = column_index + 1
        ENDDO
        row_index = row_index + 1
    ENDDO
    IF NOT employee_found THEN
        Print 'invalid employee number', input employee_number
    ENDIF
END
```

Writing out the contents of a two-dimensional array

To write out the contents of a two-dimensional array, write out the elements in the columns within a row, before moving on to the next row. This is represented in pseudocode by a DO loop within another DO loop.

In the following pseudocode algorithm, the elements of a two-dimensional array are printed to a report, by column within row, using two subscripts.

```
Write_values_of_array
    Set number_of_rows to required value
    Set number_of_columns to required value
    DO row_index = 1 to number_of_rows
        DO column_index = 1 to number_of_columns
            Print array (row_index, column_index)
        ENDDO
    ENDDO
END
```

Chapter summary

This chapter defined an array as a data structure made up of a number of variables or data items that all have the same data type and are accessed by the same name. The individual elements that make up the array are accessed by the use of an index or subscript beside the name of the array, for example scores (3).

Algorithms were developed for the most common operations on arrays, namely:

- loading a set of initial values into the elements of an array
- processing the elements of an array
- searching an array, using a linear or binary search, for a particular element
- writing out the contents of an array to a report.

Programming examples using both one- and two-dimensional arrays were developed.

Programming problems

Construct a solution algorithm for the following programming problems. Your solution should contain:

- a defining diagram
- a list of control structures required
- a pseudocode algorithm
- a desk check of the algorithm.

1 Design an algorithm that will read an array of 200 characters and display to the screen a count of the occurrences of each of the five vowels (a, e, i, o, u) in the array.

2 Design an algorithm that will accept a person's name from the screen entered as surname, first name, separated by a comma. Your program is to display the name as first name, followed by three blanks, followed by the surname.

3 Design an algorithm that will prompt for and receive 10 integers from an operator at a terminal, and then count the number of integers whose value is less than the average value of the integers. Your program is to display the average integer value and the count of integers less than the average.

4 Design an algorithm that will prompt for and receive up to 20 integers from an operator at a terminal and display to the screen the average of the integers. The operator is to input a sentinel of 999 after the required number of integers (up to 20) have been entered.

5 Design an algorithm that will read a file of student letter grades and corresponding grade points and load them into two paired arrays, as follows:

Letter grade	Grade points
A	12
B	9
C	6
D	3
F	0

Your program is to read each record on the file (which contains a letter grade followed by a grade point), validate the letter grade (which must be A, B, C, D or F), check that the grade point is numeric, and load the values into the parallel arrays. Your program is to stop processing when the file reaches EOF or the arrays are full. Print an error message if there are more records on the file than elements in the array.

6 Design an algorithm that will read a file of student records containing the student's number, name, subject number and letter grade. Your program is to use the letter grade on the student record to retrieve the corresponding grade points for that letter grade from the paired arrays that were established in Problem 5. Print a report showing each student's number and name, the subject number and the letter grade and grade point. At the end of the report, print the total number of students and the grade point average (total grade points divided by the number of students).

7 Design an algorithm that will prompt for and receive an employee number from an operator at a terminal. Your program is to search an array of valid employee numbers to check that the employee number is valid, look up a parallel array to retrieve the corresponding employee name for that number, and display the name to the screen. If the employee number is not valid, an error message is to be displayed.

8 An employee file contains records that show an employee's number, name, job code and pay code. The job codes and pay codes are three-digit codes that refer to corresponding job descriptions and pay rates, as in the following tables:

Job code	Job description
A80	Clerk
A90	Word processor
B30	Accountant
B50	Programmer
B70	Systems analyst
C20	Engineer
C40	Senior engineer
D50	Manager

Pay code	Pay rate
01	$9.00
02	$9.50
03	$12.00
04	$20.00
05	$23.50
06	$27.00
07	$33.00

Your program is to read the employee file, use the job code to retrieve the job description from the job table, use the pay code to retrieve the pay rate from the pay rate table, and print for each record the employee's number, name, job description and pay rate. At the end of the report, print the total number of employees.

9 The ACME Oil and Gas Company needs a personnel salary report for its employees, showing their expected salary increase for the next year. Each record contains the employee's number, name, gross salary, peer performance rating and supervisor performance rating. The percentage increase in salary to be applied to the gross salary is based on two factors: the peer performance rating and the supervisor performance rating, as specified in the following two-dimensional array:

Salary increase percentage table					
Peer performance rating	Supervisor performance rating				
	1	2	3	4	5
1	.013	.015	.017	.019	.021
2	.015	.017	.019	.021	.023
3	.017	.019	.021	.023	.027
4	.019	.021	.023	.025	.030
5	.021	.023	.025	.027	.040

Your program is to retrieve the percentage increase in salary, using the peer performance rating and the supervisor performance rating as indexes to look up the salary increase percentage table. Then calculate the new salary by applying the percentage increase to the gross salary figure. For each employee, print the employee's number, name, this year's gross salary and next year's gross salary. At the end of the report, print the two total gross salary figures.

10 Fred's Auto Dealership requires a program that will calculate the sales discount to be applied to a vehicle, based on its year of manufacture and type. The discount is extracted from a two-dimensional table as follows: the year of manufacture of the

vehicle is divided into six categories (2006, 2005, 2004, 2003, 2002 and 2001), and the type of car is divided into five categories (mini, small, medium, full-size and luxury). No discount is given for a vehicle older than 2001.

Year of manufacture	Discount percentage				
	Mini	**Small**	**Medium**	**Full-size**	**Luxury**
	1	2	3	4	5
2006	.050	.055	.060	.065	.070
2005	.040	.045	.050	.055	.060
2004	.030	.035	.040	.045	.050
2003	.020	.025	.030	.035	.040
2002	.010	.015	.020	.025	.030
2001	.005	.010	.015	.020	.025

Your program is to read the vehicle file, which contains the customer number and name, the make of car, year of manufacture, car type code (1, 2, 3, 4 or 5) and the sales price. Use the year of manufacture and the car type code as indexes to retrieve the discount percentage from the discount percentage table, then apply the discount percentage to the sales price to determine the discounted price of the vehicle. Print all vehicle details, including discounted price.

First steps in modularisation

8

Objectives

- To introduce modularisation as a means of dividing a problem into subtasks
- To present hierarchy charts as a pictorial representation of modular program structure
- To develop programming examples that use a simple modularised structure

Outline

8.1 Modularisation

Many solution algorithms have been presented in this book, and all were relatively simple – that is, the finished algorithm was less than one page in length. As the complexity of the programming problems increases, however, it becomes more and more difficult to consider the solution as a whole. When presented with a complex problem you may need to divide the problem into smaller parts.

To do this, first identify the major tasks to be performed, and then divide the problem into sections that represent those tasks. These sections can be considered subtasks or functions. Once the major tasks in the problem have been identified, look at each of the subtasks and identify within them further subtasks, and so on. This process of identifying first the major tasks, then further subtasks within them, is known as 'top-down design' (also known as functional decomposition or stepwise refinement).

By using this top-down design methodology, you are adopting a modular approach to program design. That is, each of the subtasks or functions will eventually become a module within a solution algorithm or program. A module, then, can be defined as a section of an algorithm that is dedicated to a single function. The use of modules makes the algorithm simpler, more systematic, and more likely to be free of errors. Since each module represents a single task, you can develop the solution algorithm task-by-task, or module-by-module, until the complete solution has been devised.

Modularisation is the process of dividing a problem into separate tasks, each with a single purpose. Top-down design methodology allows you to concentrate on the overall design of the algorithm before getting involved with the details of the lower-level modules.

The modularisation process

The division of a problem into smaller subtasks, or modules, is a relatively simple process. When you are defining the problem, write down the activities or processing steps to be performed. These activities are then grouped together to form more manageable tasks or functions, which will eventually become modules. The emphasis when defining the problem must still be on the tasks or functions that need to be performed. Each function will be made up of a number of activities, all of which contribute to the performance of a single task.

A module must be large enough to perform its task, and must include only the operations that contribute to the performance of that task. It should have a single entry, and a single exit with a top-to-bottom sequence of instructions. The name of the module should describe the work to be done as a single specific function. The convention of naming a module by using a verb followed by a two-word object is particularly important here, as it helps to identify the task or function that the module is to perform. Also, the careful naming of modules using this convention makes the algorithm and resultant code easier to follow. For example, typical module names might be:

Print_page_headings
Calculate_sales_tax
Validate_input_date

By using meaningful module names, you automatically describe the task that the module is to perform, and anyone reading the algorithm can see what the module is supposed to do.

The mainline

Since each module performs a single specific task, a mainline routine must provide the master control that ties all the modules together and coordinates their activity. This program mainline should show the main processing functions, and the order in which they are to be performed. The mainline should be easy to read, be of manageable length and show sound logic structure. Generally, you should be able to read a pseudocode mainline and see exactly what is being done in the program.

Benefits of modular design

There are a number of benefits from using modular design.

- *Ease of understanding*: each module should perform just one function.
- *Reusable code*: modules used in one program can also be used in other programs.
- *Elimination of redundancy*: using modules can help to avoid the repetition of writing out the same segment of code more than once.
- *Efficiency of maintenance*: each module should be self-contained and have little or no effect on other modules within the program.

Let us now re-look at Example 4.1 and introduce a module into the solution algorithm.

EXAMPLE 8.1   Process three characters

Design a solution algorithm that will <u>prompt</u> a terminal operator for three characters, <u>accept</u> those characters as input, <u>sort</u> them into ascending sequence and <u>output</u> them to the screen. The algorithm is to continue to read characters until 'XXX' is entered.

A Defining diagram

Input	Processing	Output
char_1	Prompt for characters	char_1
char_2	Accept three characters	char_2
char_3	Sort three characters	char_3
	Output three characters	

B Original solution algorithm

```
Process_three_characters
    Prompt the operator for char_1, char_2, char_3
    Get char_1, char_2, char_3
    DOWHILE NOT (char_1 = 'X' AND char_2 = 'X' AND char_3 = 'X')
        IF char_1 > char_2 THEN
            temp = char_1
            char_1 = char_2
            char_2 = temp
        ENDIF
        IF char_2 > char_3 THEN
            temp = char_2
            char_2 = char_3
            char_3 = temp
        ENDIF
        IF char_1 > char_2 THEN
            temp = char_1
            char_1 = char_2
            char_2 = temp
        ENDIF
        Output to the screen char_1, char_2, char_3
        Prompt operator for char_1, char_2, char_3
        Get char_1, char_2, char_3
    ENDDO
END
```

This solution looks cumbersome and involves some repetition of code, so it is an ideal candidate for modularisation, as follows.

C Solution algorithm using a module

One of the processing steps in the defining diagram is to 'sort three characters'. In the algorithm above, this sorting process is performed by three separate IF statements, one after the other. The mainline could have been simplified considerably if these three IF statements were put into a separate module called Sort_three_characters and the module was called by the mainline when required. The module would then perform the single specific task of sorting the three characters into ascending sequence. The solution algorithm would now look like this:

```
Process_three_characters
    Prompt the operator for char_1, char_2, char_3
    Get char_1, char_2, char_3
    DOWHILE NOT (char_1 = 'X' AND char_2 = 'X' AND char_3 = 'X')
        Sort_three_characters
        Output to the screen char_1, char_2, char_3
        Prompt operator for char_1, char_2, char_3
        Get char_1, char_2, char_3
    ENDDO
END

Sort_three_characters
    IF char_1 > char_2 THEN
        temp = char_1
        char_1 = char_2
        char_2 = temp
    ENDIF
    IF char_2 > char_3 THEN
        temp = char_2
        char_2 = char_3
        char_3 = temp
    ENDIF
    IF char_1 > char_2 THEN
        temp = char_1
        char_1 = char_2
        char_2 = temp
    ENDIF
END
```

The solution algorithm now consists of two modules: the mainline module Process_three_characters, and the submodule Sort_three_characters. When the mainline wants to pass control to its submodule, it simply names that module. Control will then pass to the called module, and when the processing in that module is complete, the module will pass control back to the mainline. The resultant mainline is simple and easy to read. The mainline and its module can now be represented in a hierarchy chart.

8.2 Hierarchy charts or structure charts

Once the tasks have been grouped into functions or modules, these modules can be represented graphically in a diagram. This diagram is known as a hierarchy chart, as it shows not only the names of all the modules but also their hierarchical relationship to each other.

A hierarchy chart may also be referred to as a structure chart or a visual table of contents. The hierarchy chart uses a tree-like diagram of boxes; each box represents a module in the program and the lines connecting the boxes represent the relationship of the modules to others in the program hierarchy. The chart shows no particular sequence for processing the modules; only the modules themselves in the order in which they first appear in the algorithm.

At the top of the hierarchy chart is the controlling module, or mainline. On the next level are the modules that are called directly from the mainline – that is, the modules immediately subordinate to the mainline. On the next level are the modules that are subordinate to the modules on the first level, and so on. This diagrammatic form of hierarchical relationship appears similar to an organisational chart of personnel within a large company.

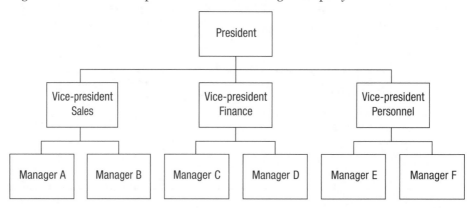

The mainline will pass control to each module when it is ready for that module to perform its task. The controlling module is said to invoke or call the subordinate module. The controlling module is therefore referred to as the 'calling module', and the subordinate module the 'called module'. On completion of its task, the called module returns control to the calling module.

The hierarchy chart for Example 8.1 is relatively simple. It shows a calling module (Process_three_characters) and a called module (Sort_three_characters):

Process_three_characters

Sort_three_characters

Example 8.1 could also have been designed to use a mainline and three modules, one for each of the main processing steps in the defining diagram, as in Example 8.2.

EXAMPLE 8.2 Process three characters

Design a solution algorithm that will <u>prompt</u> a terminal operator for three characters, <u>accept</u> those characters as input, <u>sort</u> them into ascending sequence and <u>output</u> them to the screen. The algorithm is to continue to read characters until 'XXX' is entered.

A Defining diagram

Input	Processing	Output
char_1	Prompt for characters	char_1
char_2	Accept three characters	char_2
char_3	Sort three characters	char_3
	Output three characters	

B Solution algorithm

The processing steps in the above diagram can be divided into three separate tasks: Read three characters, Sort three characters and Print three characters. Each of these tasks could then become a module in the solution algorithm, to be called from the mainline module. The solution algorithm would now look like this:

```
Process_three_characters
    Read_three_characters
    DOWHILE NOT (char_1 = 'X' AND char_2 = 'X' AND char_3 = 'X')
        Sort_three_characters
        Print_three_characters
        Read_three_characters
    ENDDO
END

Read_three_characters
    Prompt the operator for char_1, char_2, char_3
    Get char_1, char_2, char_3
END
```

```
Sort_three_characters
    IF char_1 > char_2 THEN
        temp = char_1
        char_1 = char_2
        char_2 = temp
    ENDIF
    IF char_2 > char_3 THEN
        temp = char_2
        char_2 = char_3
        char_3 = temp
    ENDIF
    IF char_1 > char_2 THEN
        temp = char_1
        char_1 = char_2
        char_2 = temp
    ENDIF
END


Print_three_characters
    Output to the screen char_1, char_2, char_3
END
```

The hierarchy chart will be made up of a mainline module and three sub-modules:

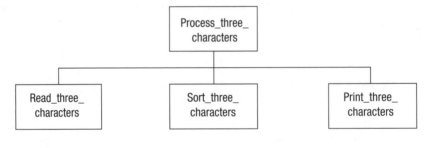

8.3 Steps in modularisation

A solution algorithm with modules requires a few more steps to be followed each time you are presented with a programming problem. Following these steps will result in effective top-down modular design.

1 Define the problem by dividing it into its three components: input, output and processing. The processing component should consist of a list of activities to be performed.
2 Group the activities into subtasks or functions to determine the modules that will make up the program. Remember that a module is dedicated to

the performance of a single task. Not all the activities may be identified at this stage. Only the modules on the first level of the hierarchy chart may be identified, with other more subordinate modules developed later.

3 Construct a hierarchy chart to illustrate the modules and their relationship to each other. Once the structure (or organisation) of the program has been developed, the order of processing of the modules can be considered.

4 Establish the logic of the mainline of the algorithm in pseudocode. This mainline should contain some initial processing before the loop, some processing within the loop, and some final processing after exiting the loop. It should contain calls to the major processing modules of the program, and should be easy to read and understand.

5 Develop the pseudocode for each successive module in the hierarchy chart. The modularisation process is complete when the pseudocode for each module on the lowest level of the hierarchy chart has been developed.

6 Desk check the solution algorithm. This is achieved by first desk checking the mainline, then each subordinate module in turn.

Your solution algorithm may contain many modules. The three most common modules are:

1 an initial processing module, containing the steps to be performed at the beginning of the algorithm, before the loop begins;

2 a processing module inside the loop containing all the steps necessary to process one record or piece of data;

3 a final processing module, containing the steps to be performed at the end of the algorithm, outside the loop.

The hierarchy chart would look like this:

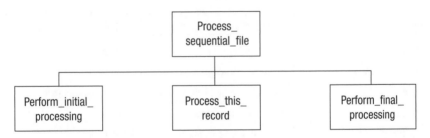

The mainline module would look like this:

```
Process_sequential_file
    Perform_initial_processing
    Read first record
    DOWHILE more records exist
        Process_this_record
        Read next record
    ENDDO
    Perform_final_processing
END
```

8.4 Programming examples using modules

The solution algorithms to the following programming examples will be developed using the above six steps in modularisation. The first example, Example 8.3, Gas Supply Billing, is a modularised version of Example 6.8.

EXAMPLE 8.3   Gas supply billing

The Domestic Gas Supply Company records its customers' gas usage figures on a customer usage file. Each record on the file contains the customer's number, name, address, and gas usage expressed in cubic metres. Design a solution algorithm that will <u>read</u> the customer usage file, <u>calculate</u> the amount owing for gas usage for each customer, and then <u>print</u> a report listing each customer's number, name, address, gas usage and the amount owing.

The company bills its customers according to the following rate: if the customer's usage is 60 cubic metres or less, a rate of $2.00 per cubic metre is applied; if the customer's usage is more than 60 cubic metres, then a rate of $1.75 per cubic metre is applied for the first 60 cubic metres and $1.50 per cubic metre for the remaining usage.

At the end of the report, print the total number of customers and the total amount owing to the company.

A Define the problem

Input	Processing	Output
customer usage records	Print heading	Heading line
• customer_number	Read usage records	customer details
• name	Calculate amount owing	• customer_number
• address	Print customer details	• name
• gas_usage	Compute total customers	• address
	Compute total amount owing	• gas_usage
	Print totals	• amount_owing
		total_customers
		total_amount_owing

B Group the activities into modules
Four modules will be used in the solution algorithm:

- a module to perform some initial processing before the loop
- a module to calculate the amount owing for each customer,

- a module to print the customer details
- a module to print the totals after exiting the loop.

C Construct a hierarchy chart

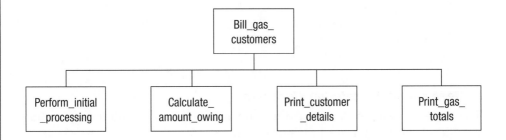

D Establish the logic of the mainline of the algorithm, using pseudocode

```
        Bill_gas_customers
1           Perform_initial_processing
2           Read customer record
3           DOWHILE more records
4               Calculate_amount_owing
5               Print_customer_details
6               Read customer record
            ENDDO
7           Print_gas_totals
        END
```

E Develop the pseudocode for each successive module in the hierarchy chart

```
        Perform_initial_processing
8           Print 'CUSTOMER USAGE FIGURES' heading
9           Set total_customers to zero
10          Set total_amount_owing to zero
        END

        Calculate_amount_owing
11          IF usage <= 60 THEN
                amount_owing = usage * $2.00
            ELSE
                amount_owing = (60 * 1.75) + ((usage – 60) * $1.50)
            ENDIF
12          add amount_owing to total_amount_owing
        END
```

```
     Print_customer_details
13       Print customer_number, name, address, gas_usage, amount_owing
14       add 1 to total_customers
     END

     Print_gas_totals
15       Print total_customers
16       Print total_amount_owing
     END
```

F Desk check the solution algorithm

The desk checking of an algorithm with modules is not different from the method developed for our previous examples:

1 Create some valid input test data.
2 List the output that the input data is expected to produce.
3 Use a desk check table to walk the data through the mainline of the algorithm to ensure that the expected output is achieved. When a submodule is called, walk the data through each line of that module as well and then return to the calling module.

1 Input data

Three test cases will be used to test the algorithm.

Customer record	gas_usage (cubic metres)
customer1	40
customer2	61
customer3	80
EOF	

2 Expected results

CUSTOMER USAGE FIGURES			
Customer Details		**Gas Usage**	**Amount Owing**
Customer1 name, address		40	$80.00
Customer2 name, address		61	$106.50
Customer3 name, address		80	$135.00
Total customers	3		
Total amount owing	$321.50		

3 Desk check table

Statement number	customer number	gas_usage	DOWHILE condition	amount_ owing	total_ amount_ owing	total_ customers	Heading
1, 8							print
9, 10					0	0	
2	customer1	40					
3			true				
4, 11				$80.00			
12					$80.00		
5, 13, 14	print	print		print		1	
6	customer2	61					
3			true				
4, 11				$106.50			
12					$186.50		
5, 13, 14	print	print		print		2	
6	customer3	80					
3			true				
4, 11				$135.00			
12					$321.50		
5, 13, 14	print	print		print		3	
6	EOF						
3			false				
7, 15, 16					print	print	

EXAMPLE 8.4   Calculate employee's pay

A company requires a program to read an employee's number, pay rate and the number of hours worked in a week. The program is then to validate the pay rate field and the hours worked field and, if valid, compute the employee's weekly pay and then print it and the input data.

Validation: According to the company's rules, the maximum hours an employee can work per week is 60 hours, and the maximum hourly rate is $25.00 per hour. If the hours worked field or the hourly rate field is out of range, the input data and an appropriate message are to be printed and the employee's weekly pay is not to be calculated.

Weekly pay calculation: Weekly pay is calculated as hours worked times pay rate. If more than 35 hours are worked, payment for the overtime hours worked is calculated at time-and-a-half.

A Define the problem

Input	Processing	Output
emp_no	Read employee details	emp_no
pay_rate	Validate input fields	pay_rate
hrs_worked	Calculate employee pay	hrs_worked
	Print employee details	emp_weekly_pay
		error_message

B Group the activities into modules

Each of the processing steps in the defining diagram will become a module in the algorithm.

C Construct a hierarchy chart

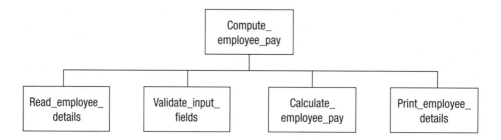

D Establish the logic of the mainline of the algorithm, using pseudocode

When each employee record is read, the hours_worked field and hourly_rate field must be validated before the weekly pay can be calculated. These validations will be performed in a module called Validate_input_fields, using a flag called valid_input_fields, which is checked in the mainline, before the weekly pay is calculated.

```
        Compute_employee_pay
1           Read_employee_details
2           DOWHILE more records
3               Validate_input_fields
4               IF valid_input_fields THEN
                    Calculate_employee_pay
                    Print_employee_details
                ENDIF
5               Read_employee_details
            ENDDO
        END
```

E Develop the pseudocode for each successive module in the hierarchy chart

```
        Read_employee_details
6           Read emp_no, pay_rate, hrs_worked
        END


        Validate_input_fields
7           Set valid_input_fields to true
8           Set error_message to blank
9           IF pay_rate > $25 THEN
                error_message = 'Pay rate exceeds $25.00'
                Print emp_no, pay_rate, hrs_worked, error_message
                valid_input_fields = false
            ENDIF
10          IF hrs_worked > 60 THEN
                error_message = 'Hours worked exceeds 60'
                Print emp_no, pay_rate, hrs_worked, error_message
                valid_input_fields = false
            ENDIF
        END
```

```
        Calculate_employee_pay
11          IF hrs_worked <= 35 THEN
                emp_weekly_pay = pay_rate * hrs_worked
            ELSE
                overtime_hrs = hrs_worked – 35
                overtime_pay = overtime_hrs * pay_rate * 1.5
                emp_weekly_pay = (pay_rate * 35) + overtime_pay
            ENDIF
        END


        Print_employee_details
12          Print emp_no, pay_rate, hrs_worked, emp_weekly_pay
        END
```

F Desk check the solution algorithm

1 Input data

Three test cases will be used to test the algorithm.

Employee Record	pay_rate	hrs_worked
employee 1	$20.00	35
employee 2	$20.00	40
employee 3	$50.00	65
EOF		

2 Expected results

Employee	Pay Rate	Hours Worked	Weekly Pay	Error Message
employee 1	$20.00	35	$700.00	
employee 2	$20.00	40	$850.00	
employee 3	$50.00	65		Pay rate exceeds $25.00
employee 3	$50.00	65		Hours worked exceeds 60

3 Desk check table

Statement number	valid_ input_ fields	pay_rate	hrs_ worked	DOWHILE condition	error_ message	emp_ weekly_ pay	ovt_hrs	ovt_pay
1, 6		$20.00	35					
2				true				
3, 7–10	true				blank			
4								
11						$700		
12		print	print			print		
5, 6		$20.00	40					
2				true				
3, 7–10	true				blank			
4								
11						$850	5	$150
12		print	print			print		
5, 6		$50.00	65					
2				true				
3, 7, 8	true				blank			
9	false	print	print		Pay rate exceeds $25			
10	false	print	print		Hours worked exceeds 60			
4								
5, 6		EOF						
2				false				

EXAMPLE 8.5   Product orders report

The Acme Spare Parts Company wants to produce a product orders report from its product orders file. Each record on the file contains the product number of the item ordered, the product description, the number of units ordered, the retail price per unit, the freight charges per unit, and the packaging costs per unit.

Your algorithm is to read the product orders file, calculate the total amount due for each product ordered and print these details on the product orders report.

The amount due for each product is calculated by multiplying the number of units ordered by the retail price of the unit. A discount of 10% is allowed on the amount due for all orders over $100.00. The freight charges and packaging costs per unit must be added to this resulting value to determine the total amount due.

The output report is to contain headings and column headings as specified in the following chart:

ACME SPARE PARTS			
ORDERS REPORT			PAGE XX
PRODUCT NO	PRODUCT DESCRIPTION	UNITS ORDERED	TOTAL AMOUNT DUE
XXXX	XXXXXXXXXX	XXX	XXXXX
XXXX	XXXXXXXXXX	XXX	XXXXX

Each detail line is to contain the product number, product description, number of units ordered and the total amount due for the order. There is to be an allowance of 45 detail lines per page.

A Define the problem

Input	Processing	Output
Product orders record	Print headings as required	Main headings
• prod_number	Read order record	column headings
• prod_description	Calculate total amount due	page number
• no_of_units	Print order details	detail lines
• retail_price		• prod_number
• freight_charge		• prod_description
• packaging_cost		• no_of_units
		• total_amount_due

B Group the activities into modules

The four steps in the processing component of the defining diagram will become the four modules in the algorithm. Note that Print_page_headings is a reusable module that is called whenever the report needs to skip to a new page.

C Construct a hierarchy chart

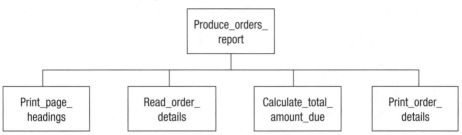

D Establish the logic of the mainline of the algorithm, using pseudocode

```
     Produce_orders_report
1        Set page_count to zero
2        Print_page_headings
3        Read_order_details
4        DOWHILE more records
5            IF line_count > 45 THEN
                 Print_page_headings
             ENDIF
6            Calculate_total_amount_due
7            Print_order_details
8            Read_order_details
         ENDDO
     END
```

E Develop pseudocode for each successive module in the hierarchy chart

The pseudocode for Print_page_headings is standard for a page heading routine that will increment the page counter, print a series of headings and reset the line counter.

```
     Print_page_headings
9        Add 1 to page_count
10       Print main heading 'ACME SPARE PARTS'
11       Print heading 'ORDERS REPORT'
12       Print column headings 1
13       Print column headings 2
14       Print blank line
15       Set line_count to zero
     END

     Read_order_details
16       Read product order record
     END
```

```
      Calculate_total_amount_due
17        amount_due = no_of_units * retail_price
18        IF amount_due > $100.00 THEN
              discount = amount_due * 0.1
          ELSE
              discount = zero
          ENDIF
19        amount_due = amount_due – discount
20        freight_due = freight_charge * no_of_units
21        packaging_due = packaging_charge * no_of_units
22        total_amount_due = amount_due + freight_due + packaging_due
      END


      Print_order_details
23        Print prod_number, prod_description, no_of_units, total_amount_due
24        add 1 to line_count
      END
```

F Desk check the solution algorithm

1 Input data

Three test cases will be used to test the algorithm. To test for correct page skipping, we would temporarily reduce the line limit from 45 to a conveniently small number – for example, two.

Record	prod_no	prod_description	no_of_units	retail_price	freight_charge	packaging_charge
1	100	Rubber hose	10	$1.00	$0.20	$0.50
2	200	Steel pipe	20	$2.00	$0.10	$0.20
3	300	Steel bolt	100	$3.00	$0.10	$0.20
EOF						

2 Expected results

```
ACME SPARE PARTS
ORDERS REPORT                                                    PAGE 1
PRODUCT NO        PRODUCT DESCRIPTION    UNITS ORDERED    TOTAL AMOUNT DUE
100               Rubber hose                 10                  $17.00
200               Steel pipe                  20                  $46.00
300               Steel bolt                 100                 $300.00
```

3 Desk check table

Statement number	DOWHILE condition	page_ count	line_ count	prod_no	no_of_ units	retail_ price	freight_ charge	pckg_ charge	total_ amount_ due
1		0							
2, 9–15		1	0						
3, 16				100	10	1.00	0.20	0.50	
4	true								
5									
6, 17–22									17.00
7, 23–24			1	print	print				print
8, 16				200	20	2.00	0.10	0.20	
4	true								
5									
6, 17–22									46.00
7, 23–24			2	print	print				print
8, 16				300	100	3.00	0.10	0.20	
4	true								
5									
6, 17–22									300.00
7, 23–24			3	print	print				print
8				EOF					
4	false								

Chapter summary

This chapter introduced a modular approach to program design. A module was defined as a section of an algorithm that is dedicated to the performance of a single function. Top-down design was defined as the process of dividing a problem into major tasks and then into further subtasks within those major tasks until all the tasks have been identified. Programming examples were provided showing the benefits of using modularisation.

Hierarchy charts were introduced as a method of illustrating the structure of a program that contains modules. Hierarchy charts show the names of all the modules and their hierarchical relationship to each other.

The steps in modularisation that a programmer must follow were listed. These were: define the problem; group the activities into subtasks or functions; construct a hierarchy chart; establish the logic of the mainline, using pseudocode; develop the pseudocode for each successive module in the hierarchy chart; and desk check the solution algorithm.

Programming examples using these six steps in modularisation were then developed in pseudocode.

Programming problems

Construct a solution algorithm for the following programming problems. To obtain your final solution, you should:

* define the problem
* group the activities into modules
* construct a hierarchy chart
* establish the logic of the mainline using pseudocode
* develop the pseudocode for each successive module in the hierarchy chart
* desk check the solution algorithm.

1 Design an algorithm that will prompt for and accept an employee's annual salary, and calculate the annual income tax due on that salary. Income tax is calculated according to the following table and is to be displayed on the screen.

Portion of salary	Income tax rate (%)
$0 to $4999.99	0
$5000 to $9999.99	6
$10 000 to $19 999.99	15
$20 000 to $29 999.99	20
$30 000 to $39 999.99	25
$40 000 and above	30

Your program is to continue to process salaries until a salary of zero is entered.

2 Design an algorithm that will prompt for and accept four numbers, sort them into ascending sequence and display them to the screen.

3 Design an algorithm that will prompt for and accept a four-digit representation of the year (for example, 2003). Your program is to determine if the year provided is a leap year and print a message to this effect on the screen. Also print a message on the screen if the value provided is not exactly four numeric digits. Continue processing until a sentinel of 0000 is entered.

4 The members of the board of a small university are considering voting for a pay increase for their 25 faculty members. They are considering a pay increase of 8%. However, before doing so, they want to know how much this pay increase will cost. Design an algorithm that will prompt for and accept the current salary for each of the faculty members, then calculate and display their individual pay increases. At the end of the algorithm, print the total faculty payroll before and after the pay increase, and the total pay increase involved.

5 Design an algorithm that will produce an employee payroll register from an employee file. Each input employee record contains the employee number, gross pay, income tax payable, union dues and other deductions. Your program is to read the employee file and print a detail line for each employee record showing employee number, gross pay, income tax payable, union dues, other deductions and net pay. Net pay is calculated as gross pay − income tax − union dues − other deductions. At the end of the report, print the total net pay for all employees.

6 Design an algorithm that will produce an inventory report from an inventory file. Each input inventory record contains the item number, open inventory amount, amount purchased and amount sold. Your program is to read the inventory file and print a detail line for each inventory record showing item number, open inventory amount, amount purchased, amount sold and final inventory amount. The final inventory amount is calculated as opening inventory amount + purchases − sales. At the end of the report, print the total open inventory amount, the total amount purchased, the total amount sold and the total final inventory amount.

7 Design an algorithm that will produce a savings account balance report from a customer savings account file. Each input savings account record contains the account number, balance forward, deposits (sum of all deposits), withdrawals (sum of all withdrawals) and interest earned. Your program is to read the savings account file and print a detail line for each savings account record showing account number, balance forward, deposits, withdrawals, interest earned and final account balance. The final account balance is calculated as balance forward + deposits − withdrawals + interest. A heading is to appear at the top of each page and allowance is to be made for 45 detail lines per page. At the end of the report, print the total balances forward, total deposits, total withdrawals, total interest earned and total final account balances.

8 Design an algorithm that will read a file of sales volume records and print a report showing the sales commission owing to each salesperson. Each input record contains salesperson number, name and that person's volume of sales for the month. The commission rate varies according to sales volume, as follows:

On sales volume ($) of	Commission rate (%)
$0.00–$200.00	5
$200.01–$1000.00	8
$1000.01–$2000.00	10
$2000.01 and above	12

The calculated commission is an accumulated amount according to the sales volume figure. For example, the commission owing for a sales volume of $1200.00 would be calculated as follows:

Commission = (200 * 5%) + ((1000 – 200) * 8%) + ((1200 – 1000) * 10%))

Your program is to print the salesperson's number, name, volume of sales and calculated commission, with the appropriate column headings.

9 Design an algorithm that will prompt for and receive your current cheque book balance, followed by a number of financial transactions. Each transaction consists of a transaction code and a transaction amount. The transaction code can be a deposit ('D') or a cheque ('C'). Your program is to add each deposit transaction amount to the balance and subtract each cheque transaction amount. After each transaction is processed, a new running balance is to be displayed on the screen, with a warning message if the balance becomes negative. When there are no more transactions, a 'Q' is to be entered for transaction code to signify the end of the data. Your algorithm is then to display the initial and final balances, along with a count of the number of cheques and deposits processed.

10 At Olympic diving competition level, 10 diving judges award a single mark (with one decimal place) for each dive attempted by a diving competitor. This mark can range from 0 to 10. Design an algorithm that will receive a score from the 10 judges and calculate the average score. The screen should display the following output:

Judge	1	2	3	4	5	6	7	8	9	10
Mark	6.7	8.1	5.8	7.0	6.6	6.0	7.6	6.1	7.2	7.0

Score for the dive 6.81

General algorithms for common business problems

Objectives

- To provide general pseudocode algorithms for four common business applications:
  - report generation with page break
  - single-level control break
  - multiple-level control break
  - sequential file update

Outline

9.1 Program structure

The aim of this chapter is to present a number of general pseudocode solutions for typical programming problems, using a modular structure.

Chapter 8 introduced a general modularised solution algorithm for the processing of sequential files. This general solution algorithm consisted of a mainline module and three subordinate modules. These are:

1 an initial processing module, containing the steps to be performed at the beginning of the algorithm, before the loop begins;
2 a processing module inside the loop containing all the steps necessary to process one record or piece of data; and
3 a final processing module, containing the steps to be performed at the end of the algorithm, outside the loop.

The hierarchy chart looked like this:

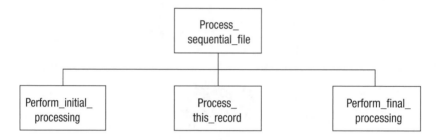

The mainline module looked like this:

```
Process_sequential_file
    Perform_initial_processing
    Read first record
    DOWHILE more records exist
        Process_this_record
        Read next record
    ENDDO
    Perform_final_processing
END
```

Let's now use this basic program structure to develop solution algorithms for four common business programming applications.

9.2 Report generation with page break

Most reports require page heading lines, column heading lines, detail lines and total lines. Reports are also required to skip to a new page after a pre-determined number of detail lines have been printed.

A typical report might look like this:

GLAD RAGS CLOTHING COMPANY			
12/5/2006	**CURRENT ACCOUNT BALANCES**		**PAGE: 1**
CUSTOMER NUMBER	**CUSTOMER NAME**	**CUSTOMER ADDRESS**	**ACCOUNT BALANCE**
12345	Sporty's Boutique	The Mall, Redfern	$300.50
12346	Slinky's Nightwear	245 Picnic Road, Pymble	$400.50
		Total customers on file	200
		Total customers with balance owing	150
		Total balance owing	$4300.00

Our general solution algorithm for processing a sequential file can be extended by the addition of three new modules to cater for these report requirements. These new modules are Print_page_headings, Print_detail_line and Accumulate_total_fields.

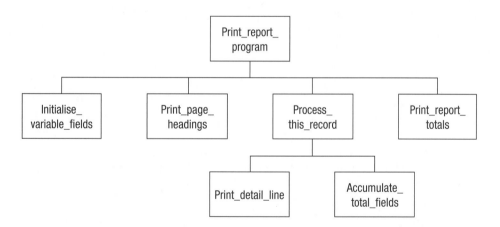

A   Hierarchy chart

Once the hierarchy chart has been established, the solution algorithm can be developed in pseudocode.

B   Solution algorithm

Mainline

    Print_report_program
        Initialise_variable_fields
        Print_page_headings
        Read first record
        DOWHILE more records exist
            IF linecount > max_detail_lines THEN
                Print_page_headings
            ENDIF
            Process_this_record
            Read next record
        ENDDO
        Print_report_totals
    END

Subordinate modules

1   Initialise_variable_fields
        set accumulators to zero
        set pagecount to zero
        set linecount to zero
        set max_detail_lines to required value
    END

2   Print_page_headings
        increment pagecount
        Print main heading lines
        Print column heading lines
        Print blank line (if required)
        set linecount to zero
    END

3   Process_this_record
        Perform necessary calculations (if any)
        Print_detail_line
        Accumulate_total_fields
    END

4   Print_detail_line
        Print detail line
        increment linecount
    END

5   Accumulate_total_fields
        increment accumulators as required
    END

6   Print_report_totals
      Print total line(s)
   END

This general pseudocode solution can now be used as a framework for any report program that requires page breaks.

9.3 Single-level control break

Printed reports that also produce control break total lines are very common in business applications. A control break total line is a summary line for a group of records that contain the same record key. This record key is a designated field on each record, and is referred to as the control field. The control field is used to identify a record or a group of records within a file. A control break occurs each time there is a change in value of the control field. Thus, control break total lines are printed each time a control break is detected.

Here is a single-level control break report.

MULTI-DISK COMPUTER COMPANY					
12/05/2006	SALES REPORT BY SALESPERSON				PAGE: 1
SALESPERSON NUMBER	SALESPERSON NAME	PRODUCT NUMBER	QTY SOLD	PRICE	EXTENSION AMOUNT
1001	Mary Smith	1032	2	$10.00	$20.00
		1033	2	$20.00	$40.00
		1044	2	$30.00	$60.00
		Sales total for Mary Smith			$120.00
1002	Jane Brown	1032	2	$10.00	$20.00
		1045	1	$35.00	$35.00
		Sales total for Jane Brown			$55.00
		Report sales total			$175.00

Note that a control break total line is printed each time the salesperson number changes.

There are two things you must consider when designing a control break program:

1 The file to be processed must have been sorted into control field sequence. (In the example above, the file was sorted into ascending sequence of salesperson number.) If the file has not been sorted, erroneous results will occur.

2 Each time a record is read from the input file, the control field on the current record must be compared with the control field on the previous record. If the control fields are different, a control break total line must be printed for the previous set of records, before the current record is processed.

The general solution algorithm, which was developed for a report generation program, can be extended by the addition of two new modules to incorporate a single-level control break. These modules are named Print_control_total_line and Reset_control_totals.

A   Hierarchy chart

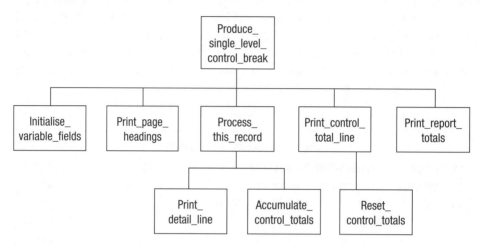

All control break report programs will require the following variables:

1 a variable named this_control_field, which will hold the control field of the record just read;
2 a variable named prev_control_field, which will hold the control field of the previous record. (To cater for the first record, the statements after the first Read statement will set the new control field to both the variables this_control_field and prev_control_field.)
3 one or more variables to accumulate the control break totals; and
4 one or more variables to accumulate the report totals.

B   Solution algorithm

Mainline

```
Produce_single_level_control_break
    Initialise_variable_fields
    Print_page_headings
    Read first record
    this_control_field = control field
    prev_control_field = control field
    DOWHILE more records exist
        IF this_control_field NOT = prev_control_field THEN
            Print_control_total_line
            prev_control_field = this_control_field
        ENDIF
        IF linecount > max_detail_lines THEN
            Print_page_headings
        ENDIF
        Process_this_record
        Read next record
        this_control_field = control field
    ENDDO
    Print_control_total_line
    Print_report_totals
END
```

There are four points in this mainline algorithm that are essential for a control break program to function correctly:

1   Each time a new record is read from the file, the new control field is assigned to the variable this_control_field.
2   When the first record is read, the new control field is assigned to both the variables this_control_field and prev_control_field. This will prevent the control totals printing before the first record has been processed.
3   The variable prev_control_field is updated as soon as a change in the control field is detected.
4   After the end of the file has been detected, the module Print_control_total_line will print the control break totals for the last record or set of records.

Subordinate modules

```
1    Initialise_variable_fields
         set control total accumulators to zero
         set report total accumulators to zero
         set pagecount to zero
         set linecount to zero
         set max_detail_lines to required value
     END
```

2   Print_page_headings
         increment pagecount
         Print main heading lines
         Print column heading lines
         Print blank line (if required)
         set linecount to zero
     END

3   Process_this_record
         Perform necessary calculations (if any)
         Print_detail_line
         Accumulate_control_totals
     END

4   Print_control_total_line
         Print control total line
         Print blank line (if required)
         increment linecount
         Reset_control_totals
     END

5   Print_report_totals
         Print report total line
     END

6   Print_detail_line
         Print detail line
         increment linecount
     END

7   Accumulate_control_totals
         increment control total accumulators
     END

8   Reset_control_totals
         add control total accumulators to report total accumulators
         set control total accumulators to zero
     END

Notice that when a control total line is printed, the module Reset_control_ totals is called. This module will add the control totals to the report totals and reset the control totals to zero for the next set of records. This general solution algorithm can now be used as a framework for any single-level control break program.

Multiple-level control break

Often reports are required to produce multiple-level control break totals. For instance, the sales report produced in Section 9.3 may require sales totals for each salesperson in the company, as well as sales totals for each department within the company.

The monthly sales report might then look like this:

		MULTI-DISK COMPUTER COMPANY				
12/05/06	SALES REPORT BY SALESPERSON					PAGE: 1
DEPT	SALESPERSON NUMBER	SALESPERSON NAME	PRODUCT NUMBER	QTY SOLD	PRICE	EXTENSION AMOUNT
01	1001	Mary Smith	1032	2	$10.00	$20.00
			1033	2	$20.00	$40.00
			1044	2	$30.00	$60.00
		Sales total for Mary Smith				$120.00
	1002	Jane Brown	1032	2	$10.00	$20.00
			1045	1	$35.00	$35.00
		Sales total for Jane Brown				$55.00
		Sales total for Dept 01				$175.00
02	1050	Jenny Ponds	1033	2	20.00	$40.00
			1044	2	30.00	$60.00
		Sales total for Jenny Ponds				$100.00
		Sales total for Dept 02				$100.00
		Report sales total				$275.00

Note that a control break total line is printed each time the salesperson number changes and each time the department number changes. Thus, there are two control fields in this file: salesperson number and department number.

The concepts that applied to a single-level control break program also apply to a multiple-level control break program:

1 The input file must be sorted into control field sequence. When there is more than one control field, the file must be sorted into a sequence of minor control field within major control field. (To produce the sales report, the sales file must have been sorted into salesperson number within department number.)

2 Each time a record is read from the file, the control field on the current record must be compared with the control field of the previous record.

If the minor control field has changed, the control totals for the previous minor control field must be printed. If the major control field has changed, the control totals for the previous minor control field and major control field must be printed.

The general solution algorithm that was developed for a single-level control break program can be extended by the addition of two new modules to incorporate a two-level control break. If three control breaks were required, another two modules would be added to the solution algorithm, and so on.

The names of the modules that produce the control totals have been changed slightly, so that they indicate which level of control break has occurred. These new module names are Print_minor_control_totals, Print_major_control_totals, Reset_minor_control_totals and Reset_major_control_totals.

A   Hierarchy chart

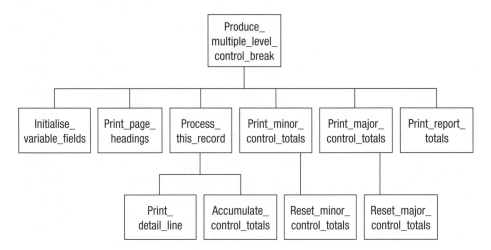

B   Solution algorithm

Mainline

```
Produce_multiple_level_control_break
    Initialise_variable_fields
    Print_page_headings
    Read first record
    this_minor_control_field = minor control field
    prev_minor_control_field = minor control field
    this_major_control_field = major control field
    prev_major_control_field = major control field
    DOWHILE more records exist
        IF this_major_control_field NOT = prev_major_control_field THEN
            Print_minor_control_totals
            prev_minor_control_field = this_minor_control_field
            Print_major_control_totals
            prev_major_control_field = this_major_control_field
        ELSE
            IF this_minor_control_field NOT = prev_minor_control_field THEN
                Print_minor_control_totals
                prev_minor_control_field = this_minor_control_field
            ENDIF
        ENDIF
        IF linecount > max_detail_lines THEN
            Print_page_headings
        ENDIF
        Process_this_record
        Read next record
        this_minor_control_field = minor control field
        this_major_control_field = major control field
    ENDDO
    Print_minor_control_totals
    Print_major_control_totals
    Print_report_totals
END
```

The points to be noted in this mainline are:

1 Each time a new record is read from the input file, the new control fields are assigned to the variables this_minor_control_field and this_major_control_field.

2 When the first record is read, the new control fields are assigned to both the current and previous control field variables. This will prevent control totals printing before the first record has been processed.

3 After the end of the input file has been detected, the two modules Print_minor_control_totals and Print_major_control_totals will print control totals for the last minor control field record, or set of records, and the last major control field set of records.

Subordinate modules

1   Initialise_variable_fields
      set minor control total accumulators to zero
      set major control total accumulators to zero
      set report total accumulators to zero
      set pagecount to zero
      set linecount to zero
      set max_detail_lines to required value
  END

2   Print_page_headings
      increment pagecount
      Print main heading lines
      Print column heading lines
      Print blank line (if required)
      set linecount to zero
  END

3   Process_this_record
      Perform necessary calculations (if any)
      Print_detail_line
      Accumulate_control_totals
  END

4   Print_minor_control_totals
      Print minor control total line
      Print blank line (if required)
      increment linecount
      Reset_minor_control_totals
  END

5   Print_major_control_totals
      Print major control total line
      Print blank line (if required)
      increment linecount
      Reset_major_control_totals
  END

6   Print_report_totals
      Print report total line
  END

7   Print_detail_line
      Print detail line
      increment linecount
  END

8   Accumulate_control_totals
         increment minor control total accumulators
     END

9   Reset_minor_control_totals
         add minor control total accumulators to major control total accumulators
         set minor control total accumulators to zero
     END

10   Reset_major_control_totals
         add major control total accumulators to report total accumulators
         set major control total accumulators to zero
     END

Because the solution algorithm has simple design and good modular structure, the processing of intermediate control field breaks as well as major and minor control field breaks can be handled easily. The solution algorithm would simply require the addition of two new modules: Print_intermed_control_totals and Reset_intermed_control_totals. The IF statement in the mainline would then be expanded to include this extra condition, as follows:

```
IF this_major_control_field NOT = prev_major_control_field THEN
    Print_minor_control_totals
    prev_minor_control_field = this_minor_control_field
    Print_intermed_control_totals
    prev_intermed_control_field = this_intermed_control_field
    Print_major_control_totals
    prev_major_control_field = this_major_control_field
ELSE
    IF this_intermed_control_field NOT = prev_intermed_control_field THEN
        Print_minor_control_totals
        prev_minor_control_field = this_minor_control_field
        Print_intermed_control_totals
        prev_intermed_control_field = this_intermed_control_field
    ELSE
        IF this_minor_control_field NOT = prev_minor_control_field THEN
            Print_minor_control_totals
            prev_minor_control_field = this_minor_control_field
        ENDIF
    ENDIF
ENDIF
```

This pseudocode algorithm can now be used to process any multiple-level control break program.

9.5 Sequential file update

Most current file transaction update systems are real-time systems; however, for batch processing applications, sequential file updating is very common. It involves updating a master file by applying update transactions to a transaction file. Both the master file and the transaction file are sequential. A new master file that incorporates the updated transactions is produced. Usually, audit reports and error reports are also printed.

A system flowchart of a sequential update program would look like this:

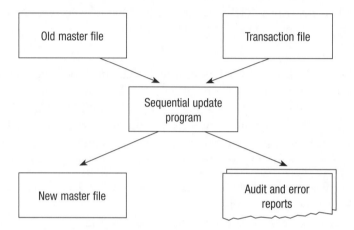

System concepts

1   Master file

A master file is a file that contains permanent and semipermanent information about the data entities it contains. The records on the master file are in sequence, according to a key field (or fields) on each record. For example, a customer master file may contain the customer's number, name, address, phone number, credit rating and current balance, and may be in sequence of customer number. In this case, customer number would be the key.

2   Transaction file

A transaction file contains all the data and activities that are included on the master file. If the transaction file has been designed specifically to update a master file, there are usually three types of update transactions on this file. These are transactions to:

- add a new record
- update or change an existing record
- delete an existing record.

For example, a customer transaction file might contain transactions that are intended to add a new customer record, change some data on an existing customer record, or delete a customer record on the customer master file. The transaction file is also in sequence according to the same key field as the master record.

3   Audit report

An audit report is a detailed list of all the transactions that were applied to the master file. It provides an accounting trail of the update activities that take place, and is used for control purposes.

4   Error report

An error report is a detailed list of errors that occurred during the processing of the update. Typical errors might be the attempted update of a record that is not on the master file, or the addition of a record that already exists. This error report will require some action to confirm and correct the identified errors.

Sequential update logic

The logic of a sequential update program is more difficult than the other problems encountered, because there are two sequential input files. Processing involves reading a record from each of the input files and comparing the keys of the two records. As a result of this comparison, processing falls generally into three categories:

1 If the key on the transaction record is less than the key on the old master record, the transaction is probably an add transaction. The details on the transaction record should be put into master record format, and the record should be written to the new master file. Another record should then be read from the transaction file.
2 If the key on the transaction record is equal to the key on the old master record, the transaction is probably an update or delete transaction. If the transaction is an update, the master record should be amended to reflect the required changes. If the transaction is a delete, the master record should not be written to the new master file. Another transaction record should then be read from the transaction file.
3 If the key on the transaction record is greater than the key on the old master record, there is no matching transaction for that master record. In this case the old master record should be written unchanged to the new master file and another record read from the old master file.

Sequential update programs also need to include logic that will handle multiple transaction records for the same master record, and the possibility of transaction records that are in error. The types of transaction record errors that can occur are:

- an attempt to add a new master record when a record with that key already exists on the master file
- an attempt to update a master record when there is no record with that key on the master file
- an attempt to delete a master record when there is no record with that key on the master file
- an attempt to delete a master record when the current balance is not equal to zero.

Balance line algorithm

The logic of the sequential update program has fascinated programmers for many years. Authors have offered many solutions to the problem, but none of these has been a truly general solution. Most solutions have been designed around a specific programming language.

A good general solution algorithm written in pseudocode was presented by Barry Dwyer in a paper entitled 'One More Time – How to Update a Master File'.[1] This algorithm has been referred to as the balance line algorithm. It handles multiple transaction records for the one master record, as well as the possibility of transaction record errors.

A modularised version of the balance line algorithm is presented in this chapter. It introduces the concept of a current record. The current record is the record that is currently being processed, ready for updating and writing to the new master file. The current record is established when the record keys on the two files are compared. The current record will be the record that has the smaller record key. Its format will be that of a new master record.

Thus, if the key on the transaction record is less than the key on the old master record, the current record will be made up of the fields on the transaction record. If the key on the transaction record is equal to or greater than the key on the old master record, the old master record will become the current record.

The current record will remain the current record until there are no more transactions to be applied to that record. It will then be written to the new master file, and a new current record will be established.

Another variable, current_record_status, is used as a program flag to indicate whether or not the current record is available for processing. If the current_record_status is active, the current record has been established and is available for updating or writing out to the new master file. If the current_record_status is inactive, the current record is not available to be up-dated or written to the new master file; for example, the current record may have been marked for deletion.

The processing of the two files will continue until end_of_job has been reached. End_of_job will occur when both the input files have no more data to be processed. Since it is not known which file will reach end of file first, the record key of each file will be set to a high value when EOF is reached. When the record key of one of the files is high, the other file will continue to be processed, as required, until the record key on that file is assigned the same high value. End_of_job occurs when the record keys on both the files are the same high value.

Let us now establish a general solution algorithm for a sequential update program. The logic provided will also include the printing of the audit and error reports.

---

1 Barry Dwyer, 'One More Time – How to Update a Master File', *Communications of the ACM*, Vol. 124, No. 1, January 1981.

A   Hierarchy chart

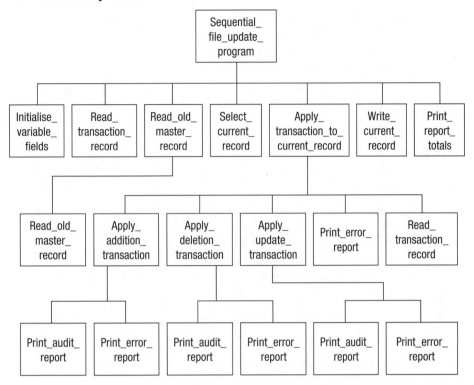

B   Solution algorithm
Mainline

```
Sequential_file_update_program
    Initialise_variable_fields
    Read_transaction_record
    Read_old_master_record
    set current_record_status to 'inactive'
    DOWHILE NOT end_of_job
        Select_current_record
        DOWHILE transaction_record_key = current_record_key
            Apply_transaction_to_current_record
        ENDDO
        IF current_record_status = 'active' THEN
            Write_current_record
            set current_record_status to 'inactive'
        ENDIF
    ENDDO
    Print_report_totals
END
```

Subordinate modules

1   Initialise_variable_fields
        set total_transaction_records to zero
        set total_old_master_records to zero
        set total_new_master_records to zero
        set total_error_records to zero
        set end_of_job to false
    END

2   Read_transaction_record
        Read transaction record
        IF NOT EOF THEN
            increment total_transaction_records
        ELSE
            set transaction_record_key to high value
            IF old_master_record_key = high value THEN
                set end_of_job to true
            ENDIF
        ENDIF
    END

3   Read_old_master_record
        Read old master record
        IF NOT EOF THEN
            increment total_old_master_records
        ELSE
            set old_master_record_key to high value
            IF transaction_record_key = high value THEN
                set end_of_job = true
            ENDIF
        ENDIF
    END

4   Select_current_record
        IF transaction_record_key < old_master_record_key THEN
            set up current record with transaction record fields
        ELSE
            set up current record with old master record fields
            set current_record_status to 'active'
            Read_old_master_record
        ENDIF
    END

```
5    Apply_transaction_to_current_record
         CASE OF transaction_type
              addition :    Apply_addition_transaction
              deletion :    Apply_deletion_transaction
              update :      Apply_update_transaction
              other :       error_message = 'invalid transaction type'
                            Print_error_report
         ENDCASE
         Read_transaction_record
     END


6    Write_current_record
         Write current record to new master file
         increment total_new_master_records
     END


7    Print_report_totals
         Print total_transaction_records
         Print total_old_master_records
         Print total_new_master_records
         Print total_error_records
     END


8    Apply_addition_transaction
         IF current_record_status = 'inactive' THEN
              set current_record_status to 'active'
              Print_audit_report
         ELSE
              error_message = 'Invalid addition; record already exists'
              Print_error_report
         ENDIF
     END


9    Apply_deletion_transaction
         IF current_record_status = 'active' THEN
              set current_record_status to 'inactive'
              Print_audit_report
         ELSE
              error_message = 'Invalid deletion, record not on master file'
              Print_error_report
         ENDIF
     END
```

```
10      Apply_update_transaction
            IF current_record_status = 'active' THEN
                apply required change(s) to current record
                Print_audit_report
            ELSE
                error_message = 'Invalid update, record not on master file'
                Print_error_report
            ENDIF
        END

11      Print_audit_report
            Print transaction details on audit report
            CASE OF transaction_type
                addition :    print 'record added'
                deletion :    print 'record deleted'
                update :      print 'record updated'
            ENDCASE
        END

12      Print_error_report
            Print transaction details on error report
            Print error_message
            increment total_error_records
        END
```

Note that end_of_job is reached when the transaction_record_key = high value AND the old_master_record_key = high value. This pseudocode algorithm can now be used to process any sequential file update program.

Chapter summary

The aim of this chapter was to develop general pseudocode algorithms to four common business applications. The applications covered were:

- report generation with page break
- single-level control break
- multiple-level control break
- sequential file update.

In each section, the application was discussed, a hierarchy chart was developed, and a general solution algorithm was presented in pseudocode. These solution algorithms can be used when writing programs that incorporate any of the above applications.

Programming problems

Using the sample solution algorithms provided in this chapter, design a solution algorithm for the following programming problems. Your solution should contain:

- a defining diagram
- a hierarchy chart
- a pseudocode algorithm
- a desk check of the solution.

1 Design an algorithm to produce a list of customers from the Glad Rags Clothing Company's customer master file. Each record on the customer master file contains the customer's number, name, address (street, city, state and postcode) and account balance.

Your program is to read the customer master file and print a report of all customers whose account balance is greater than zero. Each detail line is to contain the customer's number, name, address and account balance. Print headings and column headings at the top of each page, allowing for 35 detail lines per page, and at the end of the report, the total customers on file, the total customers with balance owing, and the total balance owing, as follows:

	GLAD RAGS CLOTHING COMPANY		
XX/XX/XX	CURRENT ACCOUNT BALANCES		PAGE: XX
CUSTOMER NUMBER	CUSTOMER NAME	ADDRESS	ACCOUNT BALANCE
XXXXX	XXXXXXXXXX	XXXXXXXXXXXXXXXXXXX	9999.99
XXXXX	XXXXXXXXXX	XXXXXXXXXXXXXXXXXXX	9999.99
	Total customers on file		999
	Total customers with balance owing		999
	Total balance owing		99999.99

2 Design an algorithm to produce a sales commission report from a company's sales file. Each record on the sales file contains the salesperson's number, name and sales amount.

Your program is to read the sales file, calculate the sales commission according to the following table, and print a sales commission report.

Sales range	Commission rate
$0–$499.99	No commission
$500.00–$749.99	2%
$750.00 and above	3%

Each detail line is to contain the salesperson's number, sales amount, commission rate and total commission. Print headings and column headings at the top of each page, allowing for 35 detail lines per page, and at the end of the report, the total commission, as follows:

SALES COMMISSIONS				PAGE: XX
SALESPERSON NUMBER	SALESPERSON NAME	SALES AMOUNT	COMMISSION RATE	COMMISSION
XXXXX	XXXXXXXXXXXXXX	9999.99	x%	999.99
XXXXX	XXXXXXXXXXXXXX	9999.99	x%	999.99
		Total Commission		**9999.99**

3 Design an algorithm that will create a validation report from a customer sales file. Each field on the sales record is to be validated as follows:

Field	Format
Customer number	Numeric
Customer name	Alphanumeric
Street	Alphanumeric
Town	Alphanumeric
Postcode	Numeric
Phone	Alphanumeric
Fax	Alphanumeric
Balance due	Numeric
Credit limit	Numeric (0–$1000)

If a field is found to be in error, print a line on the validation report showing the customer number, name, address (street, town, postcode) and an appropriate message, as indicated in the diagram below. There may be multiple messages for the one record. Print headings and column headings at the top of each page, allowing for 45 detail lines per page.

VALIDATION REPORT			
CUSTOMER SALES FILE			PAGE: XX
CUSTOMER NUMBER	CUSTOMER NAME	ADDRESS	MESSAGE
XXXX	XXXXXXXXXXXXXX	XXXXXXXXXXXXXXXXXXX	Postcode not numeric
XXXX	XXXXXXXXXXXXXX	XXXXXXXXXXXXXXXXXXX	Credit limit invalid

4 The Multi-Disk computer company requires a single-level control break program to produce a sales report by salesperson from their sales file. Design an algorithm that will read the sales file and create the sales report as shown below.

Each record on the sales file contains the salesperson's number, name, the product number of the product sold, the quantity sold and the price of the product. There may be more than one record for each salesperson, depending on the products sold that month. The sales file has been sorted into ascending sequence of salesperson number.

Your program is to read the sales file sequentially, calculate the extension amount (price * quantity sold) for each product sold and print a detail line for each record processed. Control total lines showing the sales total for each salesperson are to be printed on change of salesperson number. Print headings and column headings at the top of each page, allowing for 40 detail lines per page.

MULTI-DISK COMPUTER COMPANY					**PAGE:XX**
SALES REPORT BY SALESPERSON					**XX/XX/XX**
SALESPERSON NUMBER	**SALESPERSON NAME**	**PRODUCT NUMBER**	**QTY SOLD**	**PRICE**	**EXTENSION AMOUNT**
XXXX	XXXX XXXXXXXXX	XXXXXX	99	999.99	9999.99
		XXXXXX	99	999.99	9999.99
		XXXXXX	99	999.99	9999.99
		Sales total for xxxx xxxxxx			**99999.99**
		Report sales total			**999999.99**

5 A sales file as described in Problem 4 exists, with the addition of a further field, the department number. The sales file has been sorted into ascending sequence of salesperson number within department number. Print the same sales report, with the additional requirement of printing a sales total line on change of department number, as well as on change of salesperson number.

Print the report details as per the following sales report. Print headings and column headings at the top of each page, allowing for 40 detail lines per page.

MULTI-DISK COMPUTER COMPANY						**PAGE:XX**
SALES REPORT BY SALESPERSON						**XX/XX/XX**
DEPT	**SALESPERSON NUMBER**	**SALESPERSON NAME**	**PRODUCT NUMBER**	**QTY SOLD**	**PRICE**	**EXTENSION AMOUNT**
XX	XXXX	XXXX XXXXXXXXX	XXXXXX	99	999.99	9999.99
			XXXXXX	99	999.99	9999.99
			XXXXXX	99	999.99	9999.99
			Sales total for xxxx xxxxxxxx			**99999.99**
			Sales total for dept xx			**99999.99**
			Report sales total			**999999.99**

6 ABC University requires a single-level control break program to produce a lecturer information report by lecturer from the university's course file. Design an algorithm that will read the course file and create the lecturer information report as shown below.

Each record on the course file contains details of a lecturer's teaching load – that is, the lecturer's number, name, the course number of the course being taught, the credit hours for that course and the class size. There may be more than one record for each lecturer, depending on the number of courses he or she teaches. The course file has been sorted into ascending sequence of lecturer number.

Your program is to read the course file sequentially, calculate the lecturer's contact hours ((class size/50) * credit hours), and produce the lecturer information report. On change of lecturer number, print control total lines showing the total contact hours for each lecturer. Print headings and column headings at the top of each page, allowing for 40 detail lines per page.

		ABC UNIVERSITY			
		LECTURER INFORMATION REPORT			
LECTURER NUMBER	LECTURER NAME	COURSE NUMBER	CREDIT HOURS	CLASS SIZE	CONTACT HOURS
XXXX	XXXXXXXXXX	XXXXX	X	XXX	XXX
		XXXXX	X	XXX	XXX
		XXXXX	X	XXX	XXX
		Contact hours for lecturer xxxx			X XXX
		Contact hours for university			XX XXX

7 A course file as described in Problem 6 exists, with the addition of a further field, the university department number. The course file has been sorted into ascending sequence of lecturer number within department number. Print the same lecturer information report, with the additional requirement of printing a total contact hours line on change of department number, as well as on change of lecturer number.

Print the report details as per the following lecturer information report. Print headings and column headings at the top of each page, allowing for 40 detail lines per page.

			ABC UNIVERSITY			
			LECTURER INFORMATION REPORT			
DEPT NUMBER	LECTURER NUMBER	LECTURER NAME	COURSE NUMBER	CREDIT HOURS	CLASS SIZE	CONTACT HOURS
XXX	XXXX	XXXXXXXXXX	XXXXX	X	XXX	XXX
			XXXXX	X	XXX	XXX
			XXXXX	X	XXX	XXX
			Contact hours for lecturer xxxx			X XXX
			Contact hours for department xxx			X XXX
			Contact hours for university			XX XXX

8 A course file as described in Problem 7 exists, with the addition of a further field, the college number. The course file has been sorted into ascending sequence of lecturer number within department number within college number. The same lecturer information report is to be printed, with the additional requirement of printing a total contact hours line on change of college number, as well as on change of department number and on change of lecturer number.

Print the report details as per the following lecturer information report. Print headings and column headings at the top of each page, allowing for 40 detail lines per page.

			ABC UNIVERSITY				
			LECTURER INFORMATION REPORT				
COLLEGE NUMBER	**DEPT NUMBER**	**LECTURER NUMBER**	**LECTURER NAME**	**COURSE NUMBER**	**CREDIT HOURS**	**CLASS SIZE**	**CONTACT HOURS**
XXXXX	XXX	XXXX	XXXXXXXXXX	XXXXX	X	XXX	XXX
				XXXXX	X	XXX	XXX
				XXXXX	X	XXX	XXX
			Contact hours for lecturer xxxx				XXX
			Contact hours for department xxx				X XXX
			Contact hours for college xxxxx				XX XXX
			Contact hours for university				XX XXX

9 The XYZ Bank requires a program to sequentially update its savings account master file. A sequential file of update transactions is to be used as the input transaction file, along with the customer master file.

The customer master file contains the customer's account number, and the balance forward amount. The customer transaction update file contains three types of records, as follows:

i Deposit records containing a record code of 'D', the account number and the amount of a deposit.

ii Withdrawal records containing a record code of 'W', the account number and the amount of a withdrawal.

iii Interest records containing a record code of 'I', the account number and the amount of interest earned.

There is a deposit record for each deposit a customer made, a withdrawal record for each withdrawal, and an interest record if interest was credited during the period. The updating process consists of adding each deposit or interest to the balance forward amount on the master record, and subtracting each withdrawal.

Both files have been sorted into account number sequence. There can be multiple update transactions for any one savings account master record and a new savings account master file is to be created.

If a transaction record is in error, the transaction details are to be printed on the transaction error report, with one of the following messages:

'invalid deposit, account number not on file'

'invalid withdrawal, account number not on file'

'invalid interest record, account number not on file'

10 The Yummy Chocolates confectionery company requires a program to sequentially update its customer master file. A sequential file of update transactions is to be used as the input transaction file, along with the customer master file.

The customer master file contains the customer number, name, address (street, city, state and postcode) and account balance. The customer transaction file also contains these fields, as well as a transaction code of 'A' (add), 'D' (delete) and 'U' (update).

Both files have been sorted into customer number sequence. There can be multiple update transactions for any one customer master record and a new customer master file is to be created.

Transaction records are to be processed as follows:

i If the transaction record is an 'Add', the transaction is to be written to the new customer master file.

ii If the transaction record is a 'Delete', the old master record with the same customer number is not to be written to the new customer master file.

iii If the transaction record is an update, the old master record with the same customer number is to be updated as follows:

if customer name is present, update customer name

if street is present, update street

if town is present, update town

if state is present, update state

if postcode is present, update postcode

if balance paid is present, subtract balance paid from account balance on old customer master record.

As each transaction is processed, print the transaction details on the customer master audit report, with the message, 'record added', 'record deleted' or 'record updated' as applicable.

If a transaction record is in error, the transaction details are to be printed on the customer update errors report, with one of the following messages:

'invalid addition, customer already exists'

'invalid deletion, customer not on file'

'invalid update, customer not on file'.

Communication between modules, cohesion and coupling

You never pass parameters with me any more

Objectives

- To introduce communication between modules
- To develop solution algorithms that pass parameters between modules
- To introduce cohesion as a measure of the internal strength of a module
- To introduce coupling as a measure of the extent of information interchange between modules

Outline

10.1 Communication between modules

When designing solution algorithms, it is necessary to consider not only the division of the problem into modules but also the flow of information between the modules. The fewer and simpler the communications between modules, the easier it is to understand and maintain one module without reference to other modules. This flow of information, called 'intermodule communication', can be accomplished by the scope of the variable (local or global data) or the passing of parameters.

Scope of a variable

The scope of a variable is the portion of a program in which that variable has been defined and to which it can be referenced. If a list is created of all the modules in which a variable can be referenced, that list defines the scope of the variable. Variables can be global, where the scope of the variable is the whole program, or local, where the scope of the variable is simply the module in which it is defined.

Global data

Global data is data that can be used by all the modules in a program. The scope of a global variable is the whole program, because every module in the program can access and change that data. The lifetime of a global variable spans the execution of the whole program.

Local data

Variables that are defined within a submodule are called local variables. These local variables are not known to the calling module, or to any other module. The scope of a local variable is simply the module in which it is defined. The lifetime of a local variable is limited to the execution of the single submodule in which it is defined. Using local variables can reduce what is known as program side effects.

Side effects

A side effect is a form of cross-communication of a module with other parts of a program. It occurs when a subordinate module alters the value of a global variable inside a module. Side effects are not necessarily detrimental; however, they do tend to decrease the manageability of a program. A programmer should be aware of their impact.

Sometimes, a programmer may need to modify an existing program, and in doing so, may make a change to a global variable. This change could cause side effects or erroneous results because the new programmer is unaware of other modules that also alter that global variable.

Passing parameters

A particularly efficient method of intermodule communication is the passing of parameters or arguments between modules. Parameters are simply data items transferred from a calling module to its subordinate module at the time of calling. When the subordinate module terminates and returns control to its caller, the values in the parameters may be transferred back to the calling module. This method of communication avoids any unwanted side effects, as the only interaction between a module and the rest of the program is via parameters.

To pass parameters between modules, two things must happen:

1 The calling module must name the parameters that it wants to pass to the submodule, at the time of calling.
2 The submodule must be able to receive those parameters and return them to the calling module, if required.

In pseudocode and most programming languages, when a calling module wants to pass parameters to a submodule, it simply lists the parameters, enclosed in parentheses, beside the name of the submodule, for example:

    Print_page_headings (pageCount, lineCount)

The submodule must be able to receive those parameters, so it, too, lists the parameters that it expects to receive, enclosed in parentheses, beside the submodule name when it is defined, for example:

    Print_page_headings (pageNumber, lineNumber)

The names that the respective modules give to their parameters need not be the same – in fact, they often differ because they have been written by a different programmer – but their number, type and order must be identical. In the above example, the parameter pageCount will be passed to pageNumber, and the parameter lineCount will be passed to lineNumber. In this book, parameters will be named without underscores, to differentiate them from variables.

Formal and actual parameters

Parameter names that appear when a submodule is defined are known as formal parameters. Variables and expressions that are passed to a submodule in a particular call are called actual parameters. A call to a submodule will include an actual parameter list, one variable for each formal parameter name. There is a one-to-one correspondence between formal and actual parameters, which is determined by the relative position in each parameter list. Also, the actual parameter corresponding to a formal parameter must have the same data type as that specified in the declaration of the formal parameter.

For example, a mainline may call a module with an actual parameter list, as follows:

    Calculate_amount_owing (gasFigure, amountBilled)

while the module may have been declared with the following formal parameter list:

Calculate_amount_owing (gasUsage, amountOwing)

Although the parameter names are different, the actual and formal parameters will correspond.

Value and reference parameters

Parameters may have one of three functions:

1 To pass information from a calling module to a subordinate module. The subordinate module would then use that information in its processing, but would not need to communicate any information back to the calling module.
2 To pass information from a subordinate module to its calling module. The calling module would then use that parameter in subsequent processing.
3 To fulfil a two-way communication role. The calling module may pass information to a subordinate module, where it is amended in some fashion, then passed back to the calling module.

Value parameters

Value parameters pass a copy of the value of a parameter from one module to another. When a submodule is called, the value of each actual parameter is assigned to the corresponding formal parameter, and from then on, the two parameters are independent. The called module cannot modify the value of the parameter in any way, and, when the submodule has finished processing, the value of the parameter returns to its original value. This form of parameter passing is called 'passing by value'.

Reference parameters

Reference parameters pass the memory address of a parameter from one module to another. When a submodule is called, the reference address of the parameter is passed to the called module and that module can then use and change the value of the parameter. Each actual parameter is an 'alias' for the corresponding formal parameter; the two parameters refer to the same object, and changes made through one are visible through the other. As a result, the value of the parameter may be referenced and changed during the processing of the submodule. This form of parameter passing is called 'passing by reference'.

The requirements of the program will determine whether a parameter is passed by value or by reference. The parameter is passed by reference, if the called module is designed to change the value of the actual parameter. Conversely, the parameter is passed by value, to ensure the called routine cannot modify the parameter.

Let's look at an example that illustrates the passing of parameters by value:

EXAMPLE 10.1 Calculate percentage value

Design an algorithm that will <u>receive</u> a fraction in the form of a numerator and a denominator, <u>convert</u> that fraction to a percentage and <u>display</u> the result. Your program is to use a module to calculate the percentage.

A Defining diagram

Input	Processing	Output
numerator denominator	Get numerator, denominator Convert fraction to percentage Display percentage	percentage

B Solution algorithm

```
Calculate_percentage_value
    Prompt for numerator, denominator
    Get numerator, denominator
    Convert_fraction_value (numerator, denominator, percentage)
    IF percentage NOT = 0 THEN
        Output to screen, percentage, '%'
    ELSE
        Output to screen 'invalid fraction'
    ENDIF
END

Convert_fraction_value (numerator, denominator, calculatedPercentage)
    IF denominator NOT = 0
        calculatedPercentage = numerator / denominator * 100
    ELSE
        calculatedPercentage = 0
    ENDIF
END
```

In this example, copies of the numerator and denominator values are passed as parameters to the module Convert_fraction_value, which will use those values to calculate the percentage. When the percentage is calculated, a copy of the value in the parameter calculatedPercentage will be passed to the parameter percentage, which will be displayed to the screen. This is an example of passing by value.

Now let's look at an example that illustrates the passing of parameters by reference.

EXAMPLE 10.2 Increment two counters

Design an algorithm that will <u>increment</u> two counters from 1 to 10 and then <u>output</u> those counters to the screen. Your program is to use a module to increment the counters.

A Defining diagram

Input	Processing	Output
counter1	Increment counters	counter1
counter2	Output counters	counter2

B Solution algorithm

```
Increment_two_counters
    Set counter1, counter2 to zero
    DO I = 1 to 10
        Increment_counter (counter1)
        Increment_counter (counter2)
        Output to the screen counter1, counter2
    ENDDO
END

Increment_counter (counter)
    counter = counter + 1
END
```

In this example, the module Increment_counter is defined with a formal parameter named counter. Increment_counter is called by the mainline, first, with the actual parameter counter1, and then with the actual parameter counter2. At the first call, the reference address of counter1 is passed to the parameter counter, and its value is changed. Then the reference address of counter2 is passed to the parameter counter, and its value is also changed. The values of counter1 and counter2 are displayed on the screen and the process is repeated, so that each time the module Increment_counter is called the values in the parameters counter1 or counter2 are increased by 1. The screen output would be as follows:

```
1    1
2    2
3    3
4    4 etc.
```

This is an example of passing parameters by reference.

Hierarchy charts and parameters

Parameters that pass between modules can be incorporated into a hierarchy chart or structure chart using the following symbols:

For data parameters   For status parameters

Data parameters contain the actual variables or data items that will be passed as parameters between modules.

Status parameters act as program flags and should contain just one of two values: true or false. These program flags or switches are set to true or false, according to a specific set of conditions. They are then used to control further processing.

When designing modular programs, avoid using data parameters to indicate status as well, because this can affect the program in two ways:

1 It may confuse the reader of the program because a variable has been overloaded; that is, it has been used for more than one purpose.

2 It may cause unpredictable errors when the program is amended at some later date, as the maintenance programmer may be unaware of the dual purpose of the variable.

10.2 Programming examples using parameters

Let us now look at an example that passes both data and status parameters. This example offers an alternative solution to Example 8.4.

EXAMPLE 10.3 Calculate employee's pay

A company requires a program to <u>read</u> an employee's number, pay rate and the number of hours worked in a week. The program is then to <u>validate</u> the pay rate field and the hours worked field and, if they are valid, to <u>compute</u> the employee's weekly pay and then <u>print</u> it and the input data.

<u>Validation</u>: According to the company's rules, the maximum hours an employee can work per week is 60 hours, and the maximum hourly rate is $25.00 per hour. If the hours worked field or the hourly rate field is out of range, the input data and an appropriate message are to be <u>printed,</u> and the employee's weekly pay is not to be calculated.

Weekly pay calculation: Weekly pay is calculated as hours worked multiplied by pay rate. If more than 35 hours have been worked, payment for the overtime hours worked is calculated at time-and-a-half.

A Defining diagram

Input	Processing	Output
emp_no	Read employee details	emp_no
pay_rate	Validate input fields	pay_rate
hrs_worked	Calculate employee pay	hrs_worked
	Print employee details	emp_weekly_pay
		error_message

B Hierarchy chart

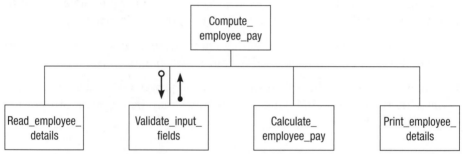

C Solution algorithm

When each employee record is read, the hours_worked and hourly_rate fields must be validated before the weekly pay can be calculated. These values will be passed, as parameters, to the module Validate_input_fields, and a third parameter, validInput, will be used as a flag to indicate whether or not the fields are valid.

```
Compute_employee_pay
    Read_employee_details
    DOWHILE more records
        Validate_input_fields (pay_rate, hrs_worked, validInput)
        IF validInput THEN
            Calculate_employee_pay
            Print_employee_details
        ELSE
            Print emp_no, pay_rate, hrs_worked, error_message
        ENDIF
        Read_employee_details
    ENDDO
END
```

```
Read_employee_details
    Read emp_no, pay_rate, hrs_worked
END

Validate_input_fields (payRate, hrsWorked, validInput)
    set validInput to true
    Set error_message to blank
    IF payRate > $25 THEN
        error_message = 'Pay rate exceeds $25.00'
        validInput = false
    ENDIF
    IF hrsWorked > 60 THEN
        error_message = 'Hours worked exceeds 60'
        validInput = false
    ENDIF
END

Calculate_employee_pay
    IF hrs_worked <= 35 THEN
        emp_weekly_pay = pay_rate * hrs_worked
    ELSE
        overtime_hrs = hrs_worked – 35
        overtime_pay = overtime_hrs * pay_rate * 1.5
        emp_weekly_pay = (pay_rate * 35) + overtime_pay
    ENDIF
END

Print_employee_details
    Print emp_no, pay_rate, hrs_worked, emp_weekly_pay
END
```

Let us now look again at Example 8.2, this time changing the solution algorithm so that parameters are used to communicate between the modules. There are two solution algorithms offered for this example, the second solution more elegant than the first.

EXAMPLE 10.4   Process three characters

Design a solution algorithm that will <u>prompt</u> a terminal operator for three characters, <u>accept</u> those characters as input, <u>sort</u> them into ascending sequence and <u>output</u> them to the screen. The algorithm is to continue to read characters until 'XXX' is entered.

A Defining diagram

Input	Processing	Output
char_1	Prompt for characters	char_1
char_2	Accept three characters	char_2
char_3	Sort three characters	char_3
	Output three characters	

B Hierarchy chart 1

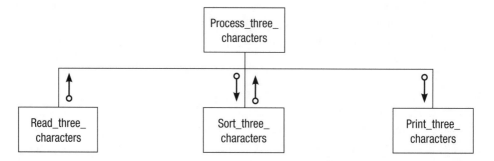

C Solution Algorithm 1

The mainline will call the module Read_three_characters, which will get the three input characters (char_1, char_2, char_3) and send them to the mainline as parameters (char1, char2, char3). These parameters will then be passed to the module Sort_three_characters, which will sort the three characters and send these sorted values back to the mainline as parameters. The three characters will then be passed to the module Print_three_characters, which will print them.

```
Process_three_characters
    Read_three_characters (char1, char2, char3)
    DOWHILE NOT (char1 = 'X' AND char2 = 'X' AND char3 = 'X')
        Sort_three_characters (char1, char2, char3)
        Print_three_characters (char1, char2, char3)
        Read_three_characters (char1, char2, char3)
    ENDDO
END

Read_three_characters (char1, char2, char3)
    Prompt the operator for char_1, char_2, char_3
    Get char_1, char_2, char_3
END
```

```
Sort_three_characters (char1, char2, char3)
    IF char1 > char2 THEN
        temp = char1
        char1 = char2
        char2 = temp
    ENDIF
    IF char2 > char3 THEN
        temp = char2
        char2 = char3
        char3 = temp
    ENDIF
    IF char1 > char2 THEN
        temp = char1
        char1 = char2
        char2 = temp
    ENDIF
END


Print_three_characters (char1, char2, char3)
    Output to the screen char1, char2, char3
END
```

The module Sort_three_characters above contains some repeated code. To avoid this, a new module, called Swap_two_characters, will be introduced, which is called by the module Sort_three_characters. The calling module (Sort_three_characters) will pass two characters at a time to the submodule (Swap_two_characters), which will swap the position of the parameters and return them to the mainline.

B Hierarchy Chart 2

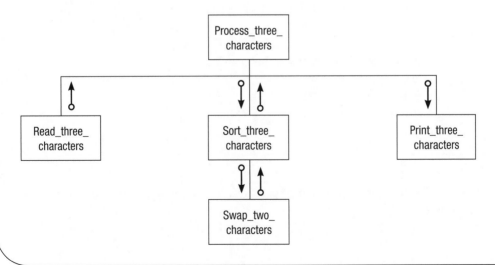

C Solution Algorithm 2

```
Process_three_characters
    Read_three_characters (char1, char2, char3)
    DOWHILE NOT (char1 = 'X' AND char2 = 'X' AND char3 = 'X')
        Sort_three_characters (char1, char2, char3)
        Print_three_characters (char1, char2, char3)
        Read_three_characters (char1, char2, char3)
    ENDDO
END

Read_three_characters (char1, char2, char3)
    Prompt the operator for char_1, char_2, char_3
    Get char_1, char_2, char_3
END

Sort_three_characters (char1, char2, char3)
    IF char1 > char_2 THEN
        Swap_two_characters (char1, char2)
    ENDIF
    IF char2 > char3 THEN
        Swap_two_characters (char2, char3)
    ENDIF
    IF char1 > char2 THEN
        Swap_two_characters (char1, char2)
    ENDIF
END

Print_three_characters (char1, char2, char3)
    Output to the screen char1, char2, char3
END

Swap_two_characters (firstChar, secondChar)
    temp = firstChar
    firstChar = secondChar
    secondChar = temp
END
```

Let us now look at a more complex example that passes a data structure as a parameter.

Example 10.5   Calculate vehicle registration costs

A program is required to calculate and print the registration cost of a new vehicle that a customer has ordered. The program is to be interactive; that is, all the input details will be provided at a terminal on the salesperson's desk. The program is to get the input details, calculate the federal tax payable, calculate the registration costs, calculate the total amount payable and then output the required information to the screen.

The input details required are:

- owner's name
- vehicle make
- vehicle model
- vehicle weight (in kg)
- body type (sedan or wagon)
- private or business code ('P' or 'B')
- wholesale price of vehicle.

The federal tax payable is calculated at the rate of $2.00 for each $100.00, or part thereof, of the wholesale price of the vehicle.

The vehicle registration cost is calculated as the sum of the following charges:

Registration fee	$27.00	
Tax levy	Private	3% of wholesale price
	Business	5% of wholesale price
Weight tax	Private	1% of vehicle weight (converted to $)
	Business	3% of vehicle weight (converted to $)
Insurance premium	Private	1% of wholesale price
	Business	2% of wholesale price

The total amount payable = federal tax + total registration charges. The information to be printed to the screen is as follows:

Vehicle make:
Vehicle model:
Body type:
Registration fee:
Tax levy:
Weight tax:
Insurance premium:
Total registration charges:
Federal tax:
Total amount payable:

The program is to process registration costs until an owner's name of 'XXX' is entered. None of the other entry details will be required after the value 'XXX' has been entered.

A Defining diagram

Input	Processing	Output
owners_name	Get input details	vehicle_make
vehicle_make	Calculate federal_tax	vehicle_model
vehicle_model	Calculate registration_costs	body_type
vehicle_weight	Calculate total_amount_payable	registration_fee
body_type	Output details to screen	tax_levy
usage_code		weight_tax
wholesale_price		insurance_premium
		total_registration_charges
		federal_tax
		total_amount_payable

Each of the five steps in the processing component will become a module in the solution algorithm.

B Hierarchy chart

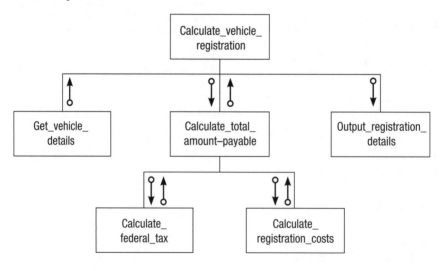

C Solution Algorithm

The module Get_vehicle_details will collect the input vehicle details into a data structure called vehicleDetails. The module Calculate_registration_costs will collect all the costs of registration into a data structure called registrationCosts. The total amount payable will also be put into the data structure registrationCosts. These data structures will be passed between modules as parameters.

The module Calculate_federal_tax will calculate the federal tax, which is payable at the rate of $2.00 for each $100.00 or part thereof of the wholesale price of the car. (A variable called tax_units is used to count the number of whole $100 units.)

```
Calculate_vehicle_registration
    Read owners_name
    DOWHILE owners_name NOT = 'XXX'
        Get_vehicle_details (vehicleDetails)
        Calculate_total_amount_payable (vehicleDetails, registrationCosts)
        Output_registration_details (vehicleDetails, registrationCosts)
        Read owners_name
    ENDDO
END


Get_vehicle_details (vehicleDetails)
    Prompt and Get vehicle_make
    Prompt and Get vehicle_model
    Prompt and Get vehicle_weight
    Prompt and Get body_type
    Prompt and Get usage_code
    Prompt and Get wholesale_price
END


Calculate_total_amount_payable (vehicleDetails, registrationCosts)
    Calculate_federal_tax (vehicleDetails, federalTax)
    Calculate_registration_costs (vehicleDetails, registrationCosts)
    total_amount_payable = federalTax + total_registration_charges
END


Calculate_federal_tax (vehicleDetails, federalTax)
    Set tax_units = zero
    DOWHILE wholesale_price > $100
        wholesale_price = wholesale_price – 100
        increment tax_units by 1
    ENDDO
    federalTax = (tax_units + 1) * $2.00
END
```

```
Calculate_registration_costs (vehicleDetails, registrationCosts)
    registration_fee = $27.00
    IF usage_code = 'P' THEN
        tax_levy = wholesale_price * 0.03
        weight_tax = vehicle_weight * 0.01
        insurance_premium = wholesale_price * 0.01
    ELSE
        tax_levy = wholesale_price * 0.05
        weight_tax = vehicle_weight * 0.03
        insurance_premium = wholesale_price * 0.02
    ENDIF
    total_registration_charges = registration_fee + tax_levy + weight_tax +
    insurance_premium
END

Output_registration_details (vehicleDetails, registrationCosts)
    Output vehicle_make
    Output vehicle_model
    Output body_type
    Output registration_fee
    Output tax_levy
    Output weight_tax
    Output insurance_premium
    Output total_registration_charges
    Output federalTax
    Output total_amount_payable
END
```

10.3 Module cohesion

A module has been defined as a section of an algorithm that is dedicated to the performance of a single function. It contains a single entry and a single exit, and the name chosen for the module should describe its function.

Programmers often need guidance in determining what makes a good module. Common queries include: 'How big should a module be?', 'Is this module too small?' and 'Should I put all the read statements in one module?'

There is a method you can use to remove some of the guesswork when establishing modules. You can look at the cohesion of the module. Cohesion is a measure of the internal strength of a module; it indicates how closely the elements or statements of a module are associated with each other. The more closely the elements of a module are associated, the higher the cohesion of the module. Modules with high cohesion are considered good modules, because of their internal strength.

Edward Yourdon and Larry Constantine established seven levels of cohesion and placed them in a scale from the weakest to the strongest.[1]

Cohesion level	Cohesion attribute	Resultant module strength
Coincidental	Low cohesion	Weakest
Logical		
Temporal		
Procedural		
Communicational		
Sequential		
Functional	High cohesion	Strongest

Each level of cohesion in the table will be discussed in this chapter, and pseudocode examples that illustrate each level will be provided.

Coincidental cohesion

The weakest form of cohesion a module can have is coincidental cohesion. It occurs when elements are collected into a module simply because they happen to fall together. There is no meaningful relationship between the elements at all, and so it is difficult to concisely define the function of the module.

Fortunately, these types of modules are rare in current programming practice. They typically used to occur as a result of one of the following conditions:

- An existing program may have been arbitrarily segmented into smaller modules because of hardware constrictions on the operation of the program.
- Existing modules may have been arbitrarily subdivided to conform to a badly considered programming standard (for example, that each module should have no more than 50 program statements).
- A number of existing modules may have been combined into one module either to reduce the number of modules in a program or to increase the number of statements in a module to a particular minimum number.

Here is a pseudocode example of a module that has coincidental cohesion:

```
File_processing
    Open employee updates file
    Read employee record
    Print_page_headings
    Open employee master file
    Set page_count to one
    Set error_flag to false
END
```

---

1 Edward Yourdon and Larry Constantine, *Structured Design: Fundamentals of a Discipline of Computer Program and System Design* (Prentice-Hall, 1979).

Notice that the instructions within the module have no meaningful relationship to each other.

Logical cohesion

Logical cohesion occurs when the elements of a module are grouped together according to a certain class of activity. That is, the elements fall into some general category because they all do the same kind of thing.

An example might be a module that performs all the read statements for three different files: a sort of 'Read_all_files' module. In such a case, the calling module would need to indicate which of the three files it required the called module to read, by sending a parameter.

A module such as this is slightly stronger than a coincidentally cohesive module, because the elements are somewhat related. However, logically cohesive modules are usually made up of a number of smaller, independent sections, which should exist independently rather than be combined together because of a related activity. Often when a module such as this is called, only a small subset of the elements within the module will be executed.

A pseudocode example for a 'Read_all_files' module might look like this:

```
Read_all_files (file_code)
    CASE of file_code
    1 : Read customer transaction record
        IF not EOF
            increment customer_transaction_count
        ENDIF
    2 : Read customer master record
        IF not EOF
            increment customer_master_count
        ENDIF
    3 : Read product master record
        IF not EOF
            increment product_master_count
        ENDIF
    ENDCASE
END
```

Notice that the three Read instructions in this module perform three separate functions.

Temporal cohesion

Temporal cohesion occurs when the elements of a module are grouped together because they are related by time. Typical examples are initialisation and finalisation modules in which elements are placed together because they perform certain housekeeping functions at the beginning or end of a program.

A temporally cohesive module can be considered a logically cohesive module, where time is the related activity. However, it is slightly stronger than a logically cohesive module because most of the elements in a time-related module are executed each time the module is called. Usually, however, the elements are not all related to the same function.

A pseudocode example of a temporally cohesive module might look like this:

```
Initialisation
    Open transaction file
    Issue prompt 'Enter today's date – DDMMYY'
    Read todays_date
    Set transaction_count to zero
    Read transaction record
    IF not EOF
        increment transaction_count
    ENDIF
    Open report file
    Print_page_headings
    Set report_total to zero
END
```

Notice that the elements of the module perform a number of functions.

Procedural cohesion

Procedural cohesion occurs when the elements of a module are related because they operate according to a particular procedure. That is, the elements are executed in a particular sequence so that the objectives of the program are achieved. As a result, the modules contain elements related more to program procedure than to program function.

A typical example of a procedurally cohesive module is the mainline of a program. The elements of a mainline are grouped together because of a particular procedural order.

The weakness of procedurally cohesive modules is that they cut across functional boundaries. That is, the procedure may contain only part of a function at one level, but multiple functions at a lower level, as in the pseudocode example below:

```
Read_student_records_and_total_student_ages
    Set number_of_records to zero
    Set total_age to zero
    Read student record
    DOWHILE more records exist
        add age to total_age
        add 1 to number_of_records
        Read student record
    ENDDO
    Print number_of_records, total_age
END
```

Note that the use of the word 'and' in the module name indicates that this module performs more than one function.

Communicational cohesion

Communicational cohesion occurs when the elements of a module are grouped together because they all operate on the same (central) piece of data. Communicationally cohesive modules are commonly found in business applications because of the close relationship of a business program to the data it is processing. For example, a module may contain all the validations of the fields of a record, or all the processing required to assemble a report line for printing.

Communicational cohesion is acceptable because it is data-related. It is stronger than procedural cohesion because of its relationship with the data, rather than the control-flow sequence.

The weakness of a communicationally cohesive module lies in the fact that usually a combination of processing for a particular piece of data is performed, as in this pseudocode example:

```
Validate_product_record
    IF transaction_type NOT = '0' THEN
        error_flag = true
        error_message = 'invalid transaction type'
        Print_error_report
    ENDIF
    IF customer_number is NOT numeric THEN
        error_flag = true
        error_message = 'invalid customer number'
        Print_error_report
    ENDIF
    IF product_no = blanks
    OR product_no has leading blanks THEN
        error_flag = true
        error_message = 'invalid product no'
        Print_error_report
    ENDIF
END
```

Sequential cohesion

Sequential cohesion occurs when a module contains elements that depend on the processing of previous elements. That is, it may contain elements in which the output data from one element serves as input data for the next. Thus, a sequentially cohesive module is like an assembly line – a series of sequential steps that perform successive transformations of data.

Sequential cohesion is stronger than communicational cohesion because it is more problem-oriented. Its weakness lies only in the fact that the module may perform multiple functions or fragments of functions.

Here is a pseudocode example of a sequentially cohesive module:

```
Process_purchases
    Set total_purchases to zero
    Prompt and Get number_of_purchases
    DO loop_index = 1 to number_of_purchases
        Promt and Get purchase
        add purchase to total_purchases
    ENDDO
    sales_tax = total_purchases * sales_tax_percent
    amount_due = total_purchases + sales_tax
END
```

Note that this module first calculates total_purchases and then uses the variable total_purchases in the subsequent calculation of amount_due.

Functional cohesion

Functional cohesion occurs when all the elements of a module contribute to the performance of a single specific task. The module can be easily named by a single verb followed by a two-word object.

Mathematically oriented modules are a good example of functional cohesion, as the elements making up the module form an integral part of the calculation.

Here is a pseudocode example of a functionally cohesive module.

```
Calculate_sales_tax
    IF product is sales tax exempt THEN
        sales_tax = 0
    ELSE
        IF product_price < $50.00 THEN
            sales_tax = product_price * 0.25
        ELSE
            IF product_price< $100.00 THEN
                sales_tax = product_price * 0.35
            ELSE
                sales_tax = product_price * 0.5
            ENDIF
        ENDIF
    ENDIF
END
```

Summary of cohesion levels

When designing an algorithm, try to form modules that have a single problem-related function. If functional cohesion is achieved, the modules will be more independent, easier to read and understand, and more maintainable than modules with less cohesion.

In some cases, it is not easy to construct a program where every module has functional cohesion. Some modules may contain lower levels of cohesion, or even a combination of types of cohesion. This may not be a problem. However, it is important that you can recognise the various cohesion levels and justify a module with a lower cohesion in a particular set of circumstances.

Your prime consideration is to produce modules and programs that are easy to understand and modify. The higher the cohesion of the modules, the more likely it is that you have achieved this aim.

10.4 Module coupling

When designing a solution algorithm, look not only at the cohesion of modules but also at the flow of information between modules. You should aim to achieve module independence – that is, modules that have fewer and simpler connections with other modules. These connections are called interfaces or couples.

Coupling is a measure of the extent of information interchange between modules. Tight coupling implies large dependence on the structure of one module by another. Because there are many connections, there are many paths along which errors can extend into other parts of the program.

Loose coupling is the opposite of tight coupling. Modules with loose coupling are more independent and easier to maintain.

Glenford Myers[2] devised a coupling scale similar to Yourdon and Constantine's cohesion scale.

Coupling level	Coupling attribute	Resultant module design quality
Common	Tight coupling	Poorest
External		
Control	↓	↓
Stamp		
Data	Loose coupling	Best

The five levels of coupling are listed in a scale from the poorest module design quality to the best. Each of the levels of coupling will be discussed, and pseudocode examples that illustrate each level will be provided. Note that these levels of coupling are not definitive. They are merely the coupling levels that Myers believes can exist in modular programs.

Common coupling

Common coupling occurs when modules reference the same global data structure. (A data structure is a collection of related data items, such as a record or an array.) When modules experience common coupling, the modules share a global data structure.

---

2 Glenford Myers, *Composite Structured Design* (Van Nostrand Reinhold, 1978).

This means that the data can be accessed and modified by any module in the program, which can make the program difficult to read.

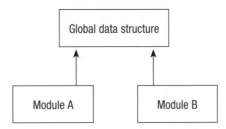

The following pseudocode example shows two modules that experience common coupling because they access the same global data structure (the customer record):

```
A     Read_customer_record
          Read customer record
          IF EOF THEN
              set EOF_flag to true
          ENDIF
      END


B     Validate_customer_record
          IF customer_number is NOT numeric THEN
              error_message = 'invalid customer number'
              Print_error_report
          ENDIF
          :
          :
      END
```

External coupling

External coupling occurs when two or more modules access the same global data variable. It is similar to common coupling except that the global data is an elementary data item, rather than a data structure. Because the global data has a simpler structure, external coupling is considered to be looser than common coupling.

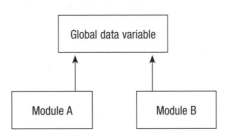

The following pseudocode example shows two modules that exhibit external coupling because they share the same global data item (sales_tax).

```
A     Calculate_sales_tax
          IF product is sales tax exempt THEN
              sales_tax = 0
          ELSE
              IF product_price < $50.00 THEN
                  sales_tax = product_price * 0.25
                  :
                  :
              ENDIF
          ENDIF
      END


B     Calculate_amount_due
          :
          :
          amount_due = total_amount + sales_tax
      END
```

Control coupling

Control coupling occurs when a module passes to another module a control variable that is intended to control the second module's logic. These control variables are referred to as program flags, or switches, and are passed between modules in the form of parameters.

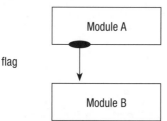

The weakness of control-coupled modules is that the passing of the control variable between modules implies that one module is aware of the internal logic of the other.

The following pseudocode example shows two modules that are control coupled because of the passing of the parameter (input_code):

```
A     Process_input_code
          Read input_code
          Choose_appropriate_action (input_code)
          :
          :
      END
```

B   Choose_appropriate_action (input_code)
           CASE OF input_code
           1 : Read employee record
           2 : Print_page_headings
           3 : Open employee master file
           4 : Set page_count to zero
           5 : error_message = 'Employee number not numeric'
           ENDCASE
      END

Stamp coupling

Stamp coupling occurs when one module passes a non-global data structure to another module in the form of a parameter.

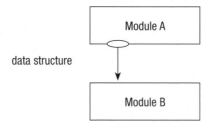

Stamp-coupled modules demonstrate loose coupling and offer good module design quality. The only relationship between the two modules is the passing of the data structure between them; there is no need for either module to know the internal logic of the other.

The following pseudocode example shows two modules that are stamp coupled because of the passing of the current_record data structure.

A   Process_transaction_record
           :
           :
           IF transaction record is for a male THEN
               Process_male_student (current_record)
           ELSE
               Process_female_student (current_record)
           ENDIF
           :
           :
      END

B   Process_male_student (current_record)
           increment male_student_count
           IF student_age > 21 THEN
               increment mature_male_count
           ENDIF
           :
           :
      END

Data coupling

Data coupling occurs when a module passes a non-global data variable to another module. It is similar to stamp coupling except that the non-global data variable is an elementary data item, not a data structure.

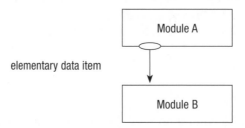

Modules that are data coupled demonstrate the loosest coupling and offer the best module design qualities. The only relationship between the two modules is the passing of one or more elementary data items between them.

The following pseudocode example shows two modules that are data coupled because they pass the elementary data items total_price and sales_tax.

```
A       Process_customer_record
            :
            :
            Calculate_sales_tax (total_price, sales_tax)
            :
        END


B       Calculate_sales_tax (total_price, sales_tax)
            IF total_price < $10.00 THEN
                sales_tax = total_price * 0.25
            ELSE
                IF total_price < $100.00 THEN
                    sales_tax = total_price * 0.3
                ELSE
                    sales_tax = total_price * 0.4
                ENDIF
            ENDIF
        END
```

A summary of coupling levels

When designing solution algorithms, you should aim towards module independence and a minimum of information interchange between modules.

If the programming language allows it, try to uncouple each module from its surroundings by:

1 passing data to a subordinate module in the form of parameters, rather than using global data

2 writing each subordinate module as a self-contained unit that can

- accept data passed to it
- operate on it without reference to other parts of the program, and
- pass information back to the calling module, if required.

Chapter summary

This chapter introduced communication between modules and parameters.

Intermodule communication was defined as the flow of information or data between modules. Local and global variables were introduced, along with the scope of a variable and the side effects of using only global data.

The passing of parameters was introduced as a form of intermodule communication, and the differences between formal and actual parameters, and value and reference parameters, was explained. Programming examples using parameters were then developed.

Module cohesion and module coupling were introduced and must be considered when designing modular programs. A program that has been well designed has modules that are independent, easy to read and easily maintained. Such modules are likely to exhibit high cohesion and loose coupling.

Cohesion is a measure of the internal strength of a module. The higher the cohesion, the stronger the module. Seven levels of cohesion were discussed, and a pseudocode example provided for each level.

Coupling is a measure of the extent of information interchange between modules. The fewer the connections between the modules, the more loosely they are coupled, offering good module design quality. Five levels of coupling were discussed, and a pseudocode example provided for each level.

Programming problems

Construct a solution algorithm for the following programming problems. To obtain your final solution, you should:

- define the problem
- group the activities into modules (also consider the data that each module requires)
- construct a hierarchy chart
- establish the logic of the mainline using pseudocode
- develop the pseudocode for each successive module in the hierarchy chart
- desk check the solution algorithm.

1 Design an algorithm that will produce a reorder list of products from a product inventory file. Each input product record contains the item number, the quantity on hand for the item, the quantity on order, the minimum inventory level for that item, and an obsolete code ('X' if the item is obsolete, blank if it is not).

Your program is to read the product file and determine which items are to be reordered. An item is to be reordered if it is not obsolete and if the quantity of the item currently on hand, plus the amount on order, is less than its minimum inventory level. Print a detail line for each item to be reordered, listing the item number, quantity on hand, quantity on order and minimum inventory level. Print headings and column headings at the top of each page, allowing for 45 detail lines per page, and at the end of the report, print the total number of items to be reordered.

2 Design an algorithm that will produce a list of selected student names from a student file. Each input student record contains the student's number, the student's name, the number of semester hours the student is currently taking, and the age of the student.

Your program is to read the student file and prepare a list of names of all full-time students (students taking 12 or more semester hours) who are 30 years of age or older. If a student appearing on the list is taking more than 20 semester hours, place three asterisks after the student's name. Print a detail line for each student selected, listing student number, name, age and number of semester hours. Print headings and column headings at the top of each page, allowing for 45 detail lines per page. Print the total number of selected students at the end of the report.

3 Design an algorithm that will produce a list of selected customers from a customer file. Each input record contains the customer's name, current monthly sales and year-to-date sales. Each time the program is run, a parameter record containing a dollar amount is read in as the first record in the file.

Your program is to read the parameter record, followed by the customer file, and prepare a list of customers whose purchases total at least $10 000 in the current month. Customers should also be included in the list if their year-to-date sales are at least as great as the amount read in as the parameter.

Print a detail line for each customer, listing customer's name, current monthly sales, year-to-date sales and the parameter amount. Print headings and column headings at the top of each page, allowing for 45 detail lines per page. Print the total number of selected customers at the end of the report.

4 Design an algorithm that will produce a tax report from an employee income file. Each input record contains the employee number and the employee's taxable income. There is one record for each employee.

Your program is to read the employee income file and calculate the tax owing on that employee's taxable income, according to the following table:

Taxable income	Tax payable
$0–14 999.99	20% of taxable income
$15 000–29 999.99	$3000 + 30% of amount greater than $15 000
$30 000–49 999.99	$7500 + 40% of amount greater than $30 000
$50 000–74 999.99	$15 500 + 50% of amount greater than $50 000
$75 000 and above	$28 000 + 75% of amount greater than $75 000

Print a detail line for each employee, listing employee number, taxable income and tax payable. Print headings and column headings at the top of each page, allowing for 45 detail lines per page. Print the total taxable income and total tax payable at the end of the report.

5 Design an algorithm that will create a data validation edit report from an inventory file. Each field on the inventory record is to be validated as follows:

Field	Format
Stock number	Numeric
Item number	Numeric (1–5000)
Description	Alphanumeric
Quantity on hand	Numeric (500–999)
Quantity on order	Numeric (500–999)
Price per unit	Numeric (10–1000)
Inventory reorder level	Numeric (50–500)

If a field is found to be in error, print a line in the data validation edit report showing the stock number, the item number and an appropriate message, as indicated in the diagram below. There may be multiple messages for the one record. Print headings and column headings at the top of each page, allowing for 45 detail lines per page.

Data validation edit report

Stock number	Item number	Message
00742	4003	Quantity on hand out of range
00853	5201	Quantity on order out of range
00932	1007	Price per unit not numeric
00932	1007	Reorder level not valid

6 Design an algorithm that will produce a list of successful applicants who have applied at the local Riff Raff department store for credit. Each input record contains the applicant's name, employment status, years in current job (if any), years at current residence, monthly wage, amount of non-mortgage debt, and number of children.

Your program is to read the applicant's file and determine whether or not each applicant will be granted credit. The store grants credit to a person who has worked in the same job for more than one year, as well as to someone who is employed and has lived at the same location for at least two years. However, credit is denied if a person owes more than two months' wages in non-mortgage debt or has more than six children.

Print a detail line for each applicant, listing the applicant's name and whether or not that applicant has been granted credit. Print headings and column headings at the top of each page, allowing for 45 detail lines per page. Print the total number of successful applicants at the end of the report.

7 Design an algorithm that will read a customer file and calculate the percentage discount allowed on a customer's purchase. Each input record contains the customer's number and name, the class code and the number of units purchased. For wholesale customers, the input record also contains the distance from the warehouse. The class code contains either 'R' for retail customers or 'W' for wholesale customers. The end-of-file is denoted by a customer number of 99999.

Your program is to read the customer file and determine the percentage discount, if any, on a customer's purchase, according to the following guidelines. Retail customers do not receive any discount, nor do wholesale customers who purchase fewer than 10 units. A 10% discount is given to wholesale customers who purchase at least 10 but fewer than 30 units and are within 50 kilometres of the distributor's warehouse. If a wholesale customer purchases between 10 and 30 units but is more than 50 kilometres away, only a 5% discount is allowed. Wholesale customers who purchase 30 or more units receive a 15% discount if they are within 50 kilometres of the warehouse, and a 10% discount if they are more than 50 kilometres away.

Print a detail line for each customer, listing the customer's number and name, the class code, the number of units purchased and the percentage discount (if any) to be applied.

Print headings and column headings at the top of each page, allowing for 45 detail lines per page.

8 The Tidy Phones Telephone Company's charges file contains records for each call made by its Metroville subscribers during a month. Each record on the file contains the subscriber's name and phone number, the phone number called, the distance from Metroville of the number called (in kilometres) and the duration of the call (in seconds).

Design a program that will read the Tidy Phones charges file and produce a telephone charges report, as follows:

```
TIDY PHONES                                                              PAGE: XX
TELEPHONE CHARGES
SUBSCRIBER NAME       SUBSCRIBER NUMBER     PHONE NUMBER CALLED      COST OF CALL
XXXX                  XXXXXXXXXX            XXX-XXXX-XXXX                  999.99
XXXX                  XXXXXXXXXX            XXX-XXXX-XXXX                  999.99
                                            TOTAL REVENUE                9999.99
```

The cost of each call is calculated as follows:

Distance from Metroville	Cost ($)/minute
less than 25 km	0.35
25 < km <75	0.65
75 < km < 300	1.00
300 < km < 1000	2.00
greater than 1000 km	3.00

Main headings and column headings are to be printed on the report, allowing 45 detail lines per page. The total revenue line is to be printed three lines after the last detail line.

9 Design an algorithm that will produce a payroll register from an employee file. Each input record contains the employee number, the hours worked that week and the rate of pay.

Your program is to read the employee file and, for each employee number, to retrieve the employee's name from a table of employee numbers and names. The table contains about 100 entries, and is in sequence of employee number, with the number 9999 used as a sentinel to mark the end of the table. If the employee number cannot be found in the table, a message is to print on the report and no more processing is to be performed for that record. The gross pay for each employee is also to be calculated as hours worked multiplied by rate of pay.

Print a detail line for each employee, listing the employee's number, name, hours worked, rate of pay and gross pay. Print headings and column headings at the top of each page, allowing for 45 detail lines per page. Print the total number of employees and total gross pay at the end of the report.

10 The Mitre-11 hardware outlets require an inventory control program that is to accept order details for an item, and generate a shipping list and a back order list.

Design an interactive program that will conduct a dialogue on the screen for the input values, and print two reports as required. The screen dialogue is to appear as follows:

ENTER Item No.	99999
Quantity on hand	999
Order quantity	999
Order number	999999

If an item number does not have precisely five digits, an error message is to appear on the screen. If the quantity on hand is sufficient to meet the order (order quantity <= quantity on hand), one line is to be printed on the shipping list. If the quantity on hand is insufficient to meet the order (order quantity > quantity on hand), the order is to be filled partially by whatever stock is available. For this situation, one line should appear on the shipping list with the appropriate number of units shipped (quantity on hand) and a message 'Order partially filled'. An entry for the balance of the order (order quantity – quantity on hand) is to be printed on the back order list.

If the quantity on hand is zero, the message 'Out of stock' is to appear on the shipping list, and an entry for the full order quantity is to be printed on the back order list.

Your program is to continue to process inventory orders until a value of zero is entered for the item number.

Report layouts for the shipping list and back order list are as follows:

MITRE-11 HARDWARE			PAGE XX
INVENTORY CONTROL SHIPPING LIST			
ORDER NO.	ITEM NO.	UNITS SHIPPED	MESSAGE
999999	99999	999	—
999999	99999	999	—

MITRE-11 HARDWARE		PAGE XX
INVENTORY CONTROL BACK ORDER LIST		
ORDER NO.	ITEM NO.	BACK ORDER QTY
999999	99999	999
999999	99999	999

An introduction to object-oriented design

11

Information hiding

Objectives

- To introduce object-oriented design
- To define objects, classes, attributes, operations and information hiding
- To introduce public and private operations, accessors and mutators
- To list the steps required to create an object-oriented solution to a problem

Outline

11.1 Introduction to object-oriented design

In this book, program design has concentrated on *what* a program has to do and the organisation of the *processes* required to achieve the desired output. In general, data has been considered only when it is required for input, output or calculations in algorithms. This is said to be a *procedural* approach to program design.

This chapter introduces another style of programming called 'object-oriented design'. Object-oriented programming uses the same concepts as procedural programming, but the primary focus is on the *things* (or objects) that make up the program rather than on the processes involved. Object-oriented programming still uses variables, modules and parameters, as well as sequence, selection and repetition structures; however, some new concepts and new terminology are also required.

Object-oriented design asks that you interact with the problem in much the same way that you interact with your world; that is, that you treat the problem as a set of separate objects that perform actions and relate to each other. An object-oriented program is a set of interacting objects, each one responsible for its own activities and data. When considering an object-oriented approach to a problem, you must:

1 analyse the objects in the program and the tasks to be performed on those objects, and
2 pass messages to objects identifying the actions to be performed.

What is an object?

There are many objects in the real world. For example, a milk jug is an object. A milk jug can be large or small, and it can be made from a range of materials, such as china, metal or plastic, so it is said to have a set of characteristics such as 'liquid capacity' and 'make'. There are also a number of tasks that a milk jug can perform, such as 'filling' and 'pouring'. The jug has a handle, which could be considered a user-friendly interface. When you hold the handle, you are 'passing a message' to the jug to indicate that an operation such as 'pouring' is to be performed.

In object-oriented programming, the milk jug is known as an 'object' and the operations to be performed are known as 'methods'. (In procedural programming, methods are the same as procedures or modules.)

What is a class?

In object-oriented programming, the term 'class' is used to describe a group of objects that share some common properties. For example, a milk jug, a water jug and a wine jug could all be objects within the class Jug. All the jugs share some common properties (they contain liquid and they have a handle) and each jug is said to be an example or 'instance' of the class Jug.

Objects and classes

An object can be defined as a container for both a set of characteristics and a set of operations that can be performed on its data. An object has the following properties:

- It has an identity that is unique for the lifetime of the object.
- It has data in the form of a set of characteristics (attributes), each of which has a value at any given point in time.
- It has a set of operations (methods) that can be performed on the data.
- It is an instance (example) of a class.

Consider another real-world object such as a car. Each car object has a unique identity in the form of its licence number, and has a set of characteristics to describe it – make, model, number of doors, body length, engine size, colour and speed. Cars also have a set of operations or actions that they can perform – accelerate, stop, brake and turn. A Ford Falcon could be an instance of the class Car.

A class, then, is considered to be a category of obects. The class defines the basic characteristics or attributes of its objects and the operations or methods that can be performed on its objects. A class has the following properties:

- It has a unique name. In this book an initial capital letter is used for the class name to identify it as a class, for example Jug and Car.
- It has data in the form of a set of characteristics or attributes, which it passes on to each object within the class.
- It has a set of operations or methods, which it passes on to each object within the class.

The process of creating objects from classes is called *instantiation,* and many objects can be instantiated from a single class. Each object will contain the same attributes, but not necessarily the same values in those attributes.

Attributes

Attributes are the set of properties or characteristics that describe a particular object. Objects of the same class will have an identical set of attributes, each with the same name and data type, but the attributes of one object may contain different data values from those of another object. For example, a milk jug and a wine jug may both have the attribute *liquid capacity*; however, the values within that attribute may be different. Furthermore, those data values may change at any point in an object's lifetime.

Methods

Objects may receive messages from other objects, asking them to perform services or operations. They may also need to perform services for themselves. Thus, objects usually have a set of operations, called 'methods', which perform these services. These methods include all the operations required to be performed on an object, and are the same as modules in procedural programming.

In pseudocode, the name of the method should be meaningful and should describe the function of the operation, such as calculateWeeklyPay() or validateStudentMark(). Convention dictates that empty parentheses are included after the names of methods to clearly distinguish them from the names of variables, and to correspond to many programming languages such as Java and C++. Parameters passed to or from the methods may be enclosed in the parentheses.

Inheritance

Object-oriented programming uses a concept called *inheritance*, which allows a new object to inherit the same attributes and methods as an existing object. For example, a cream jug may inherit the same attributes and operations as milk jug, with some additional characteristics if required. Both objects can access the same methods, such as fillJug() and pourContents().

Class diagram

Object-oriented programming requires classes, attributes and methods to be represented in a class diagram. This is similar to the way in which a defining diagram and hierarchy chart were required in procedural programming. A class diagram consists of a rectangular box divided into three sections, with the name of the class at the top, the attributes of the class in the middle and the methods at the bottom.

Class name
attribute 1
attribute 2
method 1
method 2
method 3

Although this class diagram looks new, the attribute list is similar to the input section of a defining diagram, and the method list is similar to the module names in a hierarchy chart.

Let us look at the class named Car, represented by the following diagram, which lists the name of the class, followed by its attributes and the set of operations that the class can perform.

Car
make
model
doors
bodyLength
engineSize
colour
speed
accelerate( )
stop( )
brake( )
turn(direction)

Note that the class diagram for the class Car simply lists the attributes (data) and methods (operations) for the class. It does not describe *how* or *when* the operations are to be performed.

The Ford and Toyota objects in the diagram below are instances of the Car class. Many car objects can be instantiated from the single Car class. Each car object will be able to access all the Car class operations, but the values in their attributes may be different, and can change.

RVJ635 : Car
make = 'Ford'
model = 'Falcon'
doors = 4
bodyLength = 300
engineSize = 6
colour = 'blue'
speed = 0
accelerate( )
stop( )
brake( )
turn(direction)

SVU478 : Car
make = 'Toyota'
model = 'Corolla'
doors = 5
bodyLength = 200
engineSize = 4
colour = 'red'
speed = 60
accelerate( )
stop( )
brake( )
turn(direction)

Car objects

As you can see from the examples given, object names, attributes and operations should be assigned meaningful names.

Encapsulation and information hiding

In the real world, objects are often said to be encapsulated. The word 'encapsulate' means 'to enclose together in a single indivisible unit', as if in a capsule. For example, when you turn the ignition key of a car, you expect the car to start without really needing to know the intricate workings of the engine.

Similarly, in object-oriented programming, the way an object processes its data is usually hidden from other modules or programs in the system. The object's internal processes and data can operate independently from the rest of the system. This means that objects can be used in several places in one system or across several systems, possibly at the same time, and the code inside the object can easily be maintained without impacting on the rest of the system. Conversely, changes to other parts of the system should not directly affect the object.

In object-oriented design, each object can be regarded as a 'black box' whose internal workings are hidden from all other objects. This principle of 'information hiding' simplifies the use of objects, because the rest of the system does not need to know how they are structured or how they perform their operations. Information hiding is achieved through encapsulation.

The goal of information hiding is to make the object as robust and independent as possible. It ensures that attribute values cannot accidentally be changed by other parts of the system, and carefully controls the interactions that the object has with other objects.

Let us now look again at Example 10.1, which receives a fraction and converts that fraction to a percentage.

EXAMPLE 11.1 Calculate percentage value

Design a class that will <u>receive</u> a fraction in the form of a numerator and a denominator, <u>convert</u> that fraction to a percentage and <u>print</u> the result. Your program is to use object-oriented design techniques.

In earlier chapters, to define a problem you first considered the problem statement and then converted the nouns to variables and the verbs to processes or functions to create a defining diagram, like the one below:

Input	Processing	Output
numerator	Get numerator, denominator	percentage
denominator	Convert fraction to percentage	
	Print percentage	

Object-oriented design requires that a class diagram be produced instead of a defining diagram. To create a class diagram, you need to consider the problem statement, just as you did before. In object-oriented programming, the nouns will become objects, and the verbs will become methods. (These methods correspond to the processes in the defining diagram.) The words used to describe the objects will become the attributes of the objects.

Using this guide, the input 'fraction' will become the class 'Fraction' and the numerator and denominator will become the attributes of that class. The methods will become setFraction(), convertFraction() and printPercentage(). The class diagram for the class Fraction will look like this:

Fraction
numerator
denominator
setFraction( )
convertFraction( )
printPercentage( )

As for a defining diagram, the class diagram only shows what data and methods the class will use. Let us now look again at Example 10.3, which uses a record, and construct a class diagram for that object.

EXAMPLE 11.2 Calculate employee's pay

A company requires a program to read an employee's number, pay rate and the number of hours worked in a week. The program is then to validate the pay rate field and the hours worked field and, if they are valid, to compute the employee's weekly pay and then print it and the input data.

Validation: According to the company's rules, the maximum hours an employee can work per week is 60 hours, and the maximum hourly rate is $25.00 per hour. If the hours worked field or the hourly rate field is out of range, the input data and an appropriate message are to be printed and the employee's weekly pay is not to be calculated.

Weekly pay calculation: Weekly pay is calculated as hours worked times pay rate. If more than 35 hours have been worked, payment for the overtime hours worked is calculated at time-and-a-half.

In this example, the employee record will become the class Employee and the fields on the employee record will become the attributes of the class. The modules in the hierarchy chart for Example 10.3 will become the methods in the following class diagram.

Employee
empNumber
payRate
hoursWorked
readEmployeeData( )
validateInputFields( )
calculateWeeklyPay( )
printEmployeeDetails( )

11.2 Public and private access methods

In object-oriented programming, it is necessary to consider whether the attributes and operations of an object are to have private or public access. This concept is called 'visibility'.

Private access means that the attributes and methods are invisible to the rest of the system. Usually the attributes of an object are specified as *private access*, that is, the attributes can only be accessed by methods within that class. Public attributes are not desirable as you do not want other methods or programs to change the data in your object, as this could lead to undesirable side effects.

The methods of an object are usually specified as *public access*, that is, the operations are visible to other objects. When an operation has public access, other objects can see the specifications of that operation, which is usually its name, its parameters, if any, and its return value, if any. These specifications define what the object can do and what information it requires to perform the service; however, its implementation, or how it is going to perform the service, remains hidden.

Within an object, there can also be private operations that are needed to perform the internal actions in an object and which cannot be accessed directly from outside the object.

To illustrate the concept of visibility, consider a bank account class called BankAccount, which has an attribute called accountBalance and a number of methods, as illustrated in the following BankAccount class diagram.

BankAccount
accountBalance
displayBalance( ) deposit( ) withdraw( ) calculateInterest( ) verifySufficientFunds( )

First, the attribute accountBalance, like all attributes, must be private, as it is essential that an operation in another object or program is not able to alter a customer's account balance.

Second, some of the operations of the BankAccount class must be public, for example displayBalance(), deposit() and withdraw(), as these operations help the BankAccount class to interact with external systems such as an ATM. In pseudocode, these public operations will be preceded by a + (plus) sign in the class diagram.

To display the current account balance, the public operation displayBalance() may need the services of a calculateInterest() operation. Similarly, the public operation withdraw() may need the services of a verifySufficientFunds() operation to check that the account balance is greater than the withdrawal amount. The calculateInterest() and verifySufficientFunds() operations are not visible to the user at the ATM; in fact, they are not visible to any objects outside the BankAccount class. They are internal operations of each BankAccount class because external objects do not require them, and therefore they should be declared as private. In pseudocode, these private operations will be preceded by a – (minus) sign in the class diagram.

Now let's look at the BankAccount class diagram with the methods specified as public or private.

BankAccount
–accountBalance
+displayBalance() +deposit() +withdraw() –calculateInterest() –verifySufficientFunds()

Let's now at look again at Example 11.1 and provide the class diagram and the public and private methods for the class Fraction, using pseudocode and object-oriented design techniques. Note that the pseudocode for the methods in this example is similar to the pseudocode for Example 10.1.

EXAMPLE 11.3 Calculate percentage value

Design a class that will <u>receive</u> a fraction in the form of a numerator and a denominator, <u>convert</u> that fraction to a percentage and <u>display</u> the result. Your program is to use object-oriented design techniques.

A Class diagram

The class diagram for the class Fraction is as follows:

Fraction
–numerator –denominator
+setFraction() –convertFraction() +displayPercentage()

B Methods for the Fraction class

```
class Fraction
    numerator
    denominator

setFraction (inNumerator, inDenominator)
    numerator = inNumerator
    denominator = inDenominator
END


displayPercentage()
    convertFraction(percentage)
    IF percentage NOT = 0 THEN
        Output to screen, percentage, '%'
    ELSE
        Output to screen 'invalid fraction', numerator, denominator
    ENDIF
END


convertFraction (percentage)
    IF denominator NOT = 0
        percentage = (numerator / denominator) * 100
    ELSE
        percentage = 0
    ENDIF
END
```

The attributes numerator and denominator are private in this class. There is no need to declare percentage as an attribute as it will be derived from the other attributes.

There are two public methods in this class: setFraction() and displayPercentage(). The method setFraction() is designed to receive two external values, named inNumerator and inDenominator, which are passed to the method as parameters. The method setFraction() will then assign these external values to the private attributes numerator and denominator. In this way, the data fields within the class remain private, and no outside object or program can alter their values. In pseudocode, methods that assign external values to the attributes of a class start with the word 'set'.

The public method displayPercentage() will call the private method convertFraction() and then print the percentage or an error message to the screen. The method convertFraction() will convert the fraction to a percentage and pass this value back to the calling module as a parameter. There is no need for other objects to know how this is achieved.

Instantiating objects

Object-oriented programs create objects that are members of a class. Every time an object is instantiated from a class, a special operation, or set of instructions, known as a 'constructor' method is called or invoked. Constructors are prewritten methods that have the same name as their class. When called, the constructor will create an object at a particular memory location and then assign initial values to the attributes of the new object. Default initial values are usually zero for numeric data items, and spaces (blanks) for character fields. The general pseudocode for instantiating a new object is:

```
Create object-name as new Class-name()
```

For example:

```
Create sedan as new Car()
```

The keyword 'new' refers to the creation of a new object, sedan, within the class Car. When sedan is instantiated as a new Car object, the sedan object will inherit the same attributes as car and will automatically have access to all the methods in the Car class. By convention, class names start with an upper case, or capital letter, such as Car, and object names are written in lower case, such as sedan.

Constructors may:

- have no parameters, in which case a new object is assigned all the default values for its attributes, for example Create sedan as new Car(), or
- have parameters that initialise the attributes with specific values, for example Create sedan as new Car(Ford, Falcon, 4, 300, 6, blue, 0).

If you do not want to use a default constructor, you may write your own constructor method as a list of statements that initialise the attributes, as follows:

```
Car()
    make = ''
    model = ''
    doors = 0
    bodyLength = 0
    engineSize = 0
    colour = ''
    speed = 0
END
```

A programmer-written constructor, as above, will have the same name as its class and will replace the default constructor. Let us now use a default constructor to create two new objects, called sedan and hatchback, from the class Car. In pseudocode, the constructors can be written as:

```
Create sedan as new Car()
Create hatchback as new Car()
```

These statements not only create the two new objects, they also assign default values to their attributes. All the attributes will now be visible to the object's methods, and all the methods for the class Car, such as accelerate(), stop() and brake(), can now be accessed by the new objects. When a new object uses an existing method from its class, it is written in pseudocode as the object name followed by the name of the method, separated by a period or 'dot operator', for example:

```
sedan.accelerate()
hatchback.accelerate()
```

Note that this notation can only be used to access public operations.

Accessors and mutators

Attributes are usually defined as having private access, so the values in the attributes of an object should be available to all operations used by that object, but hidden from external objects. For safety, only special public operations, known as accessors and mutators, should allow external objects to access the values in attributes.

Accessor operations pass attributes to external objects, but do not change the values. By convention, accessor names start with the word 'get', for example getFraction(). An accessor is simply a descriptive name for an operation that retrieves or gets the value of an attribute.

Mutator operations enable external values to be passed to attributes. By convention, mutator names start with the word 'set', for example setPayRate(). A mutator is simply a descriptive name for an operation that provides or sets the value of an attribute.

Messages

Objects must be able to communicate and interact with other objects, and this is achieved by the passing of messages. In most cases, a message is a call made by one object to an operation in another object. The called object takes responsibility for performing the services defined by that operation. As mentioned previously, this call is written in pseudocode as the name of the object followed by the name of the method, separated by a period or 'dot operator', for example:

```
chequeAccount.displayBalance()
```

In this example, the chequeAccount object has called the method displayBalance() to perform the service of displaying the balance of the cheque account.

In order to produce the required services, the method may need to receive information from the calling object. In some cases, the method may also return a value to the caller. In pseudocode notation, these inputs and outputs are received and sent as parameters enclosed in parentheses after the name of the method, with the sent values first in the parameter list followed by the returned values. For example, a message to a chequeAccount object requesting deposit services would take the form of the following call:

chequeAccount.deposit (amount, newBalance)

In this example, the chequeAccount object has called the method deposit() and has passed the parameter 'amount' to it. The method deposit() will deposit the amount, calculate the new cheque account balance and then return this new balance in the parameter newBalance.

11.3 Steps in creating an object-oriented solution

This chapter has introduced many new concepts and terms that are associated with object-oriented design. These concepts will now be used to create object-oriented solutions for some simple programs that use just one class.

There are three steps in creating an object-oriented solution for a problem with just one class:

1 Identify the objects and their attributes, responsibilities and operations.
2 Design the algorithms for the operations or methods, using structured design.
3 Develop a test or driver algorithm to test the solution.

To start an object-oriented design, read the problem definition carefully, looking for nouns and noun phrases. These will become the objects and the attributes of the objects in the program. To identify the operations, look closely at the verbs that describe the actions performed by the nouns. It may help to think about the responsibilities of the objects, and how these might translate into operations. These attributes, responsibilities and operations can then be represented in a class table that lists them horizontally, rather than vertically as in earlier class diagrams.

A class table

Class	Attributes	Responsibilities	Operations
class name	attribute 1 attribute 2 …		operation1() operation2() …

Let us look at some examples.

11.4 Programming examples using object-oriented design

EXAMPLE 11.4 Process exam scores

Design a class that will receive four scores from a mathematics test, calculate the total and average scores and display the total and average scores to the screen.

Step 1: Identify the objects and their attributes, responsibilities and operations

To commence the design, as before, underline the nouns and noun phrases to identify the objects and their attributes.

Design a class that will receive <u>four scores</u> from a <u>mathematics test</u>, calculate the <u>total</u> and <u>average scores</u> and display the total and average scores to the screen.

In the example, it is apparent that a MathsTest class will be required with attributes of the four scores. There is no need to make the total score or average score an attribute, because these values will be derived from the input scores. The class table will now look like this:

Class	Attributes	Responsibilities	Operations
MathsTest	score1		
	score2		
	score3		
	score4		

Now underline the verb and verb phrases to identify the responsibilities and the operations that the class is required to perform.

Design a class that will <u>receive</u> four scores from a mathematics test, <u>calculate</u> the total and average scores and <u>display</u> the total and average scores to the screen.

The underlined verbs and verb phrases indicate that the processes or responsibilities of the class are as follows: receive the four scores, calculate the total score, calculate the average score and display the results. These responsibilities can now be added to the class table:

Class	Attributes	Responsibilities	Operations
MathsTest	score1	Receive four scores	
	score2	Calculate total score	
	score3	Calculate average score	
	score4	Display final scores	

Now that the responsibilities have been established, you need to create a set of operations or methods to perform these responsibilities and to indicate whether they will have public or private access.

First, you will need a public method to receive the scores, namely setScores(). Because it will receive the scores from an external source, this method will be a mutator method, so by convention it will start with the word 'set'. You will also need a public method to display the final scores, namely displayScores(). The calculations for the total and average scores are internal, so the two methods for these operations can be private, as other objects do not need to know how these scores are calculated.

These operations can now be added to the class table:

Class	Attributes	Responsibilities	Operations
MathsTest	score1	Receive four scores	+setScores()
	score2	Calculate total score	+displayScores()
	score3	Calculate average score	-calculateTotalScore()
	score4	Display final scores	-calculateAverageScore()

Step 2: Design the algorithms for the operations, using structured design

```
Class MathsTest
    score1
    score2
    score3
    score4
```

Public operations

An algorithm is required for each operation in the class table. The mutator setScores() requires the scores to be passed to it from an external source in the form of parameters. The values in these parameters will then be passed to the attributes of the class MathsTest.

```
setScores(inScore1, inScore2, inScore3, inScore4)
    score1 = inScore1
    score2 = inScore2
    score3 = inScore3
    score4 = inScore4
END
```

The total and average scores will be displayed to the screen by the method displayScores(), which calls the private methods calculateTotalScore() and calculateAverageScore() respectively.

```
displayScores()
    calculateTotalScore(totalScore)
    calculateAverageScore(totalScore, averageScore)
    Output to screen 'Total Score is', totalScore
    Output to screen 'Average Score is', averageScore
END
```

Private operations

The private operation calculateTotalScore() will calculate the total score from the input scores and then return this value in a parameter.

```
calculateTotalScore(totalScore)
    totalScore = score1 + score2 + score3 + score4
END
```

The private operation calculateAverageScore() will receive the total score as a parameter, use this value to calculate the average score and then return this value in a parameter.

```
calculateAverageScore(totalScore, averageScore)
    averageScore = totalScore / 4
END
```

Step 3: Develop a test or driver algorithm to test the solution

The problem definition stated that a class be designed, rather than a program. This is a common task in object-oriented programming. Rather than develop a mainline algorithm that might drive an entire program, an object-oriented solution often requires a test (or driver) algorithm to test all the methods in the class.

In the test algorithm, the MathsTest class will require a constructor to create a mathsTest object and provide it with default values. This is achieved by the following statement:

```
Create mathsTest1 as new MathsTest()
```

The empty parentheses indicate that default values will be assigned to the object's attributes. The MathsTest class can now be trialled using a test algorithm called testMathsTest. This testMathsTest algorithm will simply test that all the methods in the MathsTest class work correctly, as follows:

```
testMathsTest()
    Create mathsTest1 as new MathsTest()
    inScore1 = 20
    inScore2 = 21
    inScore3 = 22
    inScore4 = 23
    mathsTest1.setScores(inScore1, inScore2, inScore3, inScore4)
    mathsTest1.displayScores()
END
```

This algorithm provides initial values for the maths test scores for the object mathsTest1. These scores are then passed as parameters to the method setScores(). The method displayScores is then called, which in turn calls calculateTotalScore() and calculateAverageScore(). This test algorithm has now tested all the methods and the expected output from this test is displayed:

Total Score is 86
Average Score is 21.5

EXAMPLE 11.5 Print student results

Design a class to manage student results in a subject. A unique student number identifies each student. During the course of the subject, each student completes three assignments (representing 40% of the final mark, but each scored out of 100) and an examination (also scored out of 100). The final mark is calculated by multiplying the sum of the assignments by 0.133, and the examination score by 0.6 and then adding the two products together.

The class should allow a user to receive a mark for an assignment or examination, validate that mark, calculate the final mark and print the final mark along with the student number for each student.

Step 1: Identify the objects and their attributes, responsibilities and operations

To commence the design, underline the nouns and noun phrases to identify the objects and their attributes.

Design a class to manage <u>student results</u> in a subject. A <u>unique student number</u> identifies each student. During the course of the subject, each student completes <u>three assignments</u> (representing 40% of the final mark, but each scored out of 100) and an <u>examination</u> (also scored out of 100). The <u>final mark</u> is calculated by multiplying the sum of the assignments by 0.133 and the examination score by 0.6 and then adding the two products together.

The class should allow a user to receive a mark for an assignment or examination, validate that mark, calculate the final mark and print the final mark along with the student number for each student.

In the example, it is apparent that a Student class will be needed, with attributes of unique student number, three assignment marks and an examination mark. There is no need to make the final mark an attribute, because it can be derived from the other attributes. The class chart will now look like this:

Class	Attributes	Responsibilities	Operations
Student	studentNumber asstOne asstTwo asstThree examMark		

Now underline the verb and verb phrases to identify the responsibilities and the operations that the object needs to perform.

Design a class to <u>manage student results</u> in a subject. A unique student number identifies each student. During the course of the subject, each student completes three assignments (representing 40% of the final mark but each scored out of 100) and an examination (also scored out of 100). The <u>final mark is calculated</u> by multiplying the sum of the assignments by 0.133 and the examination score by 0.6 and then adding the two products together.

The class should allow a user to <u>receive a mark for an assignment or examination,</u> <u>validate the mark,</u> <u>calculate the final mark</u> and <u>print the final mark</u> along with the student number for each student.

The underlined verbs and verb phrases indicate that the processes or responsibilities of the class are as follows: receive an assignment mark, receive an exam mark, validate the mark, calculate the final mark and print the final mark. These responsibilities can now be added to the class table:

Class	Attributes	Responsibilities	Operations
Student	studentNumber asstOne asstTwo asstThree examMark	Receive assignment mark Receive exam mark Validate mark Calculate final mark Print final mark	

Now that the responsibilities have been established, you need to create a set of operations or methods to perform these responsibilities and to indicate whether they will have public or private access.

First, you will need a public method to receive the assignment mark, namely setAsstMark(). Because it will receive the mark from an external source, this method will be a mutator method, so by convention, will start with the word 'set'. The method setAsstMark() requires two values when it is called, namely the assignment number and the assignment mark.

Similarly, you will also need a public method to receive the examination mark, namely setExamMark(), which requires an examination mark to be provided when it is called. You also need a public method to print the final mark, namely printFinalMark(). The operations to validate the mark and calculate the final mark will be private as other objects do not need to know how these marks are calculated.

These operations can now be added to the class table:

Class	Attributes	Responsibilities	Operations
Student	studentNumber	Receive assignment mark	+setAsstMark(asstNum, result)
	asstOne	Receive exam mark	+setExamMark(result)
	asstTwo	Validate mark	–validateMark( )
	asstThree	Calculate final mark	–calculateFinalMark( )
	examMark	Print final mark	+printFinalMark( )

Step 2: Design the algorithms for the operations, using structured design

```
Class Student
    studentNumber
    asstOne
    asstTwo
    asstThree
    examMark
```

Public operations

An algorithm is required for each operation in the object table. The mutator setAsstMark() requires two parameters to be passed to it: the assignment number (a number from 1 to 3) and the result for each assignment. The result will be validated by the private method validateMark(), before the mark for that assignment is recorded in the correct attribute.

```
setAsstMark(inAsstNum, inResult)
    validateMark(inResult, validInput)
    IF validInput THEN
        CASE OF inAsstNum
            1: asstOne = inResult
            2: asstTwo = inResult
            3: asstThree = inResult
        OTHER
            Print 'Invalid Assignment number', inAsstNum
        ENDCASE
    ENDIF
END
```

Similarly, the mutator setExamMark() will require the examination result to be passed to it. This result will also be validated by validateMark() before being used.

```
setExamMark(inResult)
    validateMark(inResult, validInput)
    IF validInput THEN
        examMark = inResult
    ENDIF
END
```

The results will be printed by the method printFinalMark(), which calls the method calculateFinalMark() to calculate the final mark before printing.

```
printFinalMark()
    calculateFinalMark(finalMark)
    Print 'Student', studentNumber, 'Final mark is', finalMark
END
```

Private operations
The valid range for the assignment and examination results can be tested in validateMark(), to ensure that no invalid marks are recorded in the attribute values. This operation will return the parameter validInput, which indicates if the input mark is valid.

```
validateMark(inResult, validInput)
    Set validInput to true
    IF (inResult < 0 OR inResult >100) THEN
        Set validInput to false
        Print 'Input mark invalid', inResult
    ENDIF
END
```

The private method calculateFinalMark() will calculate the final mark and return this value in a parameter.

```
calculateFinalMark(finalMark)
    finalMark = (asstOne + asstTwo + asstThree) * 0.133
    finalMark = finalMark + (examMark * 0.6)
END
```

Step 3: Develop a test or driver algorithm to test the solution
As in the previous example, the problem definition stated that a class be designed, rather than a program, so a test algorithm called testStudent will be developed to test all the methods in the Student class.

In the test algorithm, the Student class will require a constructor to create a student object and initialise its attributes. All the attributes will be set to zero; however the value of the studentNumber attribute will be passed as a parameter to the constructor, so a special constructor will need to be written to receive this parameter. This constructor will have the same name as its class and will replace the default constructor, as follows:

```
Student(inStudentNumber)
    studentNumber = inStudentNumber
    asstOne = 0
    asstTwo = 0
    asstThree = 0
    examMark = 0
END
```

The pseudocode to create a student object will now be:

```
Create student1 as new Student(studentNumber)
```

The Student class can now be trialled using a test algorithm called testStudent. This testStudent algorithm will simply test that all the methods in the Student class work correctly, as follows:

```
testStudent()
    studentNumber = 111000
    Create student1 as new Student(studentNumber)
    asstNum = 1
    result = 60
    student1.setAsstMark(asstNum, result)
    asstNum = 2
    result = 65
    student1.setAsstMark(asstNum, result)
    asstNum = 3
    result = 70
    student1.setAsstMark(asstNum, result)
    result = 80
    student1.setExamMark(result)
    student1.printFinalMark()
    studentNumber = 222000
    Create student2 as new Student(studentNumber)
    result = 95
    student2.setExamMark(result)
    student2.printFinalMark()
END
```

This algorithm provides values for the three assignments and the exam for the object student1, and a value for the exam only for the object student2. The testStudent algorithm then tests all the methods in the Student class and produces the following output:

```
Student 111000 Final mark is 74
Student 222000 Final Mark is 57
```

Chapter summary

Object-oriented design focuses on the objects that make up a program rather than on the processes involved. Instead of breaking up the problem into functions, the problem is broken up into the objects in the system, and the attributes and methods for each object are then identified.

An object can be defined as a container for both a set of characteristics and a set of operations that can be performed on the data. Objects encapsulate their data and operations, and can be regarded as 'black boxes' for the purposes of large system design. Objects are instantiated from classes and can inherit the same attributes and methods as an existing object.

Operations that are accessible by external objects are described as having public access, and operations that are internal to the object have private access.

The steps in designing an object-oriented solution for a simple programming problem are:

1 Identify the classes and their attributes, responsibilities and operations.
2 Design the algorithms for the operations, using structured design.
3 Develop a test or driver algorithm to test the solution.

Programming problems

1 Use object-oriented design to design a class called Circle that will receive the diameter of a circle, and calculate and display the circumference and the area of that circle.
   a Design the class table.
   b Write an algorithm for each operation.
   c Write a test or driver algorithm to test the solution.
2 Use object-oriented design to design a class called Rectangle that will receive the length and breadth of a rectangle, validate the input data and calculate and display the area of the rectangle.
   a Design the class table.
   b Write an algorithm for each operation.
   c Write a test or driver algorithm to test the solution.

3 Use object-oriented design to design a class called Book that will receive the ISBN, author, title and price of a book. Your class is to select and print the details of all books with a price of more than $50.00.

   a Design the class table.

   b Write an algorithm for each operation.

   c Write a test or driver algorithm to test the solution.

4 Use object-oriented design to design a class called MathsTest that will receive an array of 30 mathematics scores from a Mathematics exam, calculate the class average from the scores and display the class average to the screen.

   a Design the class table.

   b Write an algorithm for each operation.

   c Write a test or driver algorithm to test the solution.

5 A parts inventory record contains the following fields:

- part number (6 characters, 2 alpha and 4 numeric, e.g. AA1234)
- part description
- inventory balance.

Use object-oriented design to design a class called Inventory that will receive the input record, validate the part number and print the details of all valid inventory records that have an inventory balance equal to zero.

   a Design the class table.

   b Write an algorithm for each operation in the table.

   c Write a test or driver algorithm to test the solution.

6 Use object-oriented design to design a class called Employee that determines the weekly salary for a company's full-time employees. Each employee record contains the employee's number, name and hourly wage. Your class is to receive the employee data, validate the hourly wage and calculate the weekly salary, assuming all employees are paid for a 40 hour week. The hourly wage validation is to check that hourly wage is less than $30.00 per week. If the wage is greater than $30.00 then it is to revert to $30.00.

   a Design the class table.

   b Write an algorithm for each operation in the table.

   c Write a test or driver algorithm to test the solution.

7 Use object-oriented design to design a class called PhoneBill that calculates and prints the balance owed by each customer of a phone company during the billing period. Your PhoneBill class is to receive the customer's current balance and the total time, in minutes, of phone calls during the billing period. The input time is to be validated and the cost of calls is to be calculated at 25c per minute. Your class is to print the input balance, the phone call time, the cost of the phone calls and the total amount due.

   a Design the class table.

   b Write an algorithm for each operation in the table.

   c Write a test or driver algorithm to test the solution.

8 Use object-oriented design to design a class to manage a share portfolio. Shareholdings are identified by the company name, the number of shares purchased, the date of the purchase, the cost per share and the current price per share. You must be able to calculate the value of current shares, the profit or loss made on the stock purchased and be able to sell the shares.

    a Design the class table.

    b Write an algorithm for each operation.

    c Write a test or driver algorithm to test the class.

9 Write an algorithm for a default constructor for the Share class in Problem 8.

10 Use object-oriented design to design a class called LoanAccount that receives an account number, an account name, the amount borrowed, the term of the loan and the interest rate. The amount borrowed must be positive and less than or equal to $100 000.00, the term must be less than 30 years and the interest rate must be less than 15%. Your class is to validate the input data and print all the loan information.

    a Design the class table.

    b Write an algorithm for each operation.

    c Write a test or driver algorithm to test the class.

Object-oriented design for more than one class

12

I'd like you to welcome a new OBJECT to this CLASS

Objectives

- To describe relationships between classes
- To introduce a simplified unified modelling language
- To introduce polymorphism and operation overriding in object-oriented design
- To develop object-oriented solutions to problems using more than one class

Outline

12.1 Further object-oriented design

Chapter 11 introduced some object-oriented design concepts and terminology, and provided three steps to follow when designing an object-oriented solution to a simple problem. This chapter introduces some more concepts and terminology for problems that use more than one class, and provides an extra step to follow when designing object-oriented solutions to these problems.

A major advantage of object-oriented programming languages is their usefulness in constructing large programs; however, it would be very unusual for a program to make use of only one class. In designing programs that use more than one class, it is necessary to consider not only the individual class design but also the relationships between the classes and therefore between the objects that are instantiated from those classes.

Notations

Object-oriented design and object-oriented programming have taken some time to mature as methodologies. A notation called UML (Unified Modelling Language) has emerged from the work of Rumbaugh, Booch and Jacobsen. The notation in this chapter is based on a simplified UML standard.

UML notation allows a programmer to represent graphically the relationships between classes as well as between objects. This chapter will introduce some of the UML graphical notation used to design classes and their relationships.

Relationships between classes

When more than one class is used in a program, there can be three types of relationships between the classes:

1   Two classes may be independent of each other but one class might use the services the other provides. This relationship is called an *association*.
2   A class may be made up of other classes, or contain other classes that are part of itself. This form of relationship is called either an *aggregation* or a *composition*.
3   A class may *inherit* all the attributes and operations of a parent class, but is given a unique name, as well as its own additional attributes and operations. This form of relationship between a parent and child class is called *generalisation*.

Examples will be used to expand these relationships further.

Association

An association between two classes is required when the classes need to interact or communicate with each other for the program to achieve its purpose. For example, a Car class and a Garage class are independent, although a car may sometimes use garage services such as parking. As a result of this association, objects that are instantiated from these two classes will be able to communicate by passing or receiving messages. In some circumstances, a garage object will be created without a car object, and vice versa.

Just as instances of classes are called *objects*, instances of associations are called *links*. In a class diagram, a straight line and a small arrow indicate the direction in which to read the description of the association, although association allows communication in both directions. Classes that have an association are able to communicate by passing messages; that is, one object will make a call to an operation in another object. The numbers at each end of the association show how many objects can have this association, when it is instantiated.

The diagram above shows the association relationship between a Car class and a Garage class. The numbers indicate that there is one garage object that can be used by one or two car objects. Once an object is instantiated from each of the classes, the UML diagram may look like this:

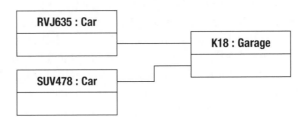

This association relationship can be described in two ways, namely, 'Two car objects use a garage object', or, in the other direction, 'A garage object is used by 1 or 2 car objects'.

Aggregation and composition

Aggregation and composition are special forms of association in which a whole class is made up of several part classes. For example, a major department store may be made up of several departments, such as Electrical Department, Manchester Department etc. These are whole–part associations: one class is the *whole* that is made up of several *parts*. The class at the *whole* end can have attributes and operations of its own, as well.

The mildest form of this association relationship is called *aggregation*, in which the *part* or *component* classes that make up the whole are able to exist without necessarily being part of the aggregation. In UML notation, an open diamond positioned at the whole end of the association represents an aggregation, as shown:

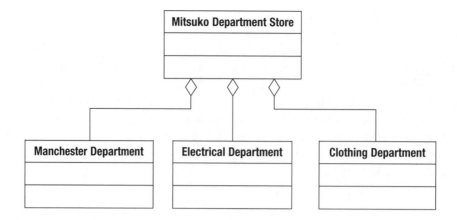

This diagram shows an aggregation relationship between the Mitsuko Department Store and the departments that make it up, namely Manchester, Electrical and Clothing.

The strongest form of association relationship is called a *composition*. Its component classes can only exist during the lifetime of the container object and cannot exist outside the composition. When the whole object is created, all of the needed component objects are created. When the whole object is destroyed, all of its component objects are also destroyed.

For example, a car is a *composition* of many parts, including an engine. So, every object of the Car class needs to have an object of the Engine class to be able to work effectively; however, an object of the Engine class cannot fulfil all of its responsibilities outside its vehicle. In UML notation, a filled diamond positioned at the whole end of the association represents a composition relationship, as shown:

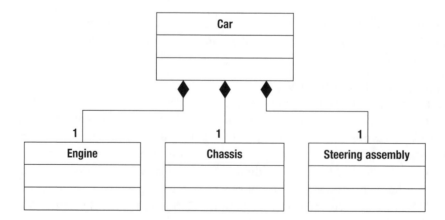

This diagram shows that an Engine, a Chassis and a Steering assembly can only exist as part of a Car, and that any Car can only have one Engine, one Chassis and one Steering assembly.

Generalisation

Sometimes, one class shares features with another class, but has enough differences to deserve its own identity. The first class then becomes a *type* of the second class. For example, cars are a type of vehicle, just as bicycles and buses are types of vehicles. Generalisation is a class hierarchy that lets us group the shared attributes and operations into a top-level class, and then to define one or more lower-level classes with extra or different attributes and operations. The top-level class, also called the *parent class* or *superclass*, has shared attributes and operations, and the *child classes* or *subclasses*, inherit these, adding their own attributes and operations to make them distinct.

Let us look at an example that uses a Vehicle class as the parent class. The Vehicle class has a set of attributes that are shared by all vehicles, such as make and model. It also has a set of operations that are shared by all vehicles, such as stop(), turn() and accelerate(). The Vehicle class may have two child classes such as Car class and Bicycle class. The Car child class will *inherit* all the attributes and operations of the Vehicle superclass, but it may have additional attributes that are particular to cars, such as trunkSize, and operations, such as openTrunk(). Similarly, the Bicycle class will inherit all the attributes and operations of the Vehicle superclass, but it may have an additional attribute such as frameType. In UML notation an open-headed arrow positioned at the parent class represents this generalisation relationship, as shown:

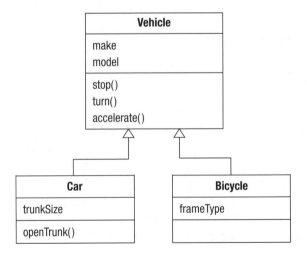

This diagram shows that Car and Bicycle are both types of Vehicle. Generalisation notation is different from association notation in UML, because it represents a type of class hierarchy instead of an association.

Polymorphism

Polymorphism, meaning *many-shaped*, refers to the use of the same method name in different classes to perform a variety of purposes. Each method is designed to work appropriately, based on the context in which it is used. Using the Vehicle example, the car and bicycle objects inherit all the same attributes and operations as a vehicle object; however, the operation to accelerate() for a car is quite different from accelerate() for a bicycle. Both objects need the operation accelerate(), but it is achieved in quite different ways for objects of each type. The Car and the Bicycle classes will each need to provide their own definition of accelerate() to be complete. This is an example of polymorphism.

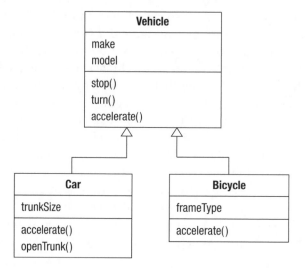

Operation overriding

Operation overriding occurs when a parent class provides an operation, but the inheriting child class defines its own version of that operation. In the above example, both Car and Bicycle inherit an accelerate() operation from their parent class Vehicle. The accelerate() operation in the Car object is different from the accelerate() operation in the Bicycle object, although it has the same name and purpose. Both operations are probably different from the accelerate() operation in Vehicle. Therefore, whenever accelerate() is called for by an object such as Car or Bicycle, the version of the operation used by that particular object will be utilised. In other words, the operation in a subclass will override the operation in the superclass. In pseudocode, the operation can be written with the dot notation, such as car.accelerate() or bicycle.accelerate().

Operation overloading

Operation overloading occurs when several operations in a single class have the same name, but will act differently according to the number of parameters that are passed to the operation when it is called. For example, a bicycle class may have two versions of the stop() operation, such as stop(handbrake) and stop(handbrake, footbrake). When a call is made to the operation stop(), the number of arguments in the call is evaluated and the correct stop() operation for the object is invoked.

Scope of the data

As soon as an object is created, the data that an object needs is brought within its scope. Attribute values are available to all the operations within the class and are visible to each operation. For example, when a vehicle object is created from the Vehicle class, values are available for its attributes (make and model) and these attributes are visible to all its operations.

12.2 Steps in creating an object-oriented solution using more than one class

In Chapter 11 there were three steps to follow when considering an object-oriented solution to a problem that uses only one class. For problems that use more than one class, there are now four steps to follow to create an object-oriented solution:

1 Identify the classes and their attributes, responsibilities and operations.
2 Determine the relationship between the objects of those classes.
3 Design the algorithms for the operations or methods, using structured design.
4 Develop a test or driver algorithm to test the solution.

To start an object-oriented design, read the problem definition carefully, looking for nouns and noun phrases. These will become the objects and the attributes of the objects in the program. To identify the operations, look closely at the verbs that describe the actions performed by the nouns. It may help to think about the responsibilities of the objects, and how these might translate into operations. These responsibilities can then be represented, along with the other sections of a class diagram, in a class table, as follows:

A class table

Class	Attributes	Responsibilities	Operations
class name	attribute 1 attribute 2 ...		operation1() operation2() ...

The relationships between the classes can also be represented using UML notation. Let us now look at some examples.

12.3 Programming examples using more than one class

EXAMPLE 12.1 Square and cube

Design a class named Square that will receive a value for the side of the square, validate that value, and calculate and display the area of the square. You are then to design a child class called Cube that will use the existing methods of its parent class to receive and validate the side of the cube and create a new method to calculate and display the volume of the cube.

Step 1: Identify the classes and their attributes, responsibilities and operations

To commence the design, underline the nouns and noun phrases to identify the objects and their attributes.

Design a class named <u>Square</u> that will receive a value for the <u>side of the square</u>, validate that value, and calculate and display the area of the square. You are then to design a child class called <u>Cube</u> that will use the existing methods of its parent class to receive and validate the <u>side of the cube</u> and create a new method to calculate and display the volume of the cube.

In this example, a Square class is required with an attribute called sideLength. A Cube class is also required, which will inherit the same attribute, so there is no need to list it again in the class table. There is no need to make the area of the square or the volume of the cube an attribute, because these values will be derived from the input side length. The class table will now look like this:

Class	Attributes	Responsibilities	Operations
Square	sideLength		
Cube			

Now underline the verb and verb phrases to identify the responsibilities and the operations that the class is required to perform.

Design a class named Square that will <u>receive a value</u> for the side of the square, <u>validate that value,</u> and <u>calculate and display the area of the square</u>. You are then to design a child class called Cube that will use the existing methods of its parent class to receive and validate the side of the cube and create a new method to <u>calculate and display the volume of the cube</u>.

The underlined verbs and verb phrases indicate that the processes or responsibilities of the Square class are as follows: receive a side length value, validate the side length value, calculate the area of the square and display the result. For the Cube class, the first two operations will be inherited, so the only new process will be to calculate and display the volume of the cube. These responsibilities can now be added to the class table, as follows:

Class	Attributes	Responsibilities	Operations
Square	sideLength	Receive side length	
		Validate side length	
		Calculate and display area	
Cube		Calculate and display volume	

Now that the responsibilities have been established, you need to create a set of operations or methods to perform these responsibilities and to indicate whether they will have public or private access.

First, you will need a public method – setSidelength() – to receive the side length. Because it will receive the side length from an external source, this method will be a mutator method and will be used by both classes.

You will also need a public method to validate the input side length, namely validateSideLength, which will also be used by both classes.

A method is required to calculate and display the area of the square, and another method is required to calculate and display the volume of the cube. These operations can now be added to the class table, as follows:

Class	Attributes	Responsibilities	Operations
Square	sideLength	Receive side length	+setSideLength()
		Validate side length	+validateSideLength()
		Calculate and display area	+calculateSquareArea()
Cube		Calculate and display volume	+calculateCubeVolume()

Step 2: Determine the relationship between the objects of those classes

The class table indicates that there are two classes, a parent Square class and a child Cube class. The following diagram shows a simplified UML notation:

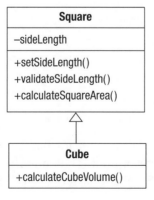

Step 3: Design the algorithms for the operations, using structured design

1   Square class

The mutator setSideLength() requires the side length to be passed to it in the form of a parameter. The value in the parameter will then be passed to the sideLength attribute.

```
setSideLength(inSidelength)
    sideLength = inSideLength
END
```

The public operation calculateSquareArea() calls a method to validate the side length and, if it is valid, calculates the area of the square and displays the result.

```
calculateSquareArea()
    validateSideLength(validInput)
    IF validInput
        squareArea = sideLength * sideLength
        Display 'Area of square of side', sidelength, 'is', squareArea
    ELSE
        Display 'Invalid input', sidelength
    ENDIF
END
```

The public operation validateSideLength() validates the sideLength attribute and returns a parameter called validInput, which indicates if the side length is valid.

```
validateSideLength(validInput)
    validInput = true
    IF sideLength NOT numeric THEN
        validInput = false
    ELSE
        IF sideLength < 0 THEN
            validInput = false
        ENDIF
    ENDIF
END
```

2   Cube class

The Cube class will inherit the existing attributes and operations of the Square class. In addition, it requires a public operation calculateCubeVolume() that calls the method validateSideLength() and, if valid, calculates and displays the volume of the cube.

```
        calculateCubeVolume()
            validateSideLength(validInput)
            IF validInput
                cubeVolume = sideLength * sideLength * sideLength
                Display 'Volume of cube of side', sidelength, 'is', cubeVolume
            ELSE
                Display 'Invalid input', sidelength
            ENDIF
        END
```

Step 4: Develop a test or driver algorithm to test the solution

A test algorithm, called testSquareCube() will be written to test the operations in both classes. In the test algorithm, the Square class will require a default constructor to create a square object and initialise the attribute sideLength. Similarly, the Cube class will require a constructor to create a cube object. This is achieved by the following statements:

```
        Create square1 as new Square()
        Create cube1 as new Cube()
```

The two classes can now be trialled using a test algorithm called test-SquareCube. This algorithm will simply test that all the methods in both classes work correctly, as follows:

```
        testSquareCube()
            Create square1 as new Square()
            Create cube1 as new Cube()
            inSideLength = 5
            square1.setSideLength(inSideLength)
            square1.calculateSquareArea()
            cube1.setSideLength(inSideLength)
            cube1.calculateCubeVolume()
        END
```

This algorithm provides an initial value for sideLength, which will be used by the objects square1 and cube1. The test algorithm then tests the methods for both classes, with the expected output as follows:

```
        Area of square of side 5 is 25
        Volume of cube of side 5 is 125
```

EXAMPLE 12.2 Calculate employee's pay

Design a parent class named Employee that will calculate the weekly pay for a company's full-time employees. The class is to receive the employee's number, name and hourly pay rate; validate the pay rate (the pay rate must be numeric and less than or equal to $30.00 per hour); and calculate the employee's weekly pay, assuming that all full-time employees work a 38 hour week.

You are then to design a child class called PartTimeEmployee that will use the existing attributes and methods of its parent class, Employee. The PartTimeEmployee class will receive an extra input value for the number of hours worked, which it must validate (number of hours worked must be valid and less than 38) and then use it to calculate the employee's weekly pay (pay rate times number of hours). For both classes, the employee's number, name and weekly pay are to be displayed.

Step 1: Identify the classes and their attributes, responsibilities and operations

To commence the design, underline the nouns and noun phrases to identify the objects and their attributes.

Design a parent class named <u>Employee</u> that will calculate the <u>weekly pay</u> for a company's full-time employees. The class is to receive the <u>employee's number, name and hourly pay rate</u>; validate the pay rate (the pay rate must be numeric and less than or equal to $30.00 per hour); and calculate the employee's <u>weekly pay</u>, assuming that all full-time employees work a 38 hour week.

You are then to design a child class called <u>PartTimeEmployee</u> that will use the existing attributes and methods of its parent class, Employee. The PartTimeEmployee class will receive an extra input value for the <u>number of hours worked</u>, which it must validate (number of hours worked must be valid and less than 38) and then use it to calculate the employee's <u>weekly pay</u> (pay rate times number of hours). For both classes, the employee's number, name and weekly pay are to be displayed.

In this example, an Employee class is required with attributes of employee number, employee name and hourly pay rate. There is also a PartTimeEmployee class, which will inherit these attributes, with an additional attribute of number of hours worked. The weekly pay is calculated by both classes and is an important part of the output, so it will become an attribute of the Employee class. The class table will now look like this:

Class	Attributes	Responsibilities	Operations
Employee	employeeNumber		
	employeeName		
	payRate		
	weeklyPay		
PartTimeEmployee	hoursWorked		

Now underline the verb and verb phrases to identify the responsibilities and the operations that the class is required to perform.

Design a parent class named Employee that will <u>calculate the weekly pay</u> for a company's full-time employees. The class is to <u>receive the employee's number, name and hourly pay rate</u>; <u>validate the pay rate</u> (the pay rate must be numeric and less than or equal to $30.00 per hour); and calculate the employee's weekly pay, assuming that all full-time employees work a 38 hour week.

You are then to design a child class called PartTimeEmployee that will use the existing attributes and methods of its parent class, Employee. The PartTimeEmployee class will receive an extra input value for the number of hours worked, which it must validate (number of hours worked must be valid and less than 38) and then use it to calculate the employee's weekly pay (pay rate times number of hours). For both classes, the employee's number, name and weekly pay are to be displayed.

The underlined verbs and verb phrases indicate that the responsibilities of the Employee class are as follows: receive employee data, validate the pay rate, calculate the weekly pay and display the complete employee data. For the PartTimeEmployee class, the operations to validate the pay rate, and display the employee data will be inherited. It will require new operations to receive and validate the number of hours worked and calculate the weekly pay. These responsibilities can now be added to the class table, as follows:

Class	Attributes	Responsibilities	Operations
Employee	employeeNumber	Receive employee data	
	employeeName	Validate pay rate	
	payRate	Calculate weekly pay	
	weeklyPay	Display employee data	
PartTimeEmployee	hoursWorked	Receive employee data	
		Validate hours worked	
		Calculate weekly pay	

Now that the responsibilities have been established, you need to create a set of operations or methods to perform these responsibilities and to indicate whether they will have public or private access.

First, both classes will need a public method to receive the employee data, namely setEmployeeData(). The two methods will have the same name; however, the method for the PartTimeEmployee class will receive an extra parameter value for the number of hours worked.

The Employee class will need a public method to validate the input pay rate, namely validatePayRate(), and the PartTimeEmployee class will need a public method to validate the number of hours worked, namely validateHoursWorked().

Both classes will need a public method to calculate the weekly pay, namely calculateWeeklyPay(). The two methods will have the same name but contain different calculations, depending on whether the employee object is full-time or part-time.

The public method to display the complete employee data, namely displayEmpData() will be used by both classes. These operations can now be added to the class table, as follows:

Class	Attributes	Responsibilities	Operations
Employee	employeeNumber	Receive employee data	+setEmployeeData()
	employeeName	Validate pay rate	+validatePayRate()
	payRate	Calculate weekly pay	+calculateWeeklyPay()
	weeklyPay	Display employee data	+displayEmpData()
PartTimeEmployee	hoursWorked	Receive employee data	+setEmployeeData()
		Validate hours worked	+validateHoursWorked()
		Calculate weekly pay	+calculateWeeklyPay()

Step 2: Determine the relationship between the objects of those classes

The class table indicates that there are two classes, a parent Employee class and a child PartTimeEmployee class. The following diagram shows a simplified UML notation:

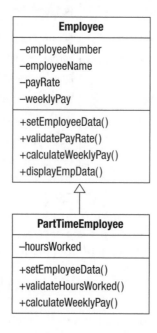

Step 3: Design the algorithms for the operations, using structured design

1   Employee class

The mutator setEmployeeData() requires input values for employee number, employee name and pay rate to be passed to it in the form of parameters. The values in the parameters will then be passed to the appropriate attributes.

```
setEmployeeData(inEmployeeNumber, inEmployeeName, inPayRate)
    employeeNumber = inEmployeeNumber
    employeeName = inEmployeeName
    payRate = inPayRate
END
```

The public operation calculateWeeklyPay() calls the method validatePayRate() to validate the input pay rate attribute and, if valid, to calculate the weekly pay.

```
calculateWeeklyPay()
    validatePayRate(validInput)
    IF validInput
        weeklyPay = payRate * 38
        displayEmpData()
    ELSE
        Display 'Invalid pay rate', payRate
    ENDIF
END
```

The public method, validatePayRate(), validates the payRate attribute and returns the parameter validInput, which indicates if the pay rate attribute is valid.

```
validatePayRate(validInput)
    validInput = true
    IF payRate NOT numeric THEN
        validInput = false
    ELSE
        IF payRate > 30 THEN
            validInput = false
        ENDIF
    ENDIF
END
```

The public method displayEmpData() is required to display the employee data, including the weekly pay. Both classes will use this method.

```
displayEmpData()
    Display employeeNumber, employeeName, weeklyPay
END
```

2 PartTimeEmployee class

The PartTimeEmployee class will inherit the existing attributes and operations of the Employee class. In addition, it requires the hoursWorked attribute to be received and validated and then used in the calculation of the weekly pay. This means that the method setEmployeeData() for this class will require four parameters instead of three. This is an example of operation overloading; that is, if the calling operation sends three parameters to the method setEmployeeData(), the Employee class method will be called, but if the calling operation sends four parameters, the PartTimeEmployee class method will be called. The pseudocode for this mutator is as follows:

```
setEmployeeData(inEmployeeNumber, inEmployeeName, inPayRate,
               inHoursWorked)
    employeeNumber = inEmployeeNumber
    employeeName = inEmployeeName
    payRate = inPayRate
    hoursWorked = inHoursWorked
END
```

Because the PartTimeEmployee class inherits all the operations of its parent class, the mutator could also have been written with an 'inherit' pseudocode statement, to avoid the repetition of code, as follows:

```
setEmployeeData(inEmployeeNumber, inEmployeeName, inPayRate,
               inHoursWorked)
    inherits Employee's setEmployeeData (inEmployeeNumber,
               inEmployeeName, inPayRate)
    hoursWorked = inHoursWorked
END
```

The public operation calculateWeeklyPay() calls the methods validatePayRate() and validateHoursWorked() to validate the input attributes and, if valid, calculates the weekly pay. This method has the same method name as the calculateWeeklyPay() method for full-time employees and so is an example of method overriding.

```
calculateWeeklyPay()
    validatePayRate(validInput)
    IF validInput
       validateHoursWorked(validInput)
       IF validInput
          weeklyPay = payRate * hoursWorked
          displayEmpdata()
       ELSE
          Display 'Invalid hours worked', hoursWorked
       ENDIF
    ELSE
       Display 'Invalid pay rate', payRate
    ENDIF
END
```

The public method validateHoursWorked() validates the hoursWorked attribute and returns the parameter validInput.

```
validateHoursWorked(validInput)
    validInput = true
    IF hoursWorked NOT numeric THEN
        validInput = false
    ELSE
        IF hoursWorked > 38 THEN
            validInput = false
        ENDIF
    ENDIF
END
```

Step 4: Develop a test or driver algorithm to test the solution

A test algorithm, called testEmployee() will be written to test the operations in both classes. In the test algorithm, the Employee class will require a constructor to create an employee object and initialise the attributes. Similarly, the PartTimeEmployee class will require a constructor to create a partTimeEmployee object. This is achieved by the following statements:

```
Create employee1 as new Employee()
Create partTimeEmployee1 as new PartTimeEmployee()
```

The two classes can now be trialled using a test algorithm called testEmployee. This algorithm will simply test that all the methods in both classes work correctly:

```
testEmployee()
    Create employee1 as new Employee()
    inEmployeeNumber = 2121
    inEmployeeName = 'Sam Jones'
    inPayRate = 25
    employee1.setEmployeeData(inEmployeeNumber, inEmployeeName,
            inPayRate)
    employee1.calculateWeeklyPay()
    Create partTimeEmployee1 as new PartTimeEmployee()
    inEmployeeNumber = 3131
    inEmployeeName = 'Peter Smith'
    inPayRate = 26
    inHoursWorked = 30
    partTimeEmployee1.setEmployeeData(inEmployeeNumber,
            inEmployeeName, inPayRate, inHoursWorked)
    partTimeEmployee1.calculateWeeklyPay()
END
```

The above test algorithm tests the methods for both classes, with the expected output as follows:

2121	Sam Jones	$950.00
3131	Peter Smith	$780.00

Data validation

The first two examples in this chapter have handled the validation of the input data as a separate operation. However an object-oriented approach to data validation places the validation of the data immediately after the data has been received, that is, in the mutator method. Validating the input data in the mutator ensures that only valid values will be passed to the attributes of the class. This next example uses this approach.

EXAMPLE 12.3 Produce employee payslips

Design a Payroll class to manage the employee payroll for a large company. The Payroll class is to read a file of employee timesheets and for each employee, call on the services of a Payslip class to calculate that employee's weekly pay and print a payslip.

The Payslip class is to receive the employee's number, pay rate and the number of hours worked in a week. The class is to validate the pay rate field and the hours worked field and, if valid, compute the employee's weekly pay and then print it and the input data onto a payslip.

Validation: According to the company's rules, the maximum hours an employee can work per week is 45 hours, and the maximum hourly rate is $30.00 per hour. If the hours worked field or the hourly rate field is out of range, the input data and an appropriate message are to be printed and the employee's weekly pay is not to be calculated.

Weekly pay calculation: Weekly pay is calculated as hours worked times pay rate. If more than 38 hours are worked, payment for the overtime hours worked is calculated at time-and-a-half.

Step 1: Identify the classes and their attributes, responsibilities and operations

To commence the design, underline the nouns and noun phrases to identify the objects and their attributes.

Design a Payroll class to manage the employee payroll for a large company. The Payroll class is to read a file of employee timesheets and for each employee, call on the services of a Payslip class to calculate that employee's weekly pay and print a payslip.

The Payslip class is to receive the employee's number, pay rate and the number of hours worked in a week. The class is to validate the pay rate field and the hours worked field and, if valid, compute the employee's weekly pay and then print it and the input data onto a payslip.

Validation: According to the company's rules, the maximum hours an employee can work per week is 45 hours, and the maximum hourly rate is $30.00 per hour. If the hours worked field or the hourly rate field is out of range, the input data and an appropriate message are to be printed and the employee's weekly pay is not to be calculated.

Weekly pay calculation: Weekly pay is calculated as hours worked times pay rate. If more than 38 hours are worked, payment for the overtime hours worked is calculated at time-and-a-half.

In this example, the Payroll class requires an attribute of the employee timesheets, and the Payslip class requires attributes of employee number, pay rate and hours worked. The weekly pay is calculated by both classes and is an important part of the output, so it will become an attribute of the Payslip class. The class table will now look like this:

Class	Attributes	Responsibilities	Operations
Payroll	employeeTimesheets		
Payslip	empNumber		
	payRate		
	hoursWorked		
	weeklyPay		

Now underline the verb and verb phrases to identify the responsibilities and the operations that the class is required to perform.

Design a Payroll class to <u>manage the employee payroll</u> for a large company. The Payroll class is to <u>read a file of employee timesheets</u> and for each employee, <u>call on the services</u> of a Payslip class to calculate that employee's weekly pay and print a payslip.

The Payslip class is to <u>receive the employee's number, pay rate and the number of hours worked</u> in a week. The class is to <u>validate the pay</u> rate field and the hours worked field and, if valid, <u>compute the employee's weekly pay</u> and then <u>print it and the input data onto a payslip</u>.

Validation: According to the company's rules, the maximum hours an employee can work per week is 45 hours, and the maximum hourly rate is $30.00 per hour. If the hours worked field or the hourly rate field is out of range, the input data and an appropriate message is to be printed and the employee's weekly pay is not to be calculated.

Weekly pay calculation: Weekly pay is calculated as hours worked times pay rate. If more than 38 hours are worked, payment for the overtime hours worked is calculated at time-and-a-half.

The underlined verbs and verb phrases indicate that the responsibilities of the Payroll class are to read the employee timesheets and manage the payroll by calling on the services of the Payslip class.

For each employee, the Payslip class is to receive the employee data, validate the pay rate, validate hours worked, calculate the weekly pay and print a payslip. These responsibilities can now be added to the class table, as follows:

Class	Attributes	Responsibilities	Operations
Payroll	employee timesheets	Read employee data	
		Manage payroll	
Payslip	empNumber	Receive employee data	
	payRate	Validate pay rate	
	hoursWorked	Validate hours worked	
	weeklyPay	Calculate weekly pay	
		Print payslip	

Now that the responsibilities have been established, you need to create a set of operations or methods to perform these responsibilities and to indicate whether they will have public or private access.

For the Payroll class, you will need public operations to read the employee timesheets, namely readTimesheetFile(), and to manage the payroll, namely runPayroll().

For the Payslip class, you will need a public method to receive the employee number and receive and validate the pay rate and the hours worked attributes. To do this, three mutators are required, namely setEmpNumber(), setPayRate() and setHoursWorked(). The flag, validInput, reports on the validity of the input and is required in many operations, so it will also need to be an attribute of the Payslip class.

Methods are also required to calculate the weekly pay, namely calculateWeeklyPay() and to print the payslip, namely printPayslip(). These operations can now be added to the class table, as follows:

Class	Attributes	Responsibilities	Operations
Payroll	employeeTimesheets	Read employee timesheet	+readTimesheetFile
		Manage payroll	+runPayroll
Payslip	empNumber	Receive employee data	+setEmpNumber()
	payRate	Validate pay rate	+setPayRate()
	hoursWorked	Validate hours worked	+setHoursWorked()
	weeklyPay	Calculate weekly pay	+calculateWeeklyPay()
	validInput	Print payslip	+printPayslip()

Step 2: Determine the relationship between the objects of those classes

The class table developed from the problem statement has two classes. An object from the Payroll class uses objects from the Payslip class. The diagram below shows this in a simplified UML notation:

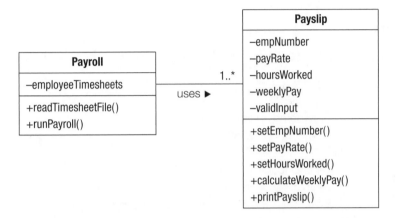

Step 3: Design the algorithms for the operations, using structured design

1 Payslip class

The mutator setEmpNumber() requires the input employee number to be passed to it in the form of a parameter. The mutators setPayRate() and setHoursWorked() receive input data, validate it and report the validity in the attribute validInput. In this way, only valid values are passed to the attributes.

```
setEmpNumber(inEmpNumber)
    empNumber = inEmpNumber
END


setPayRate(inPayRate)
    IF inPayRate > 30 THEN
        errorMessage = 'Pay rate exceeds $30.00'
        Print empNumber, inPayRate, errorMessage
        validInput = false
    ELSE
        payRate = inPayRate
    ENDIF
END
```

```
setHoursWorked(inHoursWorked)
    IF inHoursWorked > 45 THEN
        errorMessage = 'Hours worked exceeds 45'
        Print empNumber, inHoursWorked, errorMessage
        validInput = false
    ELSE
        hoursWorked = inHoursWorked
    ENDIF
END
```

A public operation calculateWeeklyPay() calculates the weekly pay.

```
calculateWeeklyPay()
    IF validInput THEN
        IF hoursWorked <= 38 THEN
            weeklyPay = payRate * hoursWorked
        ELSE
            overtimeHours = hoursWorked − 38
            overtimePay = overtimeHours * payRate * 1.5
            weeklyPay = (payRate * 38) + overtimePay
        ENDIF
    ENDIF

END
```

The public method printPayslip() prints the employee data and weekly pay onto the payslip.

```
printPayslip()
    IF validInput THEN
        Print empNumber, payRate, hoursWorked, weeklyPay
    ENDIF
END
```

2 Payroll class

The Payroll class requires a public operation to read the employee timesheets, which at this stage is just one statement, as follows:

```
readTimesheetFile
    read empNumber, payRate, hoursWorked from employee timesheet
END
```

For each record on the employee timesheet file, the Payroll class calls on the Payslip class to process that record. This call is made using a special constructor called Payslip(), to create a payslip object and initialise it with the input values from the employee timesheet file, which are passed to it as parameters. This constructor will replace the default constructor and calls the three Payslip mutators to receive and validate the input data, as follows:

```
Payslip(inEmpNumber, inPayRate, inHoursWorked)
    empNumber = ''
    payRate = 0
    hoursWorked = 0
    weeklyPay = 0
    validInput = true
    setEmpNumber(inEmpNumber)
    setPayRate(inPayRate)
    setHoursWorked(inHoursWorked)
END
```

The pseudocode to create a payslip object and invoke the Payslip constructor will now be:

```
Create payslip as new Payslip(empNumber, payRate, hoursWorked)
```

The method to manage the payroll will call this constructor and looks just like a mainline program, as follows:

```
runPayroll()
    read empNumber, payRate, hoursWorked from employee timesheet
    DOWHILE more records
        Create payslip as new Payslip(empNumber, payRate, hoursWorked)
        payslip.calculateWeeklyPay()
        payslip.printPayslip()
        read empNumber, payRate, hoursWorked from employee timesheet
    ENDDO
END
```

Step 4: Develop a test or driver algorithm to test the solution
A test algorithm, called testPayslip() will be written to test the operations in Payslip class, as follows:

```
testPayslip()
    inEmpNumber = 1122
    inPayRate = 20
    inHoursWorked = 40
    Create payslip as new Payslip(inEmpNumber, inPayRate, inHoursWorked)
    payslip.calculateWeeklyPay()
    payslip.printPayslip()
    inEmpNumber = 1133
    inPayRate = 25
    inHoursWorked = 25
    Create payslip as new Payslip(inEmpNumber, inPayRate, inHoursWorked)
    payslip.calculateWeeklyPay()
    payslip.printPayslip()
END
```

The expected output is two payslips, as follows:

Employee number	Pay rate	Hours worked	Weekly pay
1122	20	40	$820.00
1133	25	25	$625.00

Chapter summary

When object-oriented design involves more than one class, it is important to understand the relationships between the classes. An association relationship occurs when two classes are independent of each other, but one class uses the services that the other provides. An aggregation or composition relationship occurs when a class is made up of other classes. The relationship between a parent class and a child class is called generalisation.

Polymorphism refers to the same method name being used in different classes to perform a variety of purposes. Operation overriding occurs when a parent class provides an operation, but the inheriting class defines its own version of that operation. Operation overloading occurs when several operations in a single class have the same name, but will act differently according to the number of parameters that are passed to the operation when it is called.

There are four steps to be followed when designing an object-oriented solution for a programming problem that uses more than one class:

1 Identify the classes and their attributes, responsibilities and operations.
2 Determine the relationship between the objects of those classes.
3 Design the algorithms for the operations, using structured design.
4 Develop a test or driver algorithm to test the solution.

Programming problems

1 Use object-oriented design to design a parent class called Circle that will receive the diameter of a circle, and calculate and display the circumference and the area of that circle. Design a child class called Sphere that will use the existing methods of its parent class and calculate and display the volume of the sphere.
   a Design the class table and UML diagram.
   b Write an algorithm for each operation.
   c Write a test or driver algorithm to test the solution.

2 Use object-oriented design to design a parent class called Rectangle that will receive the length and breadth of a rectangle, validate the input data and calculate and display the area of the rectangle. Design a child class called RectangularPrism that will use the existing methods of its parent class and receive the height of the rectangular prism and calculate and display its volume.

   a Design the class table and UML diagram.

   b Write an algorithm for each operation.

   c Write a test or driver algorithm to test the solution.

3 Use object-oriented design to design a parent class called Book that will receive the ISBN, author, title and price of a book, and select and print the details of all books with a price of more than $50.00. Design a child class called TextBook that will use the existing methods of its parent class and receive an extra data field called grade that can be a number from 0 to 12. This class is to select and print details for all textbooks for grades 3 to 6.

   a Design the class table and UML diagram.

   b Write an algorithm for each operation.

   c Write a test or driver algorithm to test the solution.

4 Design a parent class called PhoneBill that calculates and prints the balance owed by each customer of a phone company during the billing period. Your PhoneBill class is to receive the customer's current balance and the total time, in minutes, of phone calls during the billing period. The input time is to be validated and the cost of calls is to be calculated at 25c per minute. Your class is to print the input balance, the phone call time, the cost of the phone calls and the total amount due.

   Design a child class called MobilePhone that will use all the operations of its parent class and will also receive an extra data field for the number of SMS messages sent. This class is to print all input data and phone charges, including SMS charges that are charged at 3c per message.

   a Design the class table and UML diagram.

   b Write an algorithm for each operation in the table.

   c Write a test or driver algorithm to test the solution.

5 Design a parent class called LoanAccount that receives an account number, an account name, the amount borrowed, the term of the loan and the interest rate. The amount borrowed must be positive and less than or equal to $100 000.00, the term must be less than 30 years and the interest rate must be less than 15%. Your class is to validate the input data and print all the loan information. Design a child class called PersonalLoan that uses all the methods from its parent class; however, the amount borrowed must be less than or equal to $10 000.00, the term must be for less than 5 years, and the interest rate must be between 5% and 15%.

   a Design the class table and UML diagram.

   b Write an algorithm for each operation.

   c Write a test or driver algorithm to test the class.

6 Design a class called Sales Commission that receives a sales figure and a commission rate. The class is to validate the commission rate, which must be less than 10%. Two overloaded methods named calculateCommission() are to be created. The first method receives one parameter, the sales figure and calculates the commission to be 5% of the sales figure. The second method will receive two parameters, sales figure and commission rate, and must multiply them together to calculate the commission.

   a Design the class table and UML diagram.
   b Write an algorithm for each operation in the table.
   c Write a test or driver algorithm to test the solution.

7 Design a parent class called Square that will receive data for the height and width of a square. Your class is to validate the input data and create a method called calculateSurfaceArea() to calculate the surface area. Design a child class called Cube, which has an additional attribute called depth, and create a method to override the parent method, calculateSurfaceArea.

   a Design the class table and UML diagram.
   b Write an algorithm for each operation in the table.
   c Write a test or driver algorithm to test the solution.

8 A library needs a program to keep track of the current loans. Each book has a title, an ISBN, an author, a publisher, a publication date, a call number and a unique accession number. Library patrons have a unique user code, a name, street address, and postcode, and an overdue balance that can be changed when a fine is imposed or paid. This balance, as well as the user code and the patron's name and phone number can be printed. When a loan is made, the patron's user code and the loan item's accession number are recorded, as well as the date borrowed and the due date. When a loan is overdue, a fine of $1 per day is charged to the borrower's overdue balance.

   Design a Book class and a BookLoan class that could be used by this program.

   a Design the class table and UML diagram.
   b Write an algorithm for each operation in the table.
   c Write a test or driver algorithm to test the solution.

Object-oriented design for multiple classes

13

Inheritance

Objectives

- To expand an object-oriented solution to cater for multiple classes
- To introduce interface and GUI objects

Outline

13.1 Object-oriented design for multiple classes

A number of object-oriented concepts and terminology have already been covered in the previous two chapters. This chapter develops a problem that was encountered in Chapter 12 and extends it, step by step, to cater for multiple classes. Two examples are provided, which illustrate the concept of inheritance, in which one class inherits the attributes and operations of another. Using inheritance:

1 saves time, because the Parent class contains attributes and methods that already exist; and
2 reduces errors, because the Parent class methods have already been tested and used.

The examples provided also illustrate how easy it is to extend and reuse code from existing classes, thus demonstrating the suitability of object-oriented design for larger systems.

EXAMPLE 13.1 Produce employee payslips

Design a Payroll class to manage the employee payroll of a large company. The Payroll class is to read a file of employee timesheets and, for each employee, call on the services of a Payslip class to calculate that employee's weekly pay and print a payslip.

The Payslip class is to receive the employee's number, the pay rate and the number of hours worked in a week. The class is to validate the pay rate field and the hours worked field and, if valid, compute the employee's weekly pay and then print it and the input data onto a payslip.

Validation: According to the company's rules, the maximum number of hours an employee can work per week is 45 hours, and the maximum hourly rate is $30.00 per hour. If the hours worked field or the hourly rate field is out of range, the input data and an appropriate message are to be printed and the employee's weekly pay is not to be calculated.

Weekly pay calculation: Weekly pay is calculated as hours worked times pay rate. If more than 38 hours are worked, payment for the overtime hours worked is calculated at time-and-a-half.

Design a child class to the Payslip class, called ProgrammerPayslip, to produce payslips for employees who are computer programmers and are paid differently to the company's regular employees. Programmers are not paid overtime, but are entitled to a $50 bonus for each week that the project on which they are working is running ahead of schedule. The number of days ahead of or behind schedule is obtained from another existing class called Project. An operation within the Project class, called getStatus(empNumber, daysAhead), returns the number of days ahead of or behind schedule.

A field on the input employee timesheets indicates the employee type, which is 'E' for regular employees and 'P' for programmers.

The problem definition above is the same as for Example 12.3, with an additional paragraph requesting that a child class called ProgrammerPayslip be created.

A class table, a UML diagram and a set of operations have already been developed for the original problem, so you can use these and extend them to include the extra class. Note that the new paragraph also refers to an existing class called Project. As this class already exists, its operations can be used in this program as well as other programs that may need them. This is the concept of reusability.

Step 1: Identify the classes and their attributes, responsibilities and operations

The existing class table for this problem is as follows:

Class	Attributes	Responsibilities	Operations
Payroll	employeeTimesheets	Read employee timesheet	+readTimesheetFile
		Manage payroll	+runPayroll
Payslip	empNumber	Receive employee data	+setEmpNumber()
	payRate	Validate pay rate	+setPayRate()
	hoursWorked	Validate hours worked	+setHoursWorked()
	weeklyPay	Calculate weekly pay	+calculateWeeklyPay()
	validInput	Print payslip	+printPayslip()

Now underline the nouns and verbs in the new part of the problem to identify the objects, attributes, responsibilities and operations.

Design a child class to the Payslip class, called ProgrammerPayslip, to produce payslips for employees who are computer programmers and are paid differently to the company's regular employees. Programmers are not paid overtime, but are entitled to a $50 bonus for each week that the project which they are working on is running ahead of schedule. The number of days ahead of or behind schedule is obtained from another existing class called Project. An operation within the Project class called getStatus(empNumber, daysAhead) receives the employee number and returns the number of days ahead of or behind schedule.

A field on the input employee timesheets indicates the employee type, which is 'E' for regular employees and 'P' for programmers.

The ProgrammerPayslip class is a child class of the Payslip class, so it will inherit its own copies of all attributes from the Payslip class. Programmers receive a bonus, depending on the number of days the project is ahead of schedule, so daysAhead will become an attribute of the ProgrammerPayslip class.

The ProgrammerPayslip class will also have access to all the operations of the Payslip class, with the additional requirement of calculating the bonus before calculating the weekly pay. Two new operations are required, one to calculate the bonus, calculateBonus(), and one to calculate the weekly pay, calculateWeeklyPay(), which will override the operation of the same name in the Payslip class.

The existing Project class can be considered a 'black box', charged with the responsibility of informing an external object of the number of days that the project is ahead of or behind schedule. This class and its operation getStatus(empNumber, daysAhead) should also be listed.

The class table can now be extended by adding the new classes, their attributes, responsibilities and operations.

Class	Attributes	Responsibilities	Operations
Payroll	employeeTimesheets	Read employee timesheet	+readTimesheetFile
		Manage payroll	+runPayroll
Payslip	empNumber	Receive employee data	+setEmpNumber()
	payRate	Validate pay rate	+setPayRate()
	hoursWorked	Validate hours worked	+setHoursWorked()
	weeklyPay	Calculate weekly pay	+calculateWeeklyPay()
	validInput	Print payslip	+printPayslip()
ProgrammerPayslip	daysAhead	Calculate weekly pay	+calculateWeeklyPay()
		Calculate bonus	-calculateBonus(bonus)
Project		Supply days ahead	+getStatus(empNumber, daysAhead)

Step 2: Determine the relationship between the objects of those classes

In this inheritance relationship, ProgrammerPayslip is a child class of Payslip. This is reflected by the use of an open-headed arrow in the diagram following.

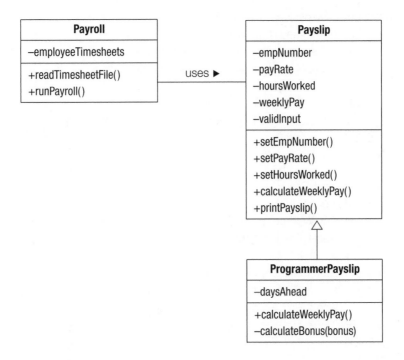

Step 3: Design the algorithms for the operations, using structured design

1 Payslip class

The Payslip class already exists with a set of attributes and operations, which are listed as follows:

```
setEmpNumber(inEmpNumber)
    empNumber = inEmpNumber
END


setPayRate(inPayRate)
    IF inPayRate > 30 THEN
        errorMessage = 'Pay rate exceeds $30.00'
        Print empNumber, inPayRate, errorMessage
        validInput = false
    ELSE
        payRate = inPayRate
    ENDIF
END
```

```
setHoursWorked(inHoursWorked)
    IF inHoursWorked > 45 THEN
        errorMessage = 'Hours worked exceeds 45'
        Print empNumber, inHoursWorked, errorMessage
        validInput = false
    ELSE
        hoursWorked = inHoursWorked
    ENDIF
END

calculateWeeklyPay()
    IF validInput THEN
        IF hoursWorked <= 38 THEN
            weeklyPay = payRate * hoursWorked
        ELSE
            overtimeHours = hoursWorked – 38
            overtimePay = overtimeHours * payRate * 1.5
            weeklyPay = (payRate * 38) + overtimePay
        ENDIF
    ENDIF
END

printPayslip()
    IF validInput THEN
        Print empNumber, payRate, hoursWorked, weeklyPay
    ENDIF
END
```

2 Project class

The Project class is already available in the system and is a 'black box', that is, the internal workings of the class are unknown. Our program must create a project object, as follows:

```
Create project as new Project()
```

and then call the operation getStatus(empNumber, daysAhead) to retrieve the daysAhead attribute, as follows:

```
project.getStatus(empNumber, daysAhead)
```

3 ProgrammerPayslip class

Each programmerPayslip object inherits the attributes and operations from the payslip object, but two new operations are required. The public method calculateWeeklyPay() will call on the private method calculateBonus(bonus) to calculate the bonus, which it will then use to calculate the weekly pay for programmers. This method will override the method of the same name in the Payslip class.

```
calculateWeeklyPay()
    IF validInput THEN
        calculateBonus(bonus)
        weeklyPay = (payRate * 38) + bonus
    ENDIF
END
```

The private operation calculateBonus(bonus) uses the daysAhead attribute to calculate the programmer's bonus, if any, and passes the bonus value to the calling module.

```
calculateBonus(bonus)
    IF daysAhead > 0 THEN
        bonus = daysAhead / 7 * $50.00
    ELSE
        bonus = 0
    ENDIF
END
```

4 Payroll class

For each record on the employee timesheet file, the Payroll class calls on either the Payslip class or the ProgrammerPayslip class to process that record. The particular call depends on the value of the employee type field in the employee timesheets. If the employee type is 'E', a payslip object is created, and if the employee type is 'P', a programmerPayslip object is created.

The public operation to read the employee timesheets must be changed to include the employee type, as follows:

```
readTimesheetFile
    Read empType, empNumber, payRate, hoursWorked from employee
            timesheet
END
```

The Payslip() constructor already exists, as follows:

```
Payslip(inEmpNumber, inPayRate, inHoursWorked)
    empNumber = ''
    payRate = 0
    hoursWorked = 0
    weeklyPay = 0
    validInput = true
    setEmpNumber(inEmpNumber)
    setPayRate(inPayRate)
    setHoursWorked(inHoursWorked)
END
```

The ProgrammerPayslip() constructor inherits this constructor and requires an extra parameter to be passed to it, namely inDaysAhead, as follows:

```
ProgrammerPayslip (inEmpNumber, inPayRate, inHoursWorked, inDaysAhead)
    Inherits Payslip (inEmpNumber, inPayRate, inHoursWorked)
    IF validInput THEN
        daysAhead = inDaysAhead
    ENDIF
END
```

Note that a child class constructor must call the parent class constructor before the child class constructor can operate. The pseudocode to create a programmerPayslip object and invoke the ProgrammerPayslip() constructor will now be:

```
Create programmerPayslip as new ProgrammerPayslip(empNumber, payRate,
        hoursWorked, daysAhead)
```

The method to manage the payroll will create a payslip or programmer-Payslip object, depending on the value of the employee type on the employee timesheet, and looks just like a mainline program, as follows:

```
runPayroll()
    Create project as new Project()
    read empType, empNumber, payRate, hoursWorked from timesheet
    DOWHILE more records
        IF empType = 'E' THEN
            Create payslip as new Payslip(empNumber, payRate, hoursWorked)
            payslip.calculateWeeklyPay()
            payslip.printPayslip()
        ELSE
            IF empType = 'P' THEN
                project.getStatus(empNumber, daysAhead)
                Create programmerPayslip as new ProgrammerPayslip
                        (empNumber, payRate, hoursWorked, daysAhead)
                programmerPayslip.calculateWeeklyPay()
                programmerPayslip.printPayslip()
            ENDIF
        ENDIF
        read empType, empNumber, payRate, hoursWorked from timesheet
    ENDDO
END
```

Step 4: Develop a test or driver algorithm to test the solution

A test algorithm, called testProgrammerPayslip(), will be written to test the operations in the ProgrammerPayslip class, as follows:

```
testProgrammerPayslip()
    inEmpNumber = 1122
    inPayRate = 20
    inHoursWorked = 38
    inDaysAhead = 14
    Create programmerPayslip1 as new ProgrammerPayslip(inEmpNumber,
            inPayRate, inHoursWorked, inDaysAhead)
    programmerPayslip1.calculateWeeklyPay()
    programmerPayslip1.printPayslip()
    inEmpNumber = 1133
    inPayRate = 25
    inHoursWorked = 38
    inDaysAhead = 0
    Create programmerPayslip2 as new ProgrammerPayslip(inEmpNumber,
            inPayRate, inHoursWorked, inDaysAhead)
    programmerPayslip2.calculateWeeklyPay()
    programmerPayslip2.printPayslip()
END
```

The expected output is two programmer payslips, as follows:

Employee number	Pay rate	Hours worked	Weekly pay
1122	20	38	$860.00
1133	25	38	$950.00

Let us now extend the problem further to include two more classes.

EXAMPLE 13.2 Produce employee payslips

Design a Payroll class to manage the employee payroll for a large company. The Payroll class is to read a file of employee timesheets and for each employee, call on the services of a Payslip class to calculate that employee's weekly pay and print a payslip.

The Payslip class is to receive the employee's number, pay rate and the number of hours worked in a week. The class is to validate the pay rate field and the hours worked field and, if valid, compute the employee's weekly pay and then print it and the input data onto a payslip.

<u>Validation</u>: According to the company's rules, the maximum hours an employee can work per week is 45 hours, and the maximum hourly rate is $30.00 per hour. If the hours worked field or the hourly rate field is out of range, the input data and an appropriate message are to be printed and the employee's weekly pay is not to be calculated.

<u>Weekly pay calculation</u>: Weekly pay is calculated as hours worked times pay rate. If more than 38 hours are worked, payment for the overtime hours worked is calculated at time-and-a-half.

Design a child class to the Payslip class, called ProgrammerPayslip, to produce payslips for employees who are computer programmers and are paid differently to the company's regular employees. Programmers are not paid overtime, but are entitled to a $50 bonus for each week that the project on which they are working is running ahead of schedule. The number of days ahead of or behind schedule is obtained from another existing class called Project. An operation within the Project class called getStatus(empNumber, daysAhead) returns the number of days ahead of or behind schedule.

Design another child class to the Payslip class, called SalesPayslip, to produce payslips for employees who are sales representatives and are paid differently to the company's regular employees. Sales representatives are not paid overtime, but are entitled to a commission of $200.00 if their weekly sales exceed $19999.99, and $100.00 if their sales are in the range of $10000.00 to $19999.99. The weekly sales figure is obtained from another existing class called Sales that is associated with each sales representative. An operation within the Sales class called getSales(empNumber, weeklySales) returns the weekly sales figure for that sales representative in dollars and cents.

A field on the input employee timesheets indicates the employee type, which is 'E' for regular employees, 'P' for programmers and 'S' for sales representatives.

The problem definition above is the same as for Example 13.1, with an additional paragraph requesting that a SalesPayslip child class be created. Note that the new paragraph also refers to an existing class called Sales. As this class already exists, its operations can be used in this program as well as other programs, and illustrates the concept of reusability.

Step 1: Identify the classes and their attributes, responsibilities and operations

The existing class table for this problem is as follows:

Class	Attributes	Responsibilities	Operations
Payroll	employeeTimesheets	Read employee timesheet	+readTimesheetFile
		Manage payroll	+runPayroll
Payslip	empNumber	Receive employee data	+setEmpNumber()
	payRate	Validate pay rate	+setPayRate()
	hoursWorked	Validate hours worked	+setHoursWorked()
	weeklyPay	Calculate weekly pay	+calculateWeeklyPay()
	validInput	Print payslip	+printPayslip()
ProgrammerPayslip	daysAhead	Calculate weekly pay	+calculateWeeklyPay()
		Calculate bonus	-calculateBonus(bonus)
Project		Supply days ahead	+getStatus(empNumber, daysAhead)

Now underline the nouns and verbs in the new part of the problem to identify the objects, attributes, responsibilities and operations.

Design another child class to the Payslip class, called SalesPayslip, to produce payslips for employees who are sales representatives and are paid differently to the company's regular employees. Sales representatives are not paid overtime, but are entitled to a commission of $200.00 if their weekly sales exceed $19999.99, and $100.00 if their sales are in the range of $10000.00 to $19999.99. The weekly sales figure is obtained from another existing class called Sales that is associated with each sales representative. An operation within the Sales class called getSales(empNumber, weeklySales) returns the weekly sales figure for that sales representative in dollars and cents.

The SalesPayslip class is a child class of the Payslip class so it will inherit its own copies of all attributes from the Payslip class. Sales representatives are paid a commission based on their weekly sales, so weeklySales will become an attribute of the SalesPayslip class.

The SalesPayslip class will also have access to all the operations of the Payslip class, with the additional requirement of calculating the commission before calculating the weekly pay. Two new operations are required, one to calculate the commission, calculateCommission(), and one to calculate the weekly pay, calculateWeeklyPay(), which will override the operation of the same name in the Payslip class.

The existing Sales class can be considered a 'black box', charged with the responsibility of informing an external object of the weekly sales figure for a sales representative. This class and its operation getSales(empNumber, weeklySales) should also be listed.

We can now extend the class table, adding the new classes, their attributes, responsibilities and operations.

Class	Attributes	Responsibilities	Operations
Payroll	employeeTimesheets	Read employee timesheet	+readTimesheetFile
		Manage payroll	+runPayroll
Payslip	empNumber	Receive employee data	+setEmpNumber()
	payRate	Validate pay rate	+setPayRate()
	hoursWorked	Validate hours worked	+setHoursWorked()
	weeklyPay	Calculate weekly pay	+calculateWeeklyPay()
	validInput	Print payslip	+printPayslip()
ProgrammerPayslip	daysAhead	Calculate weekly pay	+calculateWeeklyPay()
		Calculate bonus	-calculateBonus(bonus)
Project		Supply days ahead	+getStatus(empNumber, daysAhead)
SalesPayslip	weeklySales	Calculate weekly pay	+calculateWeeklyPay()
		Calculate commission	-calculateCommission (commission)
Sales		Supply weekly sales	+getSales(empNumber, weeklySales)

Step 2: Determine the relationship between the objects of those classes

In this inheritance relationship, ProgrammerPayslip and SalesPayslip are both child classes of Payslip. This is reflected by the use of open headed arrows in the diagram following.

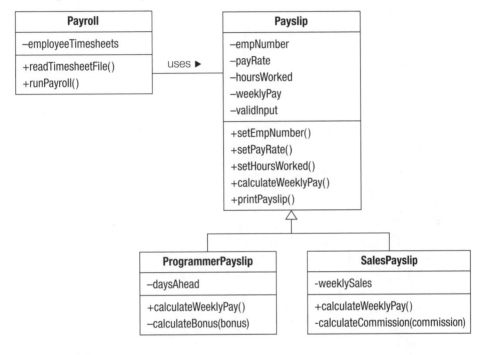

Step 3: Design the algorithms for the operations, using structured design

1 Payslip and Project classes
The Payslip and Project classes already exist with a set of attributes and operations, which were listed in Example 13.1.

2 Sales class
The Sales class is already available in the system and is a 'black box'; that is, the internal workings of the class are unknown. Our program must create a sales object:

> Create sales as new Sales()

and then call the operation getSales(empNumber, weeklySales) to retrieve the weeklySales attribute, as follows:

> sales.getSales(empNumber, weeklySales)

3 SalesPayslip class
Each salesPayslip object inherits the attributes and operations from the payslip object, but two new operations are required. The public method

calculateWeeklyPay() will call on the private method calculateCommission (commission) to calculate the commission, which it will then use to calculate the weekly pay for sales representatives. This method will override the method of the same name in the Payslip class.

```
calculateWeeklyPay()
    IF validInput THEN
        calculateCommission(commission)
        weeklyPay = (payRate * 38) + commission
    ENDIF
END
```

The private operation calculateCommission(commission) uses the weeklySales attribute to calculate the commission, if any, for the sales representative and passes the commission value to the calling module.

```
calculateCommission(commission)
    IF weeklySales > $19,999.99 THEN
        commission = $200.00
    ELSE
        IF weeklySales >= $10,000.00 THEN
            commission = $100.00
        ELSE
            commission = 0
        ENDIF
    ENDIF
END
```

4 Payroll class

For each record on the employee timesheet file, the Payroll class calls on either the Payslip class, the ProgrammerPayslip class or the SalesPayslip class to process that record. The particular call depends on the value in the employee type field on the employee timesheets. If the employee type is 'E', a payslip object is created, if the employee type is 'P', then a programmerPayslip object is created, and if the employee type is 'S', a salesPayslip object is created. The Payslip() constructor already exists, as follows:

```
Payslip(inEmpNumber, inPayRate, inHoursWorked)
    empNumber = ''
    payRate = 0
    hoursWorked = 0
    weeklyPay = 0
    validInput = true
    setEmpNumber(inEmpNumber)
    setPayRate(inPayRate)
    setHoursWorked(inHoursWorked)
END
```

The SalesPayslip() constructor inherits the Payslip() constructor and requires an extra parameter to be passed to it, namely inWeeklySales, as follows:

```
SalesPayslip (inEmpNumber, inPayRate, inHoursWorked, inWeeklySales)
    Inherits Payslip (inEmpNumber, inPayRate, inHoursWorked)
    IF validInput THEN
        weeklySales = inWeeklySales
    ENDIF
END
```

The pseudocode to create a salesPayslip object and invoke the SalesPayslip() constructor will now be:

```
Create salesPayslip as new SalesPayslip(empNumber, payRate, hoursWorked,
    weeklySales)
```

The method to manage the payroll creates a payslip, a programmerPayslip or a salesPayslip object, depending on the value of the employee type on the employee timesheet, as follows:

```
runPayroll()
    Create project as new Project()
    Create sales as new Sales()
    read empType, empNumber, payRate, hoursWorked from timesheet
    DOWHILE more records
        IF empType = 'E' THEN
            Create payslip as new Payslip(empNumber, payRate, hoursWorked)
            payslip.calculateWeeklyPay()
            payslip.printPayslip()
        ELSE
            IF empType = 'P' THEN
                project.getStatus(empNumber, daysAhead)
                Create programmerPayslip as new ProgrammerPayslip
                        (empNumber, payRate, hoursWorked, daysAhead)
                programmerPayslip.calculateWeeklyPay()
                programmerPayslip.printPayslip()
            ELSE
                IF empType = 'S' THEN
                    sales.getSales(empNumber, weeklySales)
                    Create salesPayslip as new SalesPayslip (empNumber,
                            payRate, hoursWorked, weeklySales)
                    salesPayslip.calculateWeeklyPay()
                    salesPayslip.printPayslip()
                ENDIF
            ENDIF
        ENDIF
        read empType, empNumber, payRate, hoursWorked from timesheet
    ENDDO
END
```

Step 4: Develop a test or driver algorithm to test the solution

A test algorithm, called testSalesPayslip() will be written to test the operations in the SalesPayslip class, as follows:

```
testSalesPayslip()
    inEmpNumber = 1122
    inPayRate = 20
    inHoursWorked = 38
    inWeeklySales = $20,000.00
    Create salesPayslip1 as new SalesPayslip(inEmpNumber, inPayRate,
            inHoursWorked, inWeeklySales)
    salesPayslip1.calculateWeeklyPay()
    salesPayslip1.printPayslip()
    inEmpNumber = 1133
    inPayRate = 25
    inHoursWorked = 38
    inWeeklySales = $5,000.00
    Create salesPayslip2 as new SalesPayslip(inEmpNumber, inPayRate,
            inHoursWorked, inWeeklySales)
    salesPayslip2.calculateWeeklyPay()
    salesPayslip2.printPayslip()
END
```

The expected output is two sales representative payslips, as follows:

Employee number	Pay rate	Hours worked	Weekly pay
1122	20	38	$960.00
1133	25	38	$950.00

13.2 Interface and GUI objects

An interface is a device in a program that connects the user's responses to the computer's actions. Many popular programming languages provide a graphical user interface (GUI), which enables the programmer to select the elements of the program's user interface from a pre-existing range of options. These languages are called 'visual' languages, and include Visual Basic, Visual C and Visual J. Java also shares these features.

Interface design is a subset of program design, as it concentrates on one aspect of the program's performance and implementation. Good interfaces make the program easy and comfortable to use, and combine elements of psychology, aesthetic design and good programming techniques.

Interfaces are developed from predesigned classes available in the chosen programming language. The user interface options may include windows, buttons, menus, boxes to hold text, drop-down lists and many more. Once they have been created, the interface elements can be tailored to suit the needs of the program. While some of the programs that provide GUIs are not strictly object oriented in their internal functioning, the interfaces usually are, and object-oriented approaches should be used in their design.

Each user interface element provided in the visual languages is an object with attributes and operations. The size, shape, colour, heading labels and modality of a window or form object on a screen are attributes. The programmer defines the values of these attributes when the code for the program is written. The way the window behaves in response to events that may come from the user, the program or the system is defined by the operations that the programmer has chosen to use for that window.

EXAMPLE 13.3 Library locator interface

Consider a program that supplies users with the location of a book in a library, based on its call number. The library stores materials from 000 to 250 on the ground level, from 251 to 700 on the first level, and from 701 onwards on the second level. The user will need to provide information to the program about the call number of the book he or she is seeking.

In the algorithm, this menu may appear as a case or nested IF statement. In a visual language, the inputs for these decision structures can be expressed in at least two possible ways: the user can be asked to enter a choice using text, or to click on one particular object on the screen that represents the option, such as a menu button, an option box or radio buttons.

If a typed user input is chosen, the program will have to test for invalid inputs and report them with error messages, because the user who types a call number into an input area could potentially make an error. This option requires the designer to prepare algorithms for error trapping and the programmer to write the corresponding code. However, a specific location on the correct floor can be provided with fewer objects populating the screen.

In the second approach, there is no invalid input possible. The mainline algorithm will still be a complex decision structure that calls separate modules for each choice, but that decision structure will be presented as a window containing objects that represent the menu choices. The user will select an option that matches his or her requirements and the correct location can be displayed.

To design the user interface, first plan the interface layout. This can be done on paper or on screen, according to the tools that are available. Next, using this first draft plan, create an interface object table that differs slightly from the earlier object tables. Because the purpose here is interface design, rather than program design, at this point you can ignore operations and concentrate on the appearance of the screen objects. The interface object table will allow you to specify which objects are to appear and what the initial values of some of their attributes will be. The interface object table for the sample problem could begin like this:

Object	Attributes	Initial Value
Window	Caption	'Library Locater'
	BackColor	grey
Box 1	BackColor	green
Button 1	Caption	'000–005'
Button 2	Caption	'006–120'
…	…	…
Box 2	BackColor	yellow
…	…	…
Box 3	BackColor	blue
…	…	…
Button n	Caption	'Quit'

This table becomes a reference for the programmer when development commences. Using the interface object table to set the captions and back colours, one possible interface could be:

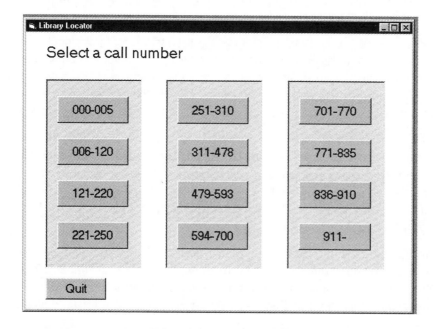

Procedural algorithms that use repetition structures often need to test for sentinel values. In the library locator example, the selection structure will occur inside a loop that is terminated when the user selects the 'Quit' option. Although the repetition algorithm will look like many procedural algorithms with a sentinel value of 'Quit', the code that is produced will potentially include no repetition structures. With thoughtful interface design, the user does not have to type in a sentinel value to leave the program. The exit condition can be represented as one of the options on the screen.

Having gone to the trouble of designing the algorithm for a programmer to implement, don't overlook the interface design. The choice of interface design can have a significant impact on the complexity of your algorithm and on the way in which your algorithm is implemented in the programming language.

Chapter summary

Most object-oriented programs need more than one class. Classes can be related to each other through association, by aggregation or composition or by inheritance. When classes are related by inheritance, all subclasses or child classes inherit the attributes and operations of the parent class and supplement them with their own attributes and operations.

Polymorphism allows several operations to have the same name, but they achieve their purposes by different methods. Using operation overriding, a child class may substitute the parent class version of an operation with its own specific version. With operation overloading, several operations of the same name may have different numbers of parameters and different algorithms.

Interface design for visual programming languages uses object-oriented design principles. Interface objects have operations and attributes. The choice of interface design can reduce the complexity of both an algorithm and the resulting program.

Programming problems

1 Use object-oriented design to design a parent class called Circle that will receive the diameter of a circle, and calculate and display the circumference and the area of that circle. Design a child class called Sphere that will use the existing methods of its parent class and calculate and display the volume of the sphere. Design another child class called Cylinder that will receive an extra value for the height of the cylinder and then use the existing methods of its parent class to calculate and display the volume of a cylinder.

   a Design the class table and UML diagram.
   b Write an algorithm for each operation.
   c Write a test or driver algorithm to test the solution.

2 Use object-oriented design to design a parent class called Book that will receive the ISBN, author, title and price of a book, and select and print records for all books with a price of more than $50.00. Design a child class called TextBook that will use the existing methods of its parent class and receive an extra data field called grade that can be a number from 0 to 12. This class is to select and print records of all textbooks of grades 3 to 6. Design another child class called PictureBook that will use the existing methods of its parent class and receive an extra data field called age that can be a number from 0 to 5. This class is to select and print records of all picture books for ages 3 to 4.

  a Design the class table and UML diagram.

  b Write an algorithm for each operation.

  c Write a test or driver algorithm to test the solution.

3 Design a parent class called LoanAccount that receives an account number, an account name, the amount borrowed, the term of the loan and the interest rate. The amount borrowed must be positive and less than or equal to $100 000.00, the term must be less than 30 years and the interest rate must be less than 15%. Your class is to validate the input data and print all the loan information. Design a child class called PersonalLoan that uses all the methods from its parent class; however, the amount borrowed must be less than or equal to $10 000.00, the term must be for less than 5 years and the interest rate must be between 5% and 15%. Design another child class called InvestmentLoan that uses all the methods from its parent class; however, the amount borrowed must be less than $500 000.00, the term must be less than 10 years and the interest rate must be less than 18%.

  a Design the class table and UML diagram.

  b Write an algorithm for each operation.

  c Write a test or driver algorithm to test the class.

4 A library needs a program to keep track of the current loans. Each book has a title, an ISBN, an author, a publisher, publication date, call number and a unique accession number. Library patrons have a unique user code, name, street address, postcode and an overdue balance that can be changed when a fine is imposed or paid. The balance, as well as the user code and the patron's name and phone number can be printed. When a loan is made, the patron's user code, the loan item's accession number, the date borrowed and the due date are recorded. When a loan is overdue, a fine of $1 per day is charged to the borrower's overdue balance.

  Design a Book class, a BookLoan class and a Patron class that could be used by this program.

  a Design the class table and UML diagram.

  b Write an algorithm for each operation in the table.

  c Write a test or driver algorithm to test the solution.

5 The library loan system in the above problem needs to be able to accommodate non-book loans, such as videos, tapes and magazines. Magazines have a title, an ISSN rather than an ISBN, a volume and number, a publisher, publication date, call number and a unique accession number. Videotapes have a title, a publisher, a publication date, a call number and a unique accession number. Overdue non-book loans are charged at $2 per day. Modify your solution design accordingly, including the class diagram, class tables and algorithms where necessary.

6 Yummy Chocolates requires an object-oriented program for an online catalogue. The catalogue is to display the details of the range of handmade chocolates. Each chocolate product has a product code, a name, a picture and the price per 100 grams. Products can be added to the catalogue, deleted and modified.

    a Design the class table and UML diagram.

    b Write an algorithm for each operation in the table.

    c Write a test or driver algorithm to test the solution.

7 Design the interface for a program that will prompt a user for his or her astrological sign and display the current prediction for the user. Prepare the interface object table and the interface layout.

8 Design an interface for the following problem. Design an algorithm that will prompt for and receive your current cheque book balance, followed by a number of financial transactions. Each transaction consists of a transaction code and a transaction amount. The transaction code can be a deposit ('D') or a cheque ('C'). Your program is to add each deposit transaction amount to the balance and subtract each cheque transaction amount. After each transaction is processed, a new running balance is to be displayed on the screen, with a warning message if the balance becomes negative. When there are no more transactions, a 'Q' is to be entered for transaction code to signify the end of the data. Your algorithm is then to display the initial and final balances, as well as a count of the number of cheques and deposits processed. Prepare the interface object table and the interface layout.

9 Design the screen interface for the following problem. The Mitre-11 hardware outlets require an inventory control program that is to accept order details for an item and then generate a shipping list and a back order list.

    Design an interactive program that will conduct a dialogue on the screen for the input values, and print two reports as required. The screen dialogue is to appear as follows:

ENTER Item No.	99999
Quantity on hand	999
Order quantity	999
Order number	999999

If an item number does not have precisely five digits, an error message is to appear on the screen. If the quantity on hand is sufficient to meet the order (order quantity <= quantity on hand), one line is to be printed on the shipping list. If the quantity on hand is insufficient to meet the order (order quantity > quantity on hand), the order is to be filled partially by whatever stock is available. For this situation, one line should appear on the shipping list with the appropriate number of units shipped (quantity on hand) and a message 'Order partially filled'. An entry for the balance of the order (order quantity – quantity on hand) is to be printed on the back order list.

If the quantity on hand is zero, the message 'Out of stock' is to appear on the shipping list, and an entry for the full order quantity is to be printed on the back order list.

Your program is to continue to process inventory orders until a value of zero is entered for the item number.

Report layouts for the shipping list and back order list are as follows:

MITRE-11 HARDWARE			PAGE XX
INVENTORY CONTROL SHIPPING LIST			
ORDER NO.	ITEM NO.	UNITS SHIPPED	MESSAGE
999999	99999	999	—
999999	99999	999	—

MITRE-11 HARDWARE		PAGE XX
INVENTORY CONTROL BACK ORDER LIST		
ORDER NO.	ITEM NO.	BACK ORDER QTY
999999	99999	999
999999	99999	999

Prepare the interface object table and the interface layout. Explain how the interface design may impact on the algorithm for this problem.

Appendix 1
Flowcharts

Outline

- Introduction to flowcharts and the three basic control structures
- Simple algorithms that use the sequence control structure
- Flowcharts and the selection control structure
- Simple algorithms that use the selection control structure
- The case structure expressed as a flowchart
- Flowcharts and the repetition control structure
- Simple algorithms that use the repetition control structure
- Further examples using flowcharts
- Flowcharts and modules

Introduction to flowcharts

This appendix introduces flowcharts as an alternative method of representing algorithms. Flowcharts are popular because they graphically represent the program logic by a series of standard geometric symbols and connecting lines. Flowcharts are relatively easy to learn and are an intuitive method of representing the flow of control in an algorithm. For simplicity, just six standard flowchart symbols will be used to represent algorithms in this text. These are:

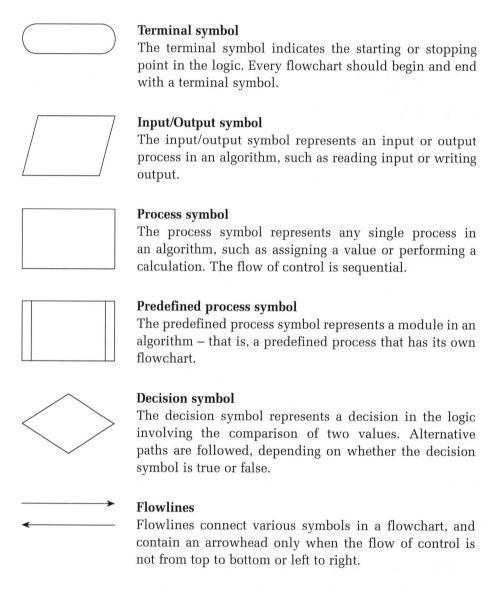

Terminal symbol

The terminal symbol indicates the starting or stopping point in the logic. Every flowchart should begin and end with a terminal symbol.

Input/Output symbol

The input/output symbol represents an input or output process in an algorithm, such as reading input or writing output.

Process symbol

The process symbol represents any single process in an algorithm, such as assigning a value or performing a calculation. The flow of control is sequential.

Predefined process symbol

The predefined process symbol represents a module in an algorithm – that is, a predefined process that has its own flowchart.

Decision symbol

The decision symbol represents a decision in the logic involving the comparison of two values. Alternative paths are followed, depending on whether the decision symbol is true or false.

Flowlines

Flowlines connect various symbols in a flowchart, and contain an arrowhead only when the flow of control is not from top to bottom or left to right.

In this appendix the three basic control structures, as set out in the Structure Theorem in pseudocode, will be explained and illustrated using flowcharts.

The three basic control structures

1   Sequence

The sequence control structure is defined as the straightforward execution of one processing step after another. A flowchart represents this control structure as a series of process symbols, one beneath the other, with one entrance and one exit.

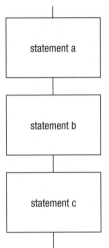

The sequence control structure can be used to represent the first four basic computer operations; namely, to receive information, put out information, perform arithmetic, and assign values. For example, a typical sequence of statements in a flowchart might read:

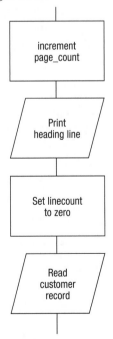

These instructions illustrate the sequence control structure as a straightforward list of steps, written one after the other, in a top-to-bottom fashion. Each instruction will be executed in the order in which it appears.

2   Selection

The selection control structure can be defined as the presentation of a condition, and the choice between two actions depending on whether the condition is true or false. This construct represents the decision-making abilities of the computer, and is used to illustrate the fifth basic computer operation; namely, to compare two variables and select one of two alternative actions. A flowchart represents the selection control structure with a decision symbol, with one line entering at the top, and two lines leaving it, following the true path or false path, depending on the condition. These two lines then join up at the end of the selection structure.

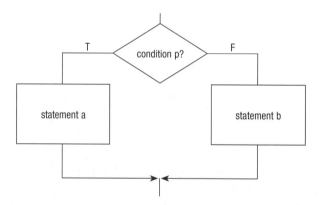

If condition p is true, the statement or statements in the true path will be executed. If condition p is false, the statement or statements in the false path will be executed. Both paths then join up to the flowline following the selection control structure. A typical flowchart might look like this:

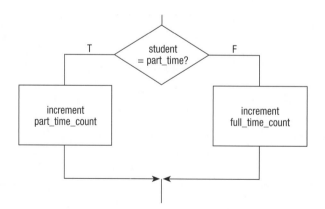

A variation of the selection control structure is the null ELSE structure, which is used when a task is performed only if a particular condition is true. The flowchart that represents the null ELSE construct has no processing in the false path.

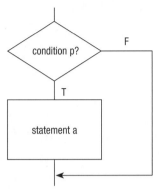

3   Repetition

The repetition control structure can be defined as the presentation of a set of instructions to be performed repeatedly, as long as a condition is true. The basic idea of repetitive code is that a block of statements is executed again and again, until a terminating condition occurs. This construct represents the sixth basic computer operation; namely, to repeat a group of actions. A flowchart represents this structure as a decision symbol and one or more process symbols to be performed while a condition is true. A flowline then takes the flow of control back to the condition in the decision symbol, which is tested before the process is repeated.

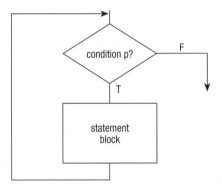

While condition p is true, the statements inside the process symbol will be executed. The flowline then returns control upwards to retest condition p. When condition p is false, control will pass out of the repetition structure down the false path to the next statement. We will now look at a flowchart that represents the repetition control structure:

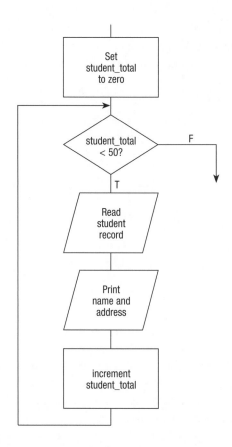

Simple algorithms that use the sequence control structure

The following examples are the same as those represented by pseudocode in Chapter 3. In each example, the problem is defined and a solution algorithm developed using a flowchart. For ease in defining the problem, the processing verbs in each example have been underlined.

EXAMPLE 3.1   Add three numbers

A program is required to <u>read</u> three numbers, <u>add</u> them together and <u>print</u> their total.

A Defining diagram

Input	Processing	Output
number1	Read three numbers	total
number2	Add numbers together	
number3	Print total number	

B Solution algorithm

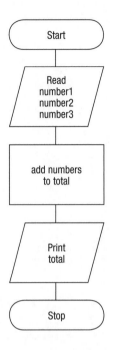

EXAMPLE 3.2   Find average temperature

A program is required to <u>prompt</u> the terminal operator for the maximum and minimum temperature readings on a particular day, <u>accept</u> those readings as integers, and <u>calculate</u> and <u>display</u> to the screen the average temperature.

A Defining diagram

Input	Processing	Output
max_temp min_temp	Prompt for temperatures Get temperatures Calculate average temperature Display average temperature	average_temp

B Solution algorithm

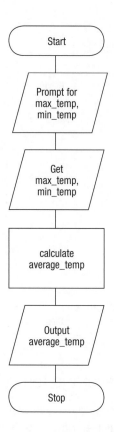

EXAMPLE 3.3 Compute mowing time

A program is required to <u>read</u> from the screen the length and width of a rectangular house block, and the length and width of the rectangular house that has been built on the block. The algorithm should then <u>compute</u> and <u>display</u> the mowing time required to cut the grass around the house, at the rate of two square metres per minute.

A Defining diagram

Input	Processing	Output
block_length	Prompt for block measurements	mowing_time
block_width	Get block measurements	
house_length	Prompt for house measurements	
house_width	Get house measurements	
	Calculate mowing area	
	Calculate mowing time	

B Solution algorithm

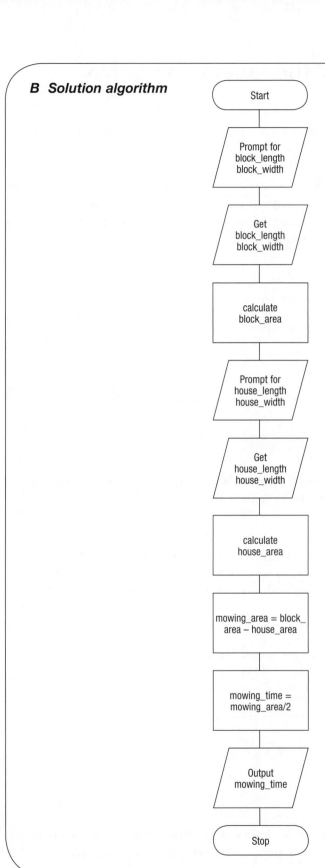

Flowcharts and the selection control structure

Each variation of the selection control structure developed in pseudocode in Chapter 4 can be represented by a flowchart.

Simple IF statement

Simple selection occurs when a choice is made between two alternative paths, depending on the result of a condition being true or false. This structure is represented in a flowchart as follows:

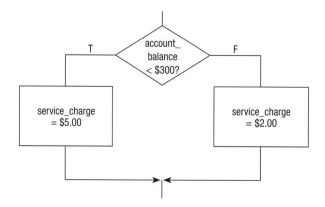

Only one of the true or false paths will be followed, depending on the result of the condition in the decision symbol.

Null ELSE statement

The null ELSE structure is a variation of the simple IF structure. It is used when a task is performed only when a particular condition is true. If the condition is false, no processing will take place, and the IF statement will be bypassed. For example:

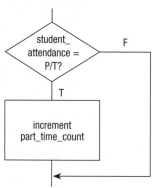

In this case, the part_time_count field will only be altered if the true path is followed, that is, when the student's attendance pattern is part-time.

Combined IF statement

A combined IF statement is one that contains multiple conditions in the decision symbol, each connected with the logical operators AND or OR. If the connector AND is used to combine the conditions, then both conditions must be true for the combined condition to be true. For example:

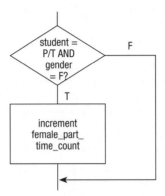

In this case, each student record will undergo two tests. Only those students who are female and whose attendance pattern is part-time will be selected, and the variable female_part_time_count will be incremented. If either condition is found to be false, the counter will remain unchanged.

Nested IF statement

The nested IF statement is used when a field is being tested for various values, with a different action to be taken for each value. In a flowchart, this is represented by a series of decision symbols, as follows.

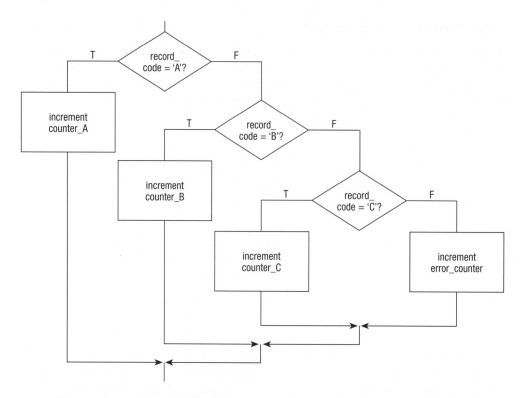

Simple algorithms that use the selection control structure

The following examples are the same as those represented by pseudocode in Chapter 4. In each example, the problem is defined and a solution algorithm developed using a flowchart. For ease in defining the problem, the processing verbs in each example have been underlined.

EXAMPLE 4.1   Read three characters

Design an algorithm that will prompt a terminal operator for three characters, accept those characters as input, sort them into ascending sequence and output them to the screen.

A Defining diagram

Input	Processing	Output
char_1	Prompt for characters	char_1
char_2	Accept three characters	char_2
char_3	Sort three characters	char_3
	Output three characters	

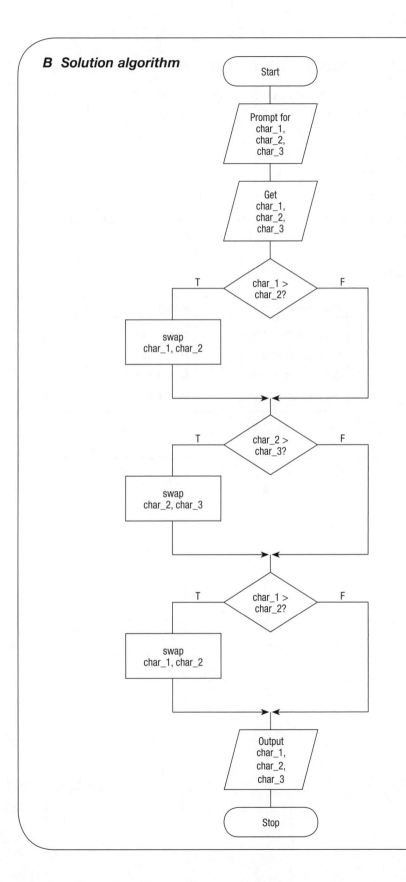

B Solution algorithm

EXAMPLE 4.2   Process customer record

A program is required to <u>read</u> a customer's name, a purchase amount and a tax code. The tax code has been validated and will be one of the following:

0   tax exempt (0%)
1   state sales tax only (3%)
2   federal and state sales tax (5%)
3   special sales tax (7%)

The program must then compute the sales tax and the total amount due, and print the customer's name, purchase amount, sales tax and total amount due.

A Defining diagram

Input	Processing	Output
cust_name	Read customer details	cust_name
purch_amt	Compute sales tax	purch_amt
tax_code	Compute total amount	sales_tax
	Print customer details	total_amt

B Solution algorithm

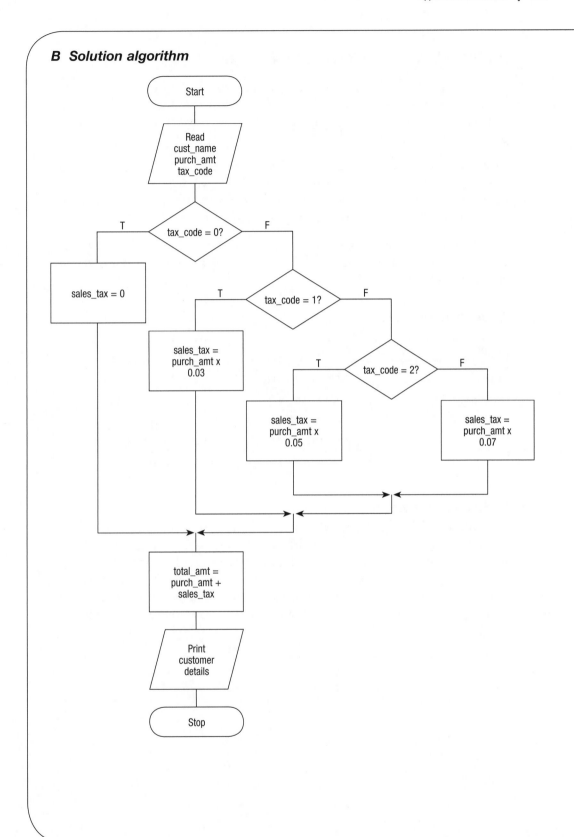

EXAMPLE 4.3   Calculate employee's pay

A program is required by a company to <u>read</u> an employee's number, pay rate and the number of hours worked in a week. The program is then to <u>validate</u> the pay rate field and the hours worked field and, if valid, <u>compute</u> the employee's weekly pay and then <u>print</u> it and the input data.

   <u>Validation</u>: According to the company's rules, the maximum hours an employee can work per week is 60 hours, and the maximum hourly rate is $25.00 per hour. If the hours worked field or the hourly rate field is out of range, the input data and an appropriate message are to be <u>printed</u> and the employee's weekly pay is not to be calculated.

   <u>Weekly pay calculation</u>: Weekly pay is calculated as hours worked times pay rate. If more than 35 hours are worked, payment for the overtime hours worked is calculated at time-and-a-half.

A Defining diagram

Input	Processing	Output
emp_no	Read employee details	emp_no
pay_rate	Validate input fields	pay_rate
hrs_worked	Calculate employee pay	hrs_worked
	Print employee details	emp_weekly_pay
		error_message

B Solution algorithm

The solution to this problem will require a series of decision symbols. First, the variables pay_rate and hrs_worked must be validated, and if either is found to be out of range, an appropriate message should be printed.

   The employee's weekly pay is only to be calculated if the variables pay_rate and hrs_worked are valid, so another variable valid_input_fields will be used to indicate to the program whether or not these input fields are valid.

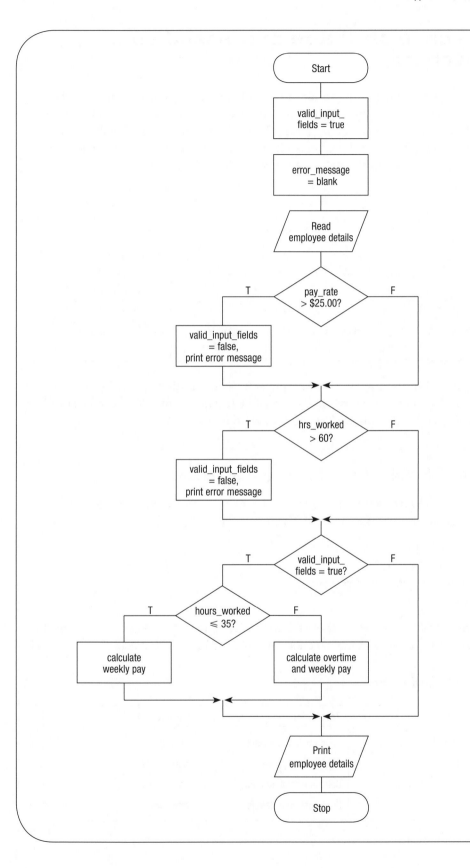

The case structure expressed as a flowchart

The case control structure is another way of expressing a nested IF statement. It is not really an additional control structure, but one that extends the basic selection control structure to be a choice between multiple values. It is expressed in a flowchart by a decision symbol with a number of paths leading from it, depending on the value of the variable, as follows:

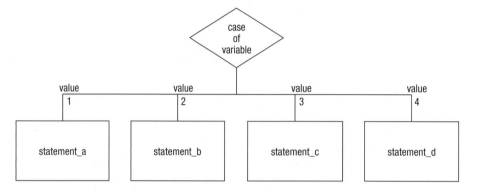

Let us now look again at Example 4.2. The solution algorithm for this example was earlier expressed as a nested IF statement. However, it could equally have been expressed as a CASE statement.

EXAMPLE 4.4   Process customer record

A program is required to <u>read</u> a customer's name, a purchase amount and a tax code. The tax code has been validated and will be one of the following:

0   tax exempt (0%)
1   state sales tax only (3%)
2   federal and state sales tax (5%)
3   special sales tax (7%)

The program must then compute the sales tax and the total amount due, and print the customer's name, purchase amount, sales tax and total amount due.

A Defining diagram

Input	Processing	Output
cust_name	Read customer details	cust_name
purch_amt	Calculate sales tax	purch_amt
tax_code	Calculate total amount	sales_tax
	Print customer details	total_amt

B Solution algorithm

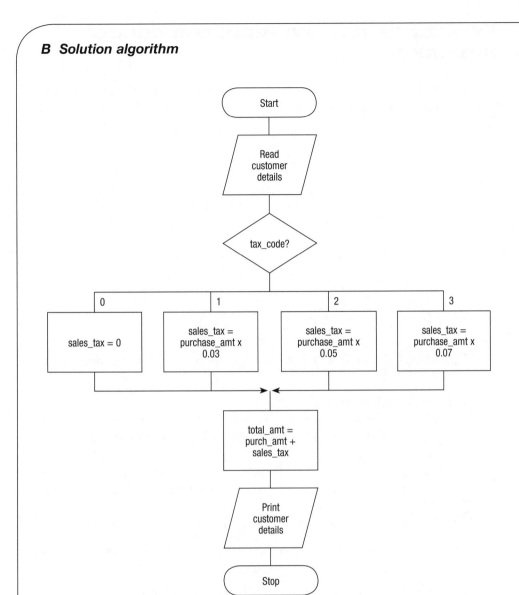

Flowcharts and the repetition control structure

In Chapter 5 the DOWHILE construct was introduced as the pseudocode representation of a repetition loop. This can be represented in a flowchart as follows:

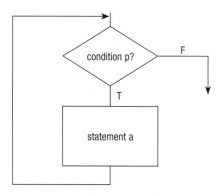

As the DOWHILE loop is a leading decision loop, the following processing takes place:

1 The logical condition p is tested.
2 If condition p is found to be true, the statements that follow the true path will be executed once. Control then returns upwards to the retesting of condition p.
3 If condition p is still true, the statements that follow the true path will be executed again, and so the repetition process continues until the condition is found to be false.
4 If condition p is found to be false, control will follow the false path.

There are two important considerations about which a programmer must be aware before designing a DOWHILE loop.

- The testing of the condition is at the beginning of the loop. This means that the programmer may need to perform some initial processing to set up the condition adequately before it can be tested.
- The only way to terminate the loop is to render the DOWHILE condition false. This means that the programmer must set up some process within the repeated processing symbols that will eventually change the condition so that the condition becomes false. Failure to do this results in an endless loop.

Simple algorithms that use the repetition control structure

The following examples are the same as those represented by pseudocode in Chapter 5. In each example, the problem is defined and a solution algorithm developed using a flowchart. For ease in defining the problem, the processing verbs in each example have been underlined.

EXAMPLE 5.1   Fahrenheit–Celsius conversion

Every day, a weather station receives 15 temperatures expressed in degrees Fahrenheit. A program is to be written that will accept each Fahrenheit temperature, convert it to Celsius and display the converted temperature to the screen. After 15 temperatures have been processed, the words 'All temperatures processed' are to be displayed on the screen.

A Defining diagram

Input	Processing	Output
f_temp (15 temperatures)	Get Fahrenheit temperatures Convert temperatures Display Celsius temperatures Display screen message	c_temp (15 temperatures)

In this example, the programmer will need:

- a DOWHILE structure to repeat the necessary processing
- a counter, called temperature_count, initialised to zero, that will control the 15 repetitions.

B Solution algorithm

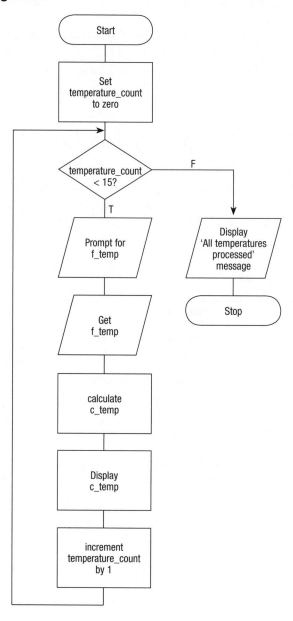

EXAMPLE 5.2   Print examination scores

A program is required to <u>read</u> and <u>print</u> a series of names and exam scores for students enrolled in a mathematics course. The class average is to be <u>calculated</u> and <u>printed</u> at the end of the report. Scores can range from 0 to 100. The last record contains a blank name and a score of 999 and is not to be included in the calculations.

A Defining diagram

Input	Processing	Output
name exam_score	Read student details Print student details Calculate average score Print average score	name exam_score average_score

The following requirements will need to be considered:

- a DOWHILE structure to control the reading of exam scores, until it reaches a score of 999
- an accumulator for total scores, namely total_score
- an accumulator for the total students, namely total_students.

B Solution algorithm

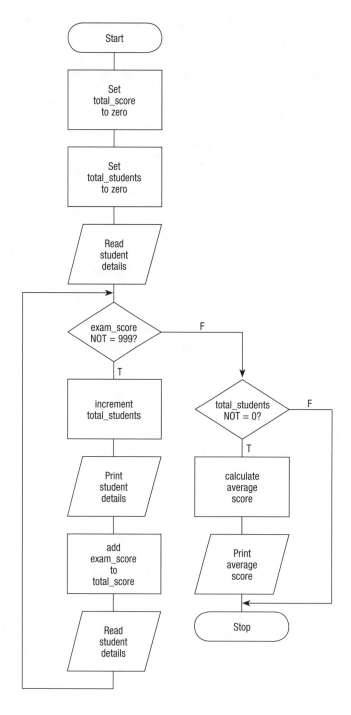

EXAMPLE 5.3   Process student enrolments

A program is required that will <u>read</u> a file of student records, and only <u>select</u> and <u>print</u> the records of those students enrolled in a course unit named Programming I. Each student record contains student number, name, address, postcode, gender and course unit number. The course unit number for Programming I is 18500. Three totals are to be <u>printed</u> at the end of the report: total females enrolled in the course, total males enrolled in the course, and total students enrolled in the course.

A Defining diagram

Input	Processing	Output
student_record	Read student records	selected student records
• student_no	Select student records	total_females_enrolled
• name	Print selected records	total_males_enrolled
• address	Compute total females enrolled	total_students_enrolled
• postcode	Compute total males enrolled	
• gender	Compute total students enrolled	
• course_unit	Print totals	

The following requirements will need to be considered:

- a DOWHILE structure to perform the repetition
- decision symbols to select the required students
- accumulators for the three total fields.

B Solution algorithm

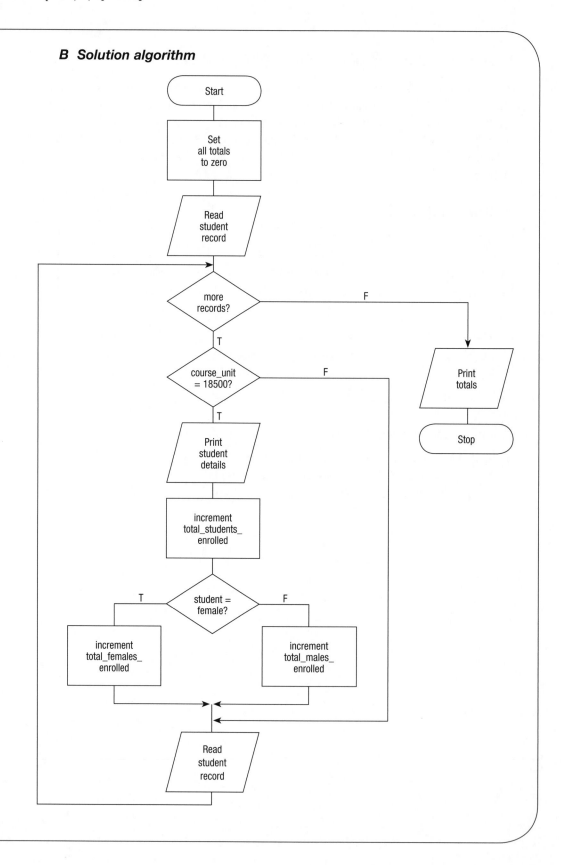

EXAMPLE 5.4   Process inventory items

A program is required to <u>read</u> a series of inventory records that contain an item number, an item description and a stock figure. The last record in the file has an item number of zero. The program is to <u>produce</u> a low stock items report, by <u>printing</u> only those records that have a stock figure of less than 20 items. A heading is to be <u>printed</u> at the top of the report and a total low stock item count <u>printed</u> at the end.

A Defining diagram

Input	Processing	Output
inventory record	Read inventory records	heading
• item_number	Select low stock items	selected records
• item_description	Print low stock records	• item_number
• stock_figure	Print total low stock items	• item_description
		• stock_figure
		total_low_stock_items

The following requirements will need to be considered:

- a DOWHILE structure to perform the repetition
- a decision symbol to select stock figures of less than 20
- an accumulator for total_low_stock_items.

B Solution algorithm

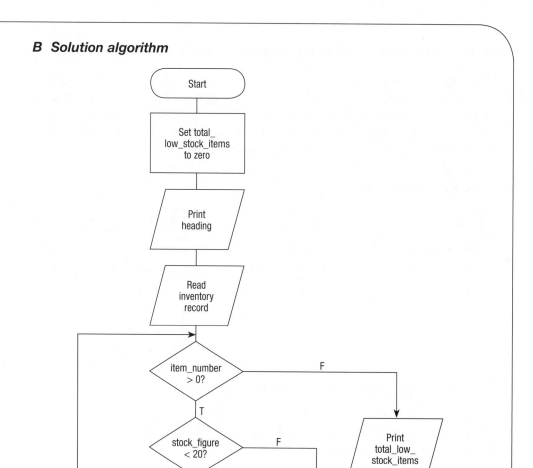

Further examples using flowcharts

The following examples are the same as those represented by pseudocode in Chapters 6 and 7. In each example, the problem is defined and a solution algorithm developed using a flowchart.

EXAMPLE 6.1   Process number pairs

Design an algorithm that will <u>prompt</u> for and <u>receive</u> pairs of numbers from an operator at a terminal and <u>display</u> their sum, product and average on the screen. If the calculated sum is over 200, an asterisk is to be <u>displayed</u> beside the sum. The program is to terminate when a pair of zero values is entered.

A Defining diagram

Input	Processing	Output
number1	Prompt for numbers	sum
number2	Get numbers	product
	Calculate sum	average
	Calculate product	'*'
	Calculate average	
	Display sum, product, average	
	Display '*'	

B Control structures required

1   A DOWHILE loop to control the repetition
2   A decision symbol to determine if an asterisk is to be displayed

C Solution algorithm

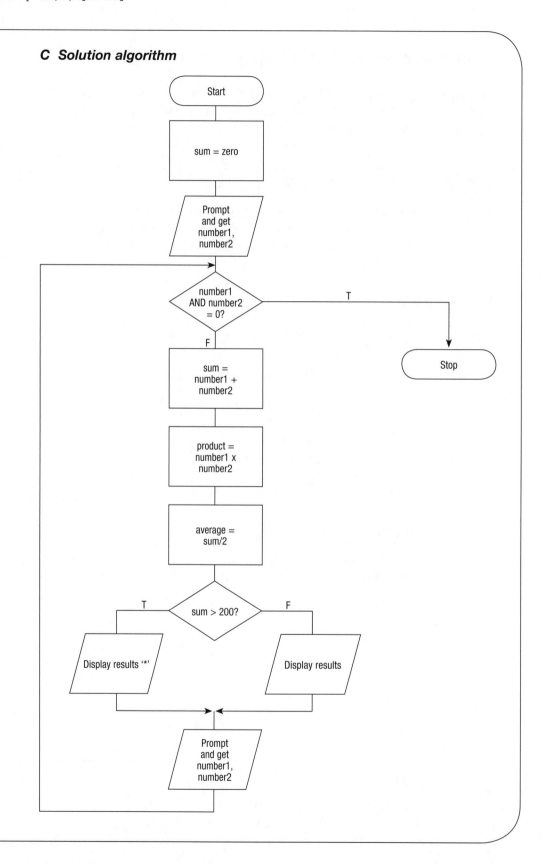

EXAMPLE 6.2   Print student records

A file of student records consists of 'S' records and 'U' records. An 'S' record contains the student's number, name, age, gender, address and attendance pattern: full-time (F/T) or part-time (P/T). A 'U' record contains the number and name of the unit or units in which the student has enrolled. There may be more than one 'U' record for each 'S' record. Design a solution algorithm that will <u>read</u> the file of student records and <u>print</u> only the student's number, name and address on a 'STUDENT LIST'.

A Defining diagram

Input	Processing	Output
'S' records	Print heading	Heading line
• number	Read student records	selected student records
• name	Select 'S' records	• number
• address	Print selected records	• name
• age		• address
• gender		
• attendance_pattern		
'U' records		

B Control structures required

1   A DOWHILE loop to control the repetition
2   A decision symbol to select 'S' records

C Solution algorithm

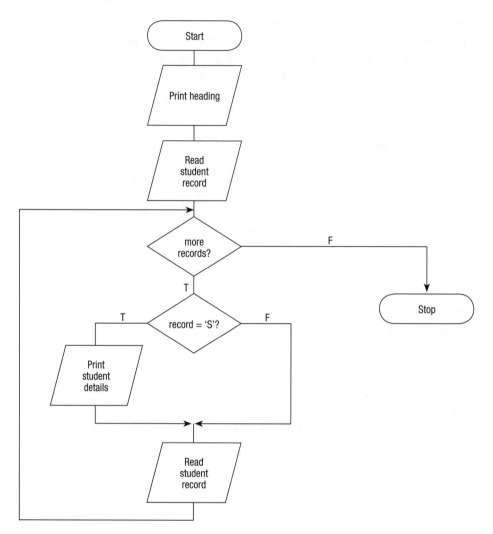

EXAMPLE 6.3 Print selected students

Design a solution algorithm that will <u>read</u> the same student file as in Example 6.2, and <u>produce</u> a report of all female students who are enrolled part-time. The report is to be headed 'FEMALE PART-TIME STUDENTS' and is to <u>show</u> the student's number, name, address and age.

A Defining diagram

Input	Processing	Output
'S' records	Print heading	Heading line
• number	Read student records	selected student records
• name	Select female P/T students	• number
• address	Print selected records	• name
• age		• address
• gender		• age
• attendance_pattern		
'U' records		

B Control structures required

1 A DOWHILE loop to control the repetition
2 Decision symbols to select 'S', female and part-time (P/T) students

C Solution algorithm

EXAMPLE 6.4   Print and total selected students

Design a solution algorithm that will <u>read</u> the same student file as in Example 6.3 and <u>produce</u> the same 'FEMALE PART-TIME STUDENTS' report. In addition, at the end of the report you are to <u>print</u> the number of students who have been selected and listed, and the total number of students on the file.

A Defining diagram

Input	Processing	Output
'S' records	Print heading	Heading line
• number	Read student records	selected student records
• name	Select female P/T students	• number
• address	Print selected records	• name
• age	Compute total students	• address
• sex	Compute total selected students	• age
• attendance_pattern	Print totals	total_students
'U' records		total_selected_students

B Control structures required

1   A DOWHILE loop to control the repetition
2   Decision symbols to select 'S', female and P/T students
3   Accumulators for total_selected_students and total_students

C Solution algorithm

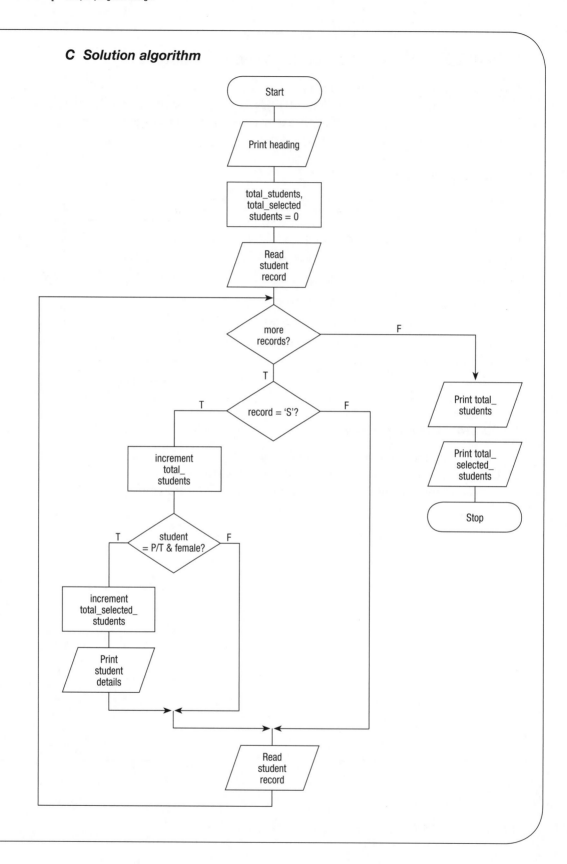

EXAMPLE 6.5 Print student report

Design an algorithm that will <u>read</u> the same student file as in Example 6.4 and, for each student, <u>print</u> the name, number and attendance pattern from the 'S' records (student records) and the unit number and unit name from the 'U' records (enrolled units records) as follows.

```
STUDENT REPORT

Student name           ...........................................
Student number         ....,......................................
Attendance             ...........................................
Enrolled units         ...........................    ...........................
                       ...........................    ...........................
                       ...........................    ...........................
```

At the end of the report, print the total number of students enrolled.

A Defining diagram

Input	Processing	Output
'S' records	Print heading	Heading line
• number	Read student records	detail lines
• name	Print 'S' record details	• name
• attendance_pattern	Print 'U' record details	• number
'U' records	Compute total students	• attendance_pattern
• unit_number	Print total students	• unit_number
• unit_name		• unit_name
		total_students

B Control structures required

1 A DOWHILE loop to control the repetition
2 Decision symbols to select 'S' or 'U' records
3 An accumulator for total_students

C Solution algorithm

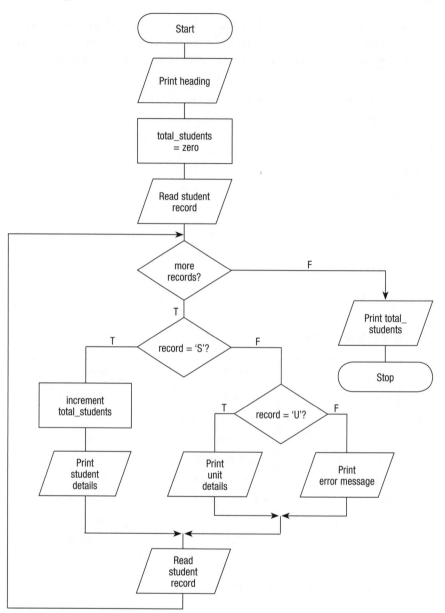

EXAMPLE 6.6 Produce sales report

Design a program that will <u>read</u> a file of sales records and <u>produce</u> a sales report. Each record in the file contains a customer's number and name, a sales amount and a tax code. The tax code is to be applied to the sales amount to determine the sales tax due for that sale, as follows:

Tax code	Sales tax
0	tax exempt
1	3%
2	5%

The report is to print a heading 'SALES REPORT', and detail lines listing the customer number, name, sales amount, sales tax and the total amount owing.

A Defining diagram

Input	Processing	Output
sales record	Print heading	Heading line
• customer_number	Read sales records	detail lines
• name	Calculate sales tax	• customer_number
• sales_amt	Calculate total amount	• name
• tax_code	Print customer details	• sales_amt
		• sales_tax
		• total_amount

B Control structures required

1 A DOWHILE loop to control the repetition
2 A case structure to calculate the sales_tax

Assume that the tax_code field has been validated and will only contain a value of 0, 1 or 2.

C Solution algorithm

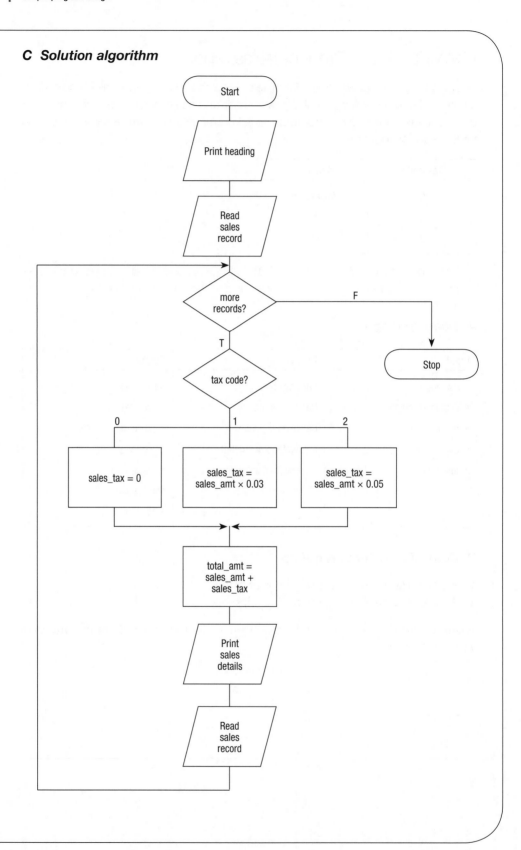

EXAMPLE 6.7 Student test results

Design a solution algorithm that will <u>read</u> a file of student test results and <u>produce</u> a student test grades report. Each test record contains the student number, name and test score (out of 50). The program is to <u>calculate</u> for each student the test score as a percentage and to <u>print</u> the student's number, name, test score (out of 50) and letter grade on the report. The letter grade is determined as follows:

A = 90–100%
B = 80–89%
C = 70–79%
D = 60–69%
F = 0–59%

A Defining diagram

Input	Processing	Output
Student test records	Print heading	Heading line
• student_number	Read student records	student details
• name	Calculate test percentage	• student_number
• test_score	Calculate letter grade	• name
	Print student details	• test_score
		• grade

B Control structures required
1 A DOWHILE loop to control the repetition
2 Decision symbols to calculate the grade

C Solution algorithm

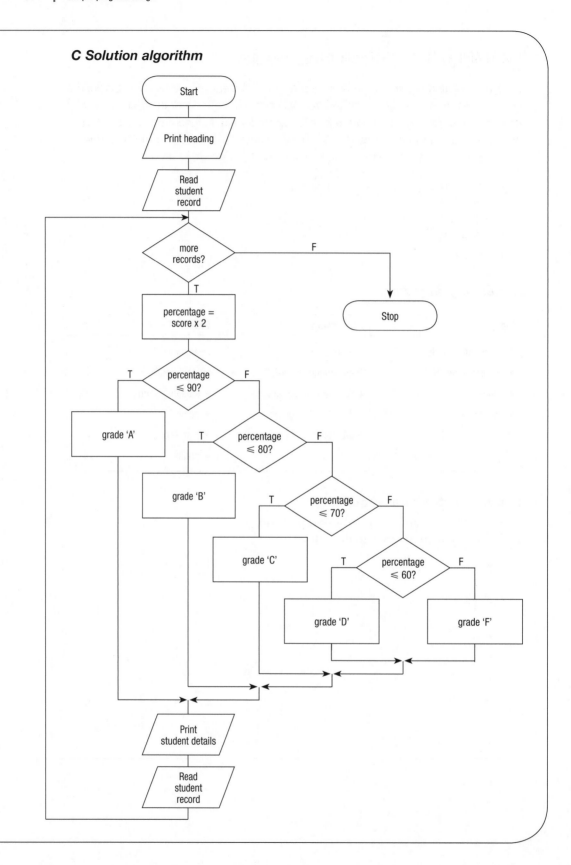

EXAMPLE 6.8 Gas supply billing

The Domestic Gas Supply Company records its customers' gas usage figures on a customer usage file. Each record on the file contains the customer's number, name and address, and their gas usage expressed in cubic metres. Design a solution algorithm that will <u>read</u> the customer usage file, <u>calculate</u> the amount owing for gas usage for each customer, and <u>print</u> a report listing each customer's number, name, address, gas usage and the amount owing.

The company bills its customers according to the following rate: if the customer's usage is 60 cubic metres or less, a rate of $2.00 per cubic metre is applied; if the customer's usage is more than 60 cubic metres, then a rate of $1.75 per cubic metre is applied for the first 60 cubic metres and $1.50 per cubic metre for the remaining usage.

At the end of the report, print the total number of customers and the total amount owing to the company.

A Defining diagram

Input	Processing	Output
customer usage records	Print heading	Heading line
• customer_number	Read usage records	customer details
• name	Calculate amount owing	• customer_number
• address	Print customer details	• name
• gas_usage	Compute total customers	• address
	Compute total amount owing	• gas_usage
	Print totals	• amount_owing
		total_customers
		total_amount_owing

B Control structures required

1 A DOWHILE loop to control the repetition
2 A decision symbol to calculate the amount_owing
3 Accumulators for total_customers and total_amount_owing

C Solution algorithm

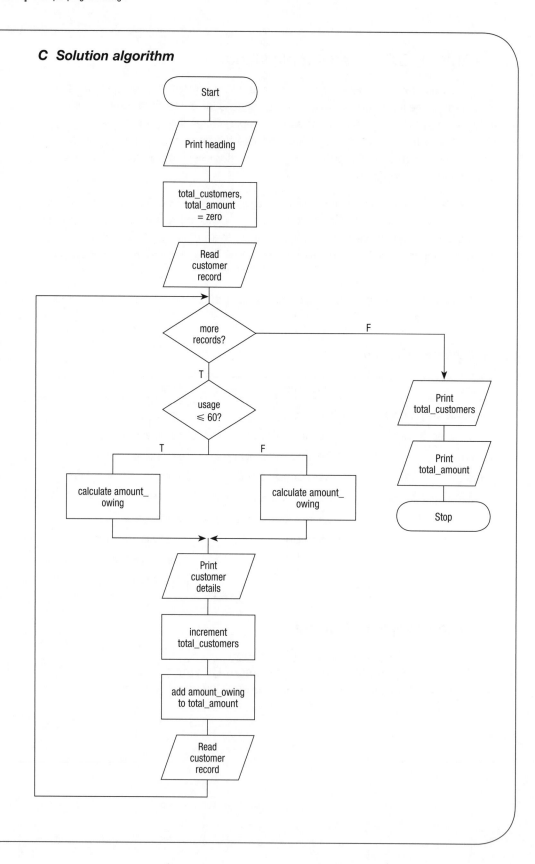

EXAMPLE 7.6   Process exam scores

Design a program that will <u>prompt</u> for and <u>receive</u> 18 examination scores from a mathematics test, <u>calculate</u> the class average, and <u>display</u> all the scores and the average score to the screen.

A Defining diagram

Input	Processing	Output
18 exam scores	Prompt for scores Get scores Calculate average score Display scores Display average score	18 exam scores average_score

B Control structures required

1 An array to store the exam scores – that is, 'scores'
2 An index to identify each element in the array
3 A DO loop to accept the scores
4 Another DO loop to display the scores to the screen

C Solution algorithm

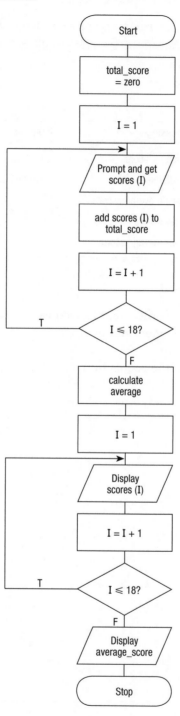

EXAMPLE 7.7   Process integer array

Design an algorithm that will <u>read</u> an array of 100 integer values, <u>calculate</u> the average integer value, and <u>count</u> the number of integers in the array that are greater than the average integer value. The algorithm is to <u>display</u> the average integer value and the count of integers greater than the average.

A Defining diagram

Input	Processing	Output
100 integer values	Read integer values	average
	Calculate integer average	integer_count
	Calculate integer count	
	Display integer average	
	Display integer count	

B Control structures required

1 An array of integer values – 'numbers'
2 A DO loop to calculate the average of the integers
3 A DO loop to count the number of integers greater than the average

C Solution algorithm

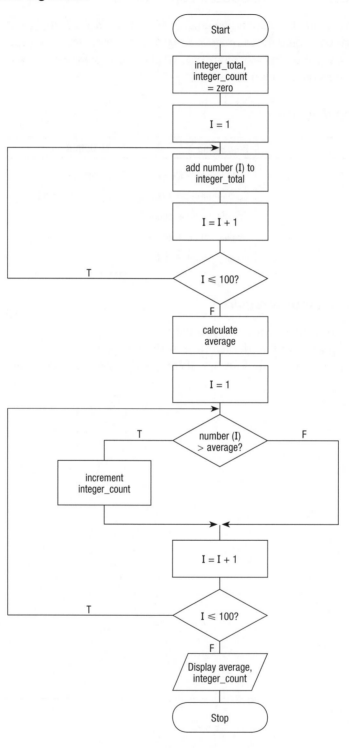

EXAMPLE 7.8   Validate sales number

Design an algorithm that will <u>read</u> a file of sales transactions and <u>validate</u> the sales numbers on each record. As each sales record is read, the sales number on the record is to be verified against an array of 35 sales numbers. Any sales number not found in the array is to be <u>flagged</u> as an error.

A Defining diagram

Input	Processing	Output
sales records • sales_number	Read sales records Validate sales numbers Print error message	error_message

B Control structures required

1 A previously initialised array of sales numbers – 'sales_numbers'
2 A DOWHILE loop to read the sales file
3 A DOWHILE loop to perform a linear search of the array for the sales number
4 A variable element_found that will stop the search when the sales number is found

C Solution algorithm

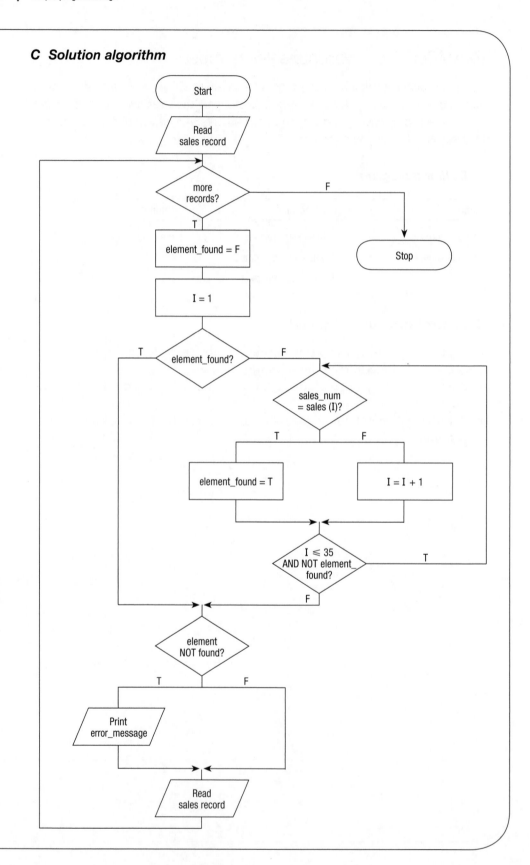

EXAMPLE 7.9   Calculate freight charge

Design an algorithm that will <u>read</u> an input weight for an item to be shipped, <u>search</u> an array of shipping weights and <u>retrieve</u> a corresponding freight charge. In this algorithm, two paired arrays, each containing six elements, have been established and initialised. The array, shipping_weights, contains a range of shipping weights in grams, and the array, freight_charges, contains a corresponding array of freight charges in dollars, as follows.

Shipping weights (grams)	Freight charges
1–100	3.00
101–500	5.00
501–1000	7.50
1001–3000	12.00
3001–5000	16.00
5001–9999	35.00

A Defining diagram

Input	Processing	Output
entry weight	Prompt for entry weight Get entry weight Search shipping weights array Compute freight charge Display freight charge	freight_charge error_message

B Control structures required

1   Two arrays, 'shipping_weights' and 'freight_charges', already initialised
2   A DOWHILE loop to search the shipping_weights array and hence retrieve the freight charge
3   A variable element_found that will stop the search when the entry weight is found

C Solution algorithm

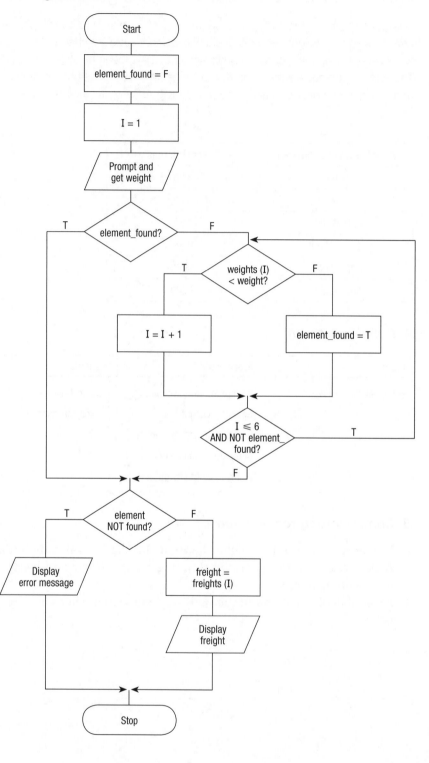

Flowcharts and modules

When designing a modular solution to a problem, using a flowchart, the predefined process symbol is used to designate a process or module. This keeps flowcharts simple, because, as in pseudocode, the main flowchart contains the name of the process, or module, and each process has its own separate flowchart.

Let's now look at the examples from Chapter 8, to see how flowcharts that contain modules are drawn.

EXAMPLE 8.1   process three characters

Design a solution algorithm that will <u>prompt</u> a terminal operator for three characters, <u>accept</u> those characters as input, <u>sort</u> them into ascending sequence and <u>output</u> them to the screen. The algorithm is to continue to read characters until 'XXX' is entered.

A Defining diagram

Input	Processing	Output
char_1	Prompt for characters	char_1
char_2	Accept three characters	char_2
char_3	Sort three characters	char_3
	Output three characters	

B Hierarchy chart

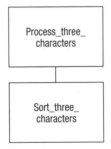

C Solution algorithm using a predefined process symbol

The flowchart solution consists of two flowcharts: a main flowchart called Process_three_characters and a process flowchart called Sort_three_characters. When the main flowchart wants to pass control to its process module, it simply names that process in a predefined process symbol. Control then passes to the process flowchart, and when the processing in that flowchart is complete, the module will pass control back to the main flowchart. The solution flowchart is simple and easy to read.

Process_three_characters

Sort_three_characters

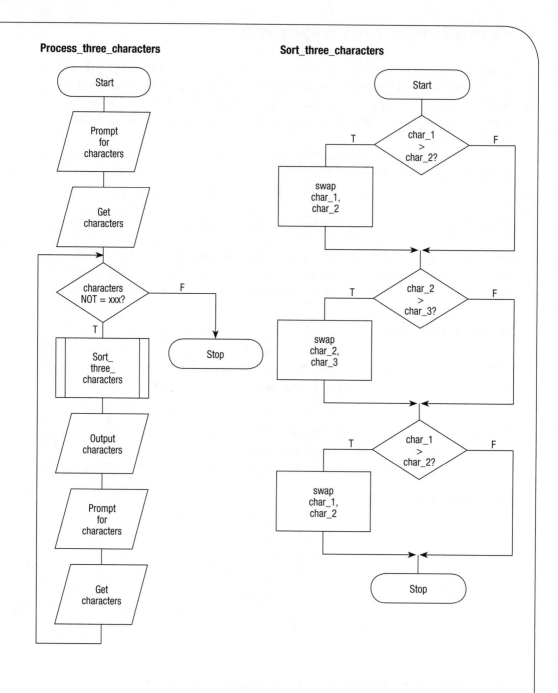

EXAMPLE 8.2 Process three characters

Design a solution algorithm that will <u>prompt</u> a terminal operator for three characters, <u>accept</u> those characters as input, <u>sort</u> them into ascending sequence and <u>output</u> them to the screen. The algorithm is to continue to read characters until 'XXX' is entered.

A Defining diagram

Input	Processing	Output
char_1	Prompt for characters	char_1
char_2	Accept three characters	char_2
char_3	Sort three characters	char_3
	Output three characters	

B Hierarchy chart

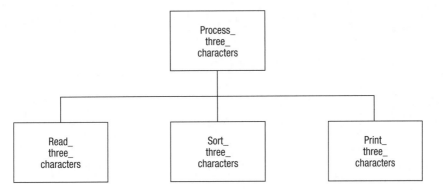

C Solution algorithm

There are four modules in this algorithm, a mainline module and three subordinate modules, which will be represented by a flowchart, as follows:

Process_three_characters

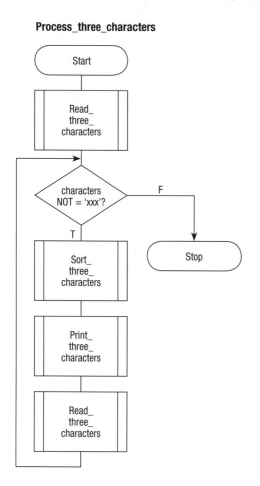

Read_three_characters

Print_three_characters

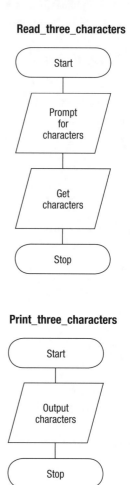

Example 8.2 continued next page

Example 8.2 continued from previous page

Sort_three_characters

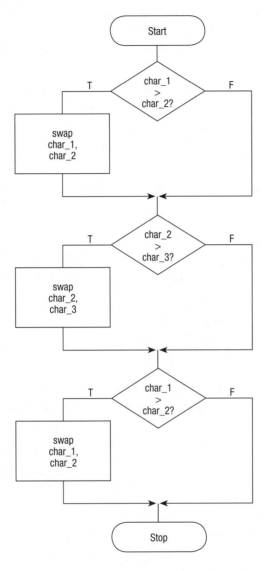

EXAMPLE 8.3   Gas supply billing

The Domestic Gas Supply Company records its customers' gas usage figures on a customer usage file. Each record on the file contains the customer's number, name, address, and gas usage expressed in cubic metres. Design a solution algorithm that will <u>read</u> the customer usage file, <u>calculate</u> the amount owing for gas usage for each customer, and <u>print</u> a report listing each customer's number, name, address, gas usage and the amount owing.

The company bills its customers according to the following rate: if the customer's usage is 60 cubic metres or less, a rate of $2.00 per cubic metre is applied; if the customer's usage is more than 60 cubic metres, then a rate of $1.75 per cubic metre is applied for the first 60 cubic metres and $1.50 per cubic metre for the remaining usage.

At the end of the report, print the total number of customers and the total amount owing to the company.

A Defining diagram

Input	Processing	Output
customer usage records	Print heading	Heading line
• customer_number	Read usage records	customer details
• name	Calculate amount owing	• customer_number
• address	Print customer details	• name
• gas_usage	Compute total customers	• address
	Compute total amount owing	• gas_usage
	Print totals	• amount_owing
		total_customers
		total_amount_owing

B Hierarchy chart

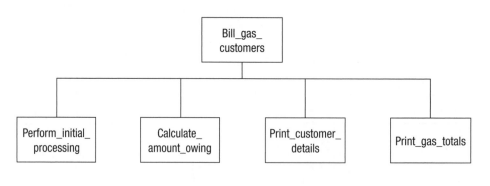

C *Solution algorithm*

Bill_gas_customers

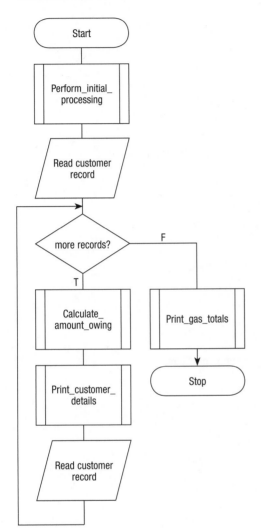

Perform_initial_processing

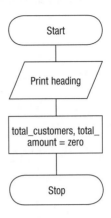

Example 8.3 continued next page

Example 8.3 continued from previous page

Calculate_amount_owing

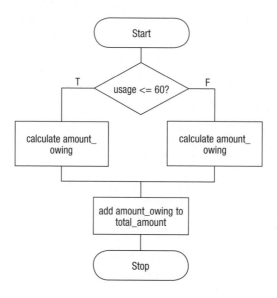

Print_customer_details

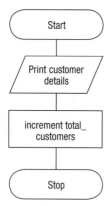

Print_gas_totals

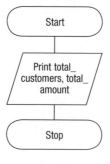

EXAMPLE 8.4   Calculate employee's pay

A company requires a program to <u>read</u> an employee's number, pay rate and the number of hours worked in a week. The program is then to <u>validate</u> the pay rate field and the hours worked field and, if valid, <u>compute</u> the employee's weekly pay and then <u>print</u> it and the input data.

<u>Validation</u>: According to the company's rules, the maximum hours an employee can work per week is 60 hours, and the maximum hourly rate is $25.00 per hour. If the hours worked field or the hourly rate field is out of range, the input data and an appropriate message are to be <u>printed</u> and the employee's weekly pay is not to be calculated.

<u>Weekly pay calculation</u>: Weekly pay is calculated as hours worked times pay rate. If more than 35 hours are worked, payment for the overtime hours worked is calculated at time-and-a-half.

A Define the problem

Input	Processing	Output
emp_no	Read employee details	emp_no
pay_rate	Validate input fields	pay_rate
hrs_worked	Calculate employee pay	hrs_worked
	Print employee details	emp_weekly_pay
		error_message

B Hierarchy chart

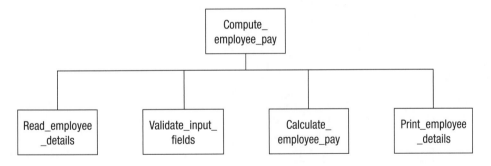

C Solution algorithm

Compute_employee_pay

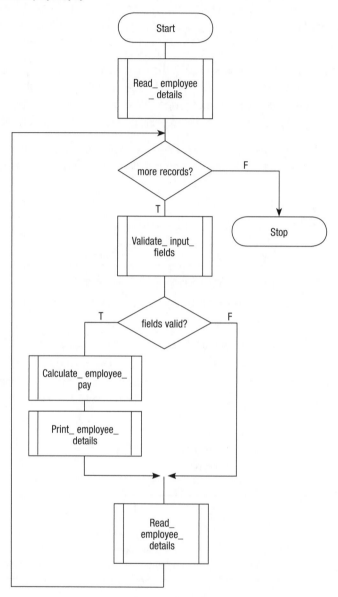

Example 8.4 continued next page

Example 8.4 continued from previous page

Validate_input_fields

Read_employee_details

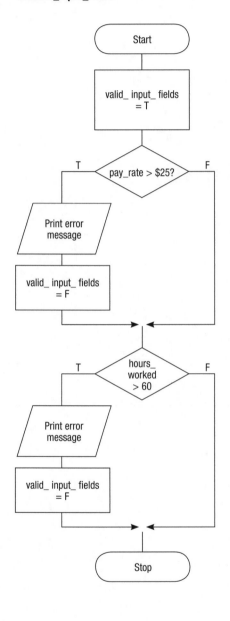

Calculate_employee_pay

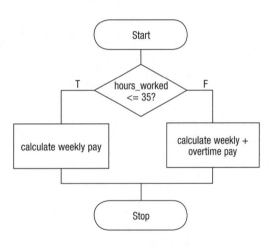

Print_employee_details

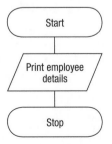

Appendix 2
Special algorithms

Outline

- Sorting algorithms
- Dynamic data structures

This appendix contains a number of algorithms that are not included in the body of the book but may be required at some time in your career.

The first section contains three sorting algorithms: bubble sort, insertion sort and selection sort. The second section introduces three dynamic data structures – queues, stacks and linked lists – and provides algorithms to manipulate them.

Sorting algorithms

Bubble sort algorithms

This algorithm sorts an integer array into ascending order using a bubble sort method.

On each pass, the algorithm compares each pair of adjacent items in the array. If the pair is out of order, they are switched; otherwise they remain in the original order. So, at the end of the first pass, the largest element in the array will have bubbled to the last position in the array.

The next pass will work only with the remaining elements, and will move the next largest element to the second-last position in the array and so on.

In the algorithm:

Array = array to be sorted

number_of_elements = number of elements in the array

elements_switched = flag to record if the elements have been switched in the current pass

temp = temporary area for holding an array element that is being switched

I = index for outer loop

J = index for inner loop.

Assume that the contents of Array and number_of_elements have already been established.

```
Bubble_sort_algorithm
    set I to number_of_elements
    set elements_switched to true
    DOWHILE (elements_switched AND I ≥ 2)
        set J to 1
        set elements_switched to false
        DOWHILE J <= I – 1
            IF Array (J) > Array (J + 1) THEN
                temp = Array (J)
                Array (J) = Array (J + 1)
                Array (J + 1) = temp
                elements_switched = true
            ENDIF
            J = J + 1
        ENDDO
        I = I – 1
    ENDDO
END
```

Insertion sort algorithm

This algorithm sorts an integer array into ascending order using an insertion sort method.

In the algorithm, the array is scanned until an out-of-order element is found. The scan is then temporarily halted while a backward scan is made to find the correct position to insert the out-of-order element. Elements bypassed during this backward scan are moved up one position to make room for the element being inserted. This method of sorting is more efficient than the bubble sort.

In the algorithm:

Array = array to be sorted
number_of_elements = number of elements in the array
temp = temporary area for holding an array element while correct position is being searched
I = current position of the element
J = index for inner loop.

Assume that the contents of Array and number_of_elements have been established.

```
Insertion_sort_algorithm
    set I to 1
    DOWHILE I <= (number_of_elements – 1)
        IF Array (I) > Array (I + 1) THEN
            temp = Array (I + 1)
            J = I
            DOWHILE (J ≥ 1 AND Array (J) > temp)
                Array (J + 1) = Array (J)
                J = J – 1
            ENDDO
            Array (J + 1) = temp
        ENDIF
        I = I + 1
    ENDDO
END
```

Selection sort algorithm

This algorithm sorts an integer array into ascending sequence using a selection sort method.

On the first pass the algorithm finds the smallest element in the array and moves it to the first position in the array by switching it with the element originally in that position. Each successive pass moves one more element into position. After the number of passes is one number less than the number of elements in the array, the array will be in order.

In the algorithm:

Array = array being sorted
number_of_elements = number of elements in the array
smallest_element = area for holding the smallest element found in that pass
current_smallest_position = the value of the current position in which to place the smallest element
I = index for outer loop
J = index for inner loop.

Assume that the contents of Array and number_of_elements have been established.

```
Selection_sort_algorithm
    Set current_smallest_position to 1
    DOWHILE current_smallest_position <= (number_of_elements – 1)
        Set I to current_smallest_position
        smallest_element = Array (I)
        Set J = I + 1
        DOWHILE J <= number_of_elements
            IF Array (J) < smallest_element THEN
                I = J
                smallest_element = Array (J)
            ENDIF
            J = J + 1
        ENDDO
        Array (I) = Array (current_smallest_position)
        Array (current_smallest_position) = smallest_element
        Add 1 to current_smallest_position
    ENDDO
END
```

Dynamic data structures

An array is called a static data structure, because in common programming languages the maximum number of elements must be specified when the array is declared. A dynamic data structure is one in which the number of elements can expand or contract as the problem requires. The elements in these data structures are called nodes.

In building dynamic data structures, pointers are used to create new nodes, and link nodes dispose of those no longer needed. A pointer is a variable whose memory cell contains the address in memory where a data item resides. Therefore, a pointer provides an indirect reference to a data item.

This section covers several examples of dynamic data structures, including queues, stacks and linked lists. Algorithms that manipulate these structures are also provided.

Queues

A queue is a data structure holding data items that are processed on a first-in-first-out basis, like a line of people going through a cafeteria: the first one in the line is the first to reach the cash register and get out of the line.

There are two operations that can be performed on a queue: a node can be added to the end of a queue, and a node can be removed from the head of a queue.

Some programming languages do not support the notion of dynamic data structures, and so do not provide a pointer type. In such cases, the easiest way of representing a queue in an algorithm is by declaring it to be an array.

The effect of a pointer is then achieved by using an integer variable to hold the subscript of the array element representing the node that is currently being operated on. Pointers are required to locate the position of the head of the queue and the tail of the queue, as these must be known. Most queues are designed so that the head of the queue wraps around to the tail when required.

Names used in the algorithms are:

Queue = queue to be manipulated
max_size = maximum number of items in the queue
queue_counter = current number of items in the queue
queue_head = position of the head of the queue
queue_tail = position at which the next item will be inserted in the queue.

The pseudocode to add an item and to delete an item from a queue is:

```
Add_item_to_tail_of_queue
    IF (queue_tail = queue_head AND queue_counter > 0) THEN
        Print error message ('queue overflow')
    ELSE
        Queue (queue_tail) = new item
        queue_tail = queue_tail + 1
        IF queue_tail > max_size THEN
            queue_tail = 1
        ENDIF
        queue_counter = queue_counter + 1
    ENDIF
END


Remove_item_from_head_of_queue
    IF queue_counter = 0 THEN
        Print error message ('queue is empty')
    ELSE
        required value = Queue (queue_head)
        queue_head = queue_head + 1
        IF queue_head > max_size THEN
            queue_head = 1
        ENDIF
        queue_counter = queue_counter – 1
    ENDIF
END
```

It is not necessary to alter the data item that is 'removed' from the queue, because it will simply be overwritten if its place is required.

Stacks

A stack is a data structure holding data items that are processed on a last-in-first-out basis, like a stack of trays in a cafeteria: when a tray is required, it is removed from the top of the stack, and when one is added to the stack, it is also placed on the top. These operations on stack data structures are often called 'pop' (for removing the top element) and 'push' (for adding a new element to the stack).

Once again, the easiest way of representing this stack in an algorithm is by declaring it to be an array.

In the algorithms:

Stack = stack to be manipulated
max_size = the maximum size of the stack
top_of_stack = the position of the top of the stack.

```
Add_item_to_top_of_stack (Push)
    IF top_of_stack NOT = max_size THEN
        top_of_stack = top_of_stack + 1
        Stack (top_of_stack) = new item
    ELSE
        Print error message ('stack overflow')
    ENDIF
END


Remove_item_from_top_of_stack (Pop)
    IF top_of_stack NOT = zero THEN
        value required = Stack (top_of_stack)
        top_of_stack = top_of_stack – 1
    ELSE
        Print error message ('stack underflow')
    ENDIF
END
```

Once again, it is not necessary to alter the data item that is 'removed' from the stack, as it will be overwritten when the next item is added.

Linked lists

A (linear) linked list is a data structure holding a series of elements or cells that contain both a data item and a pointer to the next element in the list. A linked list can be illustrated as follows:

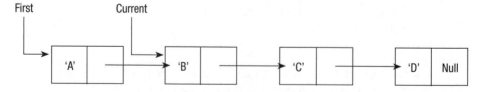

In the diagram, the pointer called 'First' points to the first cell in the list and the pointer called 'Current' points to the current cell in the list. The pointer in the last cell is labelled 'Null', as it indicates the end of the list. Null does not point to a data value.

The advantage of such a data structure is that the elements in the list may be added or deleted by manipulating the pointers rather than by physically moving the data. The data structure thus can be maintained in a logical sequence, without that logical sequence being physically implemented.

Again, where the programming language does not support a pointer type, the easiest way of representing a linked list is by using a technique of 'parallel arrays', as described in chapter 7. Here, one array holds the items in the list and the other array holds, at corresponding positions, the 'link' to the (logically) next item – that is, the value of the subscript of the next item. An integer variable is needed to hold the subscript of the 'first' item (in logical order), and some convention must be adopted whereby an impossible subscript value is understood to be a Null pointer.

Names used in the algorithms are:

Items = an array holding the list values
Links = an array holding subscripts of the next items
first = the subscript of the first item in the list
current = the subscript of the list item currently being operated on
last = the subscript of the item 'previous' to the 'current' item
continue = a Boolean variable set to true to indicate that the search for a value is to continue.

Pseudocode examples that manipulate a singly linked linear list follow:

1 Traverse a list, printing its value

```
Traverse_and_print
    current = first
    DOWHILE current NOT = Null
        Print items (current)
        current = Links (current)
    ENDDO
END
```

2 Search a list for a particular value ('value')

```
Search_list_for_value
    current = first
    continue = true
    DOWHILE (continue AND current NOT = Null)
        IF items (current) NOT = value THEN
            last = current
            current = Links (current)
        ELSE
            continue = false
        ENDIF
    ENDDO
END
```

Note that continue will still be true if the value was not in the list, in which case current will be Null.

3 Remove a designated value from the list. (This algorithm follows on from the one above, where the value was located.)

```
Remove_value_from_list
    IF NOT continue THEN (i.e. the value was found on the list)
        IF current = first THEN
            first = Links (current)
        ELSE
            Links (last) = Links (current)
        ENDIF
    ENDIF
END
```

In practice, the position of the space just freed would be recorded for later use. This would require the definition of an integer variable 'free' to hold the subscript of the first element of free space. Then, after a remove operation, the free list would be updated with the statements:

Links (current) = free
free = current

More complex linked structures, such as binary trees and graphs, and the algorithms to manipulate them are beyond the present scope of this book. They may be found in more advanced programming texts and introductory Computer Science texts.

Appendix 3
Translating pseudocode into computer languages: quick reference chart

Outline

BASIC/VB/VBA
PASCAL/DELPHI
C/C++

Pseudocode	VB, VBA	Pascal/Delphi	C++
Data types Integer Floating Point Boolean Character String	**Integer, Long** **Single, Double** **Boolean** **Char** (*VB.Net only*) **string**	**Integer** **Single, Double** **Boolean** **Char** **string**	**int, long** **float, double** **bool** **char** **string**

Module declaration
Name
  statement/s
END
	SUB *Name(parameters if any)*
	  statement/s
	END SUB
	
	FUNCTION
	Name(parameters if any) **AS** *datatype*
	
	  statement/s
	  Name = returnValue
	END FUNCTION
		PROCEDURE *Name(parameters if any)*;
		BEGIN
		  statement/s;
		END;
		
		FUNCTION
		Name(parameters if any):
		  datatype;
		BEGIN
		  statement/s;
		  Name := returnValue;
		        or
		  RESULT := *returnValue*;
		END;
			void *Name(parameters if any)*
			{
			  statement/s;
			};
			
			datatype Name(parameters if any)
			{
			  statement/s;
			  return *value*;
			    };

Variable declaration	**DIM** *variableName* **AS** *datatype*	**VAR** *variableName1, ...: datatype*;	*datatype variableName1, ...*;
Constant declaration *CONSTNAME = value*	**CONST** *CONSTNAME* **AS** *datatype = value*	**CONST** *CONSTNAME = value*;	**const** *datatype CONSTNAME = value*;

Pseudocode	VB, VBA	Pascal/Delphi	C++
Conditional operators *operand = operand* *operand* **NOT** *= operand* *operand < operand* *operand > operand* *operand <= operand* *operand >= operand*	*operand = operand* *operand* **<>** *operand* *operand < operand* *operand > operand* *operand <= operand* *operand >= operand*	*(operand = operand)* *(operand <> operand)* *(operand < operand)* *(operand > operand)* *(operand <= operand)* *(operand >= operand)*	*(operand = = operand)* *(operand != operand)* *(operand < operand)* *(operand > operand)* *(operand <= operand)* *(operand >= operand)*
Logical operators *operand* **AND** *operand* *operand* **OR** *operand* *operand* **NOT** *operand*	*operand* **AND** *operand* *operand* **OR** *operand* **NOT** *(operand)*	*(operand* **AND** *operand)* *(operand* **OR** *operand)* **NOT** *(operand)*	*(operand* **&&** *operand)* *(operand* || *operand)* *! (operand)*

IF *(condition)* **THEN** *True statement/s block*
ELSE
    False statement/s block
ENDIF
	IF *(condition)* THEN
	  True statement/s block
	ELSE
	    False statement/s block
	ENDIF
		IF *(condition)* **THEN**
		  BEGIN
		    True statement/s block;
		  END
		  ELSE
		    BEGIN
		    False statement/s block;
		  END;
			if *(condition)*
			  {
			    True statement/s block;
			  }
			else
			  {
			    False statement/s block;
			  };

Pseudocode	VB, VBA	Pascal/Delphi	C++
| ```
CASE OF single_variable
    value_1 : statement block_1
    value_2 : statement          block_2
    ...
    value_n : statement          block_n
    ...
    value_other : statement block_
other
ENDCASE
``` | ```
SELECT CASE single_variable
    CASE value_1 : statement block_1
    CASE value_2 : statement block_2
    CASE value_n : statement block_n
    CASE ELSE : statement block_other
END SELECT
``` | ```
CASE single_variable OF
    value_1 : statement block_1;
    value_2 : statement block_2;
    ...
    value_n : statement block_n;

ELSE
    statement block_other;
END;
``` | ```
switch (single_variable)
{
    case value_1:
    statement/s;
        break;
    case value_2:
    statement/s;
        break;
    ...
    case value_n:
        statement/
    s;
        break;
    default: statement/s;
};
``` |
| ```
DOWHILE (condition)
statement/s
ENDDO
``` | ```
DO WHILE (condition) statement/s
LOOP

or
WHILE (condition)
    statement/s
WEND
``` | ```
WHILE (condition) DO
    BEGIN
        statement/s;
    END;
``` | ```
while (condition)
{
    statement/s;
};
``` |

Pseudocode	VB, VBA	Pascal/Delphi	C++
DO *statement/s* **WHILE** (*condition*)	**DO** *statement/s* **LOOP WHILE** (*condition*)	**REPEAT** *statement/s;* **UNTIL NOT** (*condition*);	**do** { *statement/s;* } **while** (*condition*);
REPEAT *statement/s* **UNTIL** (*condition*)	**DO** *statement/s* **LOOP UNTIL** (*condition*)	**REPEAT** *statement/s;* **UNTIL** (*condition*);	**do** { *statement/s;* } **while** !(*condition*);

DO *counter = begin* **TO** *end*
statement/s
ENDDO
	FOR *counter = begin* **TO** *end*
	statement/s
	NEXT *counter*
		FOR *counter* := *begin* **TO** *end* **DO**
		  BEGIN
		    statement/
		    s;
		  END;
			for(*counter = begin; counter <= end;*
			counter++)
			{
			  statement/s;
			};

Record structures
recordName
  fieldname1
  fieldname2
  ...
  fieldnameN
	TYPE *recordNameType*
	  field1 **AS** *datatype*
	  field2 **AS** *datatype*
	  ...
	  fieldN **AS** *datatype*
	END TYPE
		TYPE
		  recordName = **RECORD**
		    field1: datatype;
		    field2: datatype;
		    ...
		    fieldN: datatype;
		  END;
			struct *recordNameType*
			{
			  datatype field1;
			  datatype field2;
			  ...
			  datatype fieldN;
			};

Pseudocode	VB, VBA	Pascal/Delphi	C++

Sequential Files – Reading
Initial processing
READ *variableName*
DOWHILE NOT EOF
 	
...
    READ *variableName*
ENDDO
Final processing
	OPEN "*sourcefile*" **FOR INPUT AS** *fileNo*
	...
	DO WHILE NOT EOF(*fileNo*)
	    INPUT #fileNo, field1, field2,...
	,*fieldN*
	                          ...
	LOOP
	....
	CLOSE *#fileNo*
	
	Note: You can't do a priming read as VB uses a read ahead method.
		Program *Name*(**Input**, **Output**, *fileHandle*)
		VAR *fileHandle* : **TEXTFILE**;
		...
		BEGIN
		    ASSIGNFILE(*fileHandle*,"*sourcefile*");
		    RESET (*fileHandle*); {**Open** for Reading}
		    WHILE NOT (**EOF**(*fileHandle*)) **DO**
		    BEGIN
		                          ...
		READLN(*fileHandle*, *variable*);
		    END;
		    ...
		    CLOSEFILE(*fileHandle*);
		END.
			#include <**fstream.h**>
			...
			ifstream *inFileHandle*;
			...
			inFileHandle.**open**("*sourcefile*");
			...
			inFileHandle >> *variableName*;
			while (!*inFileHandle*.**eof**())
			{
			    ...
			    inFileHandle >> *variableName*;
			};
			inFileHandle.**close**();

Sequential files – Writing
 	
WRITE ***variableName***
	OPEN "*sourcefile*" FOR
	OUTPUT AS *fileNo*
	    ...
	    OUTPUT #*fileNo*, field1, field2,...
	,*fieldN*
	    ...
	CLOSE *#fileNo*
		Program *Name*(**Input**, **Output**, *fileHandle*)
		VAR fileHandle : **TEXTFILE**;
		...
		BEGIN
		
		    ASSIGNFILE(*fileHandle*,"*sourcefile*");
		    REWRITE (*fileHandle*); {Open for Writing}
		    WRITELN(*fileHandle*, *variable* **or** *value*);
		    ...
		    CLOSEFILE(*fileHandle*);
		END.
			#include <**fstream.h**>
			...
			ofstream *outFileHandle*;
			...
			outFileHandle.**open**("*sourcefile*");
			    ...
			                          outFileHandle<<*variableName*<<"";
			    ...
			outFileHandle.**close**();

Pseudocode	VB, VBA	Pascal/Delphi	C++
Declaring arrays ***One-dimensional*** *SET arrayName (maxNumElements)*	**DIM** *arrayName (begin* **TO** *end)* **AS** *datatype*	**VAR** *arrayName :* **ARRAY**[*begin .. end*] **OF** *datatype;*	*datatype arrayName* [*maxNumElements*];
Declaring arrays ***Two-dimensional*** *SET arrayName (row, column)*	**DIM** *arrayName (begin* **TO** *maxrow, begin* **TO** *maxcolumn)* **AS** *datatype*	**VAR** *arrayName :* **ARRAY**[*begin .. maxrow, begin .. maxcolumn*] **OF** *datatype;*	*datatype arrayName [row][columns*];
Processing Array Elements ***Assigning a value*** *arrayName (index) = value*	*arrayName (index) = value*	*arrayName [index] := value;*	*arrayName [index] = value;*
Reading a Value *variableName = arrayName (index)*	*variableName = arrayName (index)*	*variableName := arrayName [index];*	*variableName = arrayName [index];*

This chart is supplied courtesy of Victor Cockrell, Curtin University, Western Australia

Glossary

actual parameter
A parameter that is passed to a subordinate module in a particular call.

accessor
A descriptive name for an operation that retrieves or 'gets' the value of an attribute.

algorithm
A set of detailed, unambiguous and ordered instructions developed to describe the processes necessary to produce the desired output from given input.

array
A data structure made up of a number of variables that all have the same data type and are accessed by the same name.

attribute
A characteristic or property of an object.

audit report
A detailed list of all transactions that occurred during the life of the program.

binary search
A search that involves halving the number of elements to search for each time the logic is executed, until an element is found or its absence is detected.

Boolean variable
A variable that can contain only one of two possible values: true or false.

CASE control structure
A structure that extends the basic selection control structure from a choice between two values to a choice from multiple values.

class
A template or pattern that defines the basic attributes, relationships and operations available to its objects.

cohesion
A measure of the internal strength of a module – that is, how closely the elements or statements of a module are associated with each other. The higher the cohesion, the better the module.

constant
A data item with a name and a value that remain the same during the execution of a program.

constructor
A set of instructions that creates an object and initialises its attributes.

control structures
The Structure Theorem states that it is possible to write any program using only three basic control structures:

1   *Sequence*: the straightforward execution of one processing step after another.

2   *Selection*: the presentation of a condition, and the choice between two actions, depending on whether the condition is true or false.

3   *Repetition*: the presentation of a set of instructions to be performed repeatedly, as long as a condition is true.

counted repetition
A loop in an algorithm where the exact number of loop iterations is known in advance.

coupling
A measure of the extent of information interchange between modules. The fewer the connections between modules, the more loosely they are coupled. The looser the coupling, the better the module.

data-driven design
A design methodology based on the idea that the data in a program is more stable than the processes involved.

data structure
A collection of elementary data items.

data type
A set of values and a set of operations that can be performed on those values.

defining diagram
A diagram that arranges the input, output and processing components of a problem into separate columns. It is constructed when the programmer defines the problem.

desk checking
A method of manually tracing through the logic of a program with some chosen test data.

direct access file
A file where data is stored and retrieved randomly, using a key or index.

dynamic data structure
A structure in which the number of elements can expand or contract as the problem requires.

elementary data item
One containing a single variable that is always treated as a unit.

error report
A detailed list of the errors that occurred during the life of the program.

event-driven design
A design methodology based on the idea that an event can cause a program to change from one known state to another.

file
A collection of related records.

flowchart
A graphical representation of program logic, using a series of standard geometric symbols and lines.

formal parameter
A parameter that appears when a subordinate module is defined.

functional decomposition
The division of a problem into separate tasks or functions as the first step towards designing the solution algorithm. Each function will be dedicated to the performance of a single specific task.

global data
Data that is known to the whole program.

graphical user interface (GUI)
An interface that enables the programmer to select the program's interface from a pre-existing range of options.

hierarchy chart
A diagram that shows the name of each module in the solution algorithm and its hierarchical relationship to the other modules.

information hiding
A term used in object-oriented design whereby the structure of the data and the performance of its operations are 'hidden' from the user.

instantiation
The process of creating objects from classes. Each object will contain the same attributes, but not necessarily the same values in those attributes.

interface
A device in a program connecting a user's responses with the program's actions.

intermodule communication
The flow of information or data between modules.

leading decision loop
A loop in an algorithm in which the condition is tested before any statements are executed.

linear search
A search that involves looking at the elements one by one until an element is found or the end of the input is reached.

linked list
A data structure that holds a series of elements containing both a data item and a pointer to the next item in the list.

literal
A constant whose name is the written representation of its value.

local data
Data that is defined within the module in which it will be referenced and is not known outside that module.

mainline
The controlling module of a solution algorithm, which ties all the modules together and coordinates their activity.

master file
A file that contains permanent and semipermanent information about the data entities it contains.

modular design
Grouping tasks together because they all perform the same function. Modular design is directly connected to top-down development, as the tasks into which you divide the problem will actually form the future modules of the program.

module
A section of an algorithm that is dedicated to the performance of a single task or function.

multidimensional array
An array constructed in such a way that two or more subscripts are required to locate an element in the array.

mutator
A descriptive name for an operation that provides or 'sets' the value of an attribute.

object
A container for a set of data, and the operations that need to be performed on that data.

object-oriented design
A methodology that views the system as a collection of interacting objects, rather than functions, whose internal structure is hidden from the user.

operation

A set of services that an object can perform. Public operations are those producing services requested by other objects. Private operations are those performing internal operations in an object and cannot be accessed directly from outside the object.

operation overriding

A term used in object-oriented design to refer to the situation in which a parent class provides an operation, but the inheriting child class defines its own version of that operation.

overloading

A term used in object-oriented design to refer to operations in a single class that have the same name.

paired arrays

Two arrays that contain the same number of elements and whose elements correspond in the same position.

parameter

A variable, literal or constant, that is used to communicate between the modules of a program.

- Data parameters contain the actual variables or data items that will be passed between modules.

- Status parameters act as program flags and should contain just one of two values: true or false.

pointer

A variable whose memory cell contains the address in memory where a data item resides.

polymorphism

A term used in object-oriented design to refer to the use of operations of the same name for a variety of purposes.

priming read

A statement that appears immediately before the DOWHILE condition in a solution algorithm.

private access

The attributes and methods that are invisible to the rest of the system. In a class diagram a minus sign is used in front of the name.

public access

Operations that are visible to other objects. Other objects can see the specifications of that operation. In a class diagram a plus sign is used in front of the name.

procedure-driven design

A design methodology based on the idea that the most important feature of a program is its processes or functions.

pseudocode
A subset of English that has been formalised and abbreviated to look like a high-level computer language. Keywords and indentation are used to signify particular control structures.

queue
A data structure holding data items that are processed on a first-in-first-out basis.

record
A collection of data items or fields that all bear some relationship to each other.

reference parameter
A parameter whose reference address is passed to a subordinate module and thus can be modified.

scope of a variable
The portion of a program in which a variable has been defined and can be referred to; that is, a list of all the modules in which that variable can be referenced.

sentinel
A special record placed at the end of valid data to signify the end of that data. It is also known as a trailer record.

sequential file
A file where the data is stored and retrieved sequentially.

sequential file update
An update of a sequential master file, using a sequential file of update transactions.

side effect
An event that occurs when a subordinate module alters the value of a global variable inside that module.

stack
A data structure holding data items that are processed on a last-in-first-out basis.

string
A collection of characters.

Structure Theorem
The Structure Theorem states that it is possible to write any computer program by using only three basic control structures. These control structures are simple sequence, selection and repetition.

structured programming
A method of writing programs so that each instruction obeys the Structure Theorem. Structured programming also incorporates top-down development and modular design.

top-down design

The division of a problem into separate tasks as the first step towards designing the solution algorithm. The programmer develops an algorithm that incorporates the major tasks first, and only considers the more detailed steps when all the major tasks have been completed.

trailing decision loop

A loop in an algorithm in which the condition is tested at the end of the loop, after the statements in the loop have been executed once.

transaction file

A file that contains transactions designed to update a master file.

value parameter

A parameter whose value is passed to a subordinate module, but which cannot be modified.

variable

A collection of memory cells that store a particular data item.

visibility

A term used in object-oriented design to refer to the public or private nature of an operation. An operation is visible if it can interact with the rest of the program.

Index